THE BIRTH AND DEATH OF JESUS CHRIST

DON T. PHILLIPS

"The Birth and Death of Jesus Christ," by Don T. Phillips. ISBN: 978-1-62137-523-4 (hardcover).

Published 2014 by Virtualbookworm.com Publishing Inc., P.O. Box 9949, College Station, TX 77842, US.

Manufactured in the United States of America.

Table of Contents

OBITUARY

On Nisan 14, April 5 in 30 AD; Jesus Christ of Nazareth died in Jerusalem at Golgotha, which is called the *Place of the Skull*. He had just turned 34 years old. Jesus Christ was tried and convicted of treason by Pontius Pilate. After a short hearing, He was sentenced to die a most cruel death by being nailed to a cross where He hung until he breathed His last breath. He was born in the town of Bethlehem during the reign of Herod the Great, and He was survived by his Mother Mary and several other brothers and sisters. He was never married but He is survived by *many sons and daughters*. Jesus Christ was said by many to be the long awaited Jewish Messiah; by others to be the Son of God; and by still others simply a good man. He taught and ministered throughout all Judea for a period of 3.5 years, during which He healed the sick; made the lame to walk; and cured all manner of illnesses; including leprosy. It is written that He even raised the dead. It was generally agreed that He was a kind and loving man, who preached of love, repentance and the forgiveness of sins. Those who followed after Christ following His death believe that He was raised from the dead after 3 days and 3 nights, and ascended into heaven where He now sits upon the right hand of God the Father. He preached of a new covenant made between God and all people by which eternal life and salvation would be offered by grace to all who might believe upon His holy name. Some say that the world has been changed forever by this man who was self-proclaimed to be the Son of God. He spoke of an eternal kingdom which would be established by Him when He comes again; one which will be built upon righteousness and the glory of His appearing... Let it be so.

When the even was come, there came a rich man of Arimathaea, named Joseph, who also himself was Jesus' disciple: He went to Pilate, and begged the body of Jesus. Then Pilate commanded the body to be delivered. And when Joseph had taken the body, he wrapped it in a clean linen cloth, and laid it in his own new tomb, which he had hewn out in the rock: and he rolled a great stone to the door of the sepulcher, and departed.

Matthew 27: 57-60

DEDICATION

This book is dedicated to:

Dr. Bruce M. Wood….. A Pastor's Pastor

And First Lady

Connie Wood… An inspiration to all

Dr. Bruce M. Wood and Connie Wood

Aldersgate United Methodist Church

College Station, Texas

"…. Do not be afraid, for I know that you are looking for Jesus who was crucified. He is not here; He has risen, just as He said.

Come and see the place where He lay…."

Matthew 16: 5-6

PREFACE

Almost 6000 years have elapsed since Adam and Eve left the Garden of Eden and entered into a world that had been stained with sin. Thousands of important events have taken place since that day, but two in particular are more important than all the rest. In the fullness of time, God send the archangel Gabriel to a young virgin named Mary with the news that by divine appointment she would supernaturally conceive and bear a son. His name would be Jesus, and He would be the Son of God. His birth was predicted by the prophet Isaiah more than 500 years before He was born.

For unto us a child is born, unto us a son is given: and the government shall be upon his shoulder: and his name shall be called Wonderful, Counselor, The mighty God, The everlasting Father, The Prince of Peace. **Isaiah 9:1**

The birth of Jesus Christ was a miraculous event which changed the world, but an even more miraculous and glorious event was yet to come. Conceived of God, born of a virgin, raised in poverty and clothed in the body of an ordinary man; Jesus Christ grew in wisdom and grace until in due time He came to the River Jordan to be baptized into a ministry of reconciliation and salvation for all who would believe upon His name.

After an earthly ministry of 3.5 years, the birth of Christ was overshadowed by the single most important event that would ever occur.... the death of Jesus Christ on the Cross of Calvary. How strange it might seem to a sinful and wicked world that the death of someone would be the most important thing that ever occurred.

The death of Jesus Christ was no ordinary death. Christ willingly went to the cross of Calvary to die for the sins of the world. He was the perfect Passover Lamb who suffered and died for everyone who would ever live, either before or after. The price was great but the promise was greater. All who would believe that He was the only Son of God and accept Him as their personal Lord and Savior would receive the gift of eternal life; not by works lest anyone should boast, but by grace.

I became curious some years ago about when (year and month) my Lord and Savior Jesus Christ was born and died. To my surprise, there were no verified secular, archeological or biblical records of when these two landmark events took place. As I began to search the scriptures for clues, and to research ancient documents for recorded dates; I soon found myself engulfed in a plethora of conflicting opinions and scholarly investigations. After several years of analyzing both biblical and archeological documents, I finally arrived at the conclusions which are contained in this manuscript. I have no doubt that the results I now present will be rejected by many and accepted by many. Until we can set down underneath the shade of an olive tree with Jesus Christ and ask Him, we will likely never have definitive proof concerning when He was born and died.

In a sense it is extremely important that we find the truth....for the truth is what we seek. However, in a broader sense it is not important at all. What is important is that Jesus Christ was the Son of God, who willingly left His heavenly home and dwelt among mankind in a tabernacle of flesh. He died for our sins on the cross of Calvary so that all who would believe upon His glorious name might find forgiveness of their sins and gain eternal life. Oh what love and grace He bestows upon all who would follow after Him.

The sacrificial death of Jesus Christ changed the relationship between God and man forever. The Law which was given to Moses on Mt. Sinai was called the Old Covenant, and it was replaced by a New Covenant on the Hill of Golgotha. Salvation would now be offered to Jews and gentiles alike, and forgiveness of sins would no longer be based upon a Levitical sacrificial system but upon Grace: Whosoever will believe that Jesus Christ is the one and only Son of God, and accept Him as their Lord and Savior, will be forgiven of all their sins and receive eternal life.

This promise was guaranteed and sealed by the death and resurrection of Jesus Christ. So is it really important that we try to find out when this greatest of all events happened? To me it is.... and perhaps it may also be important to all who would read this book. So, we will seek the truth and in doing so discover many important signs and wonders. Come join me in this search!

May God richly bless you and keep you until that day when He returns again to gather us to His side. And so we will forever be with Him in His majesty and glory. Amen.

Don T. Phillips
June 1, 2014

"Behold, I show you a mystery. We shall not all sleep but we shall all be changed. In a moment, in the twinkling of an eye, at the last trump: for the trumpet shall sound, and the dead shall be raised incorruptible, and we shall be changed."

I Corinthians 15: 51-52

CHAPTER 1

THE HEBREW CALENDAR

In the time of Christ, the nation of Israel was an agricultural society. The people also kept sheep, goats and a few cattle; but every year they planted, sowed and reaped. The primary crops were wheat, barley, grapes, olives and nuts. Just as today, the success of growing food for one's family heavily depended upon when to plant and when to harvest crops. In fact, the Seven Feasts of Israel were established around the agricultural cycles, although each has prophetic implications. We discuss both the historical and spiritual aspects of each of the Seven Feasts of Israel in Chapter 2.

In order to understand and determine when the Christ child was born, it is necessary to understand both the Hebrew Calendar and the way that time was measured by the ancient Hebrews.

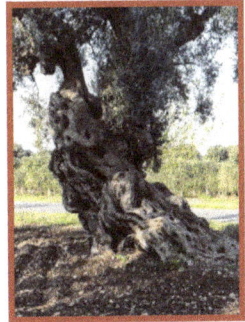

The Jewish calendar was constructed to keep accurate track of the summer and winter solstices and the different planting seasons. We will show later that as far back as the reign of King David, the Jewish Levitical priesthood possessed a detailed understanding of how the moon and sun interacted to divide time into months, years and the four seasons. There are two primary ways that all societies measure time. The first is to use a calendar based upon the amount of time that it takes the moon to cycle from one new moon to the next and back again. This *lunar cycle* takes approximately 29.5 days (29 days, 12 hours 3.33 seconds.). The mean tropical

solar year is about 365.2422 days long. The calendar in use today is called the Gregorian calendar and almost exactly equals 365.2422 days. The Gregorian calendar did not come into use until 1582 when it was introduced by Pope Gregory XII. In 45 BC, a calendar called the *Julian calendar* was introduced by Julius Caesar in 45 BC. Prior to that a calendar called the old Roman calendar was in use. The new Julian calendar had a regular (common) year of 365 days divided into 12 months, with a leap day added to the month of February every four years (leap year). This made the Julian year 365.25 days long. The slight error between 365.2422 days and 365.25 seems to be negible, but every 128 years this inaccuracy will cause the Julian calendar to drop behind the solar year by one day. By 1582 the Julian calendar had a 10 day error! In October of 1582 BC Pope Gregory XIII decided it was time to correct this error and reform the Julian calendar by adding back the 10 days. Hence, the Julian calendar day of Thursday, October 4, 1582 was changed to Friday, October 15. The cycle of weekdays was not affected. New rules were introduced which determined leap years, and when Easter would be celebrated. This correction and refinement of the original Roman calendar was called the *Gregorian calendar*. The Gregorian calendar is very accurate, losing only 1 day every 3,236 years against the length of a solar year as compared to the Julian calendar which lost 1 day every 128 years.

Name of calendar	When introduced	Average year	Approximate error introduced
Gregorian calendar	AD 1582	365.2425 days	27 seconds (1 day every 3,236 years)
Julian calendar	45 BC	365.25 days	11 minutes (1 day every 128 years)

The ancient Jewish calendar was a *lunar* calendar that was accurate and used rules similar to the modern Jewish calendar. It is built around 12 months alternating between 29 and 30 days. Since the average length of the lunar month is 29.530589 days, it is convenient to have months alternate between 29 and 30 days. This results in a Jewish 12 month year of 354 days. However, the *seasons* are determined by the rotation of the earth around the sun, and this cycle is 365.2422 days. It can be easily recognized that a Jewish lunar year of 354 days will fall short of a solar year by about 11.25 days every year. If left to continue, in 3 years the lunar calendar would fall short of a solar calendar by about 34 days. It is clear that if not adjusted, after about 18 years January 1 on a lunar calendar would actually be midsummer.

The Ancient Hebrew Calendar

Calendar Months	Nisan	Iyar	Sivan	Tammuz	Av	Elul	Tishri	Heshvan	Kislev	Tevet	Shevat	Adar	Adar II
Religious Year	1	2	3	4	5	6	7	8	9	10	11	12	
Civil Year	7	8	9	10	11	12	1	2	3	4	5	6	
Length	30	29	30	29	30	29	30	29	30	29	30	29	29
Gregorian Months	March/April	April/May	May/June	June/July	July/Aug	Aug/Sept	Sept/Oct	Oct/Nov	Nov/Dec	Dec/Jan	Jan/Feb	Feb/Mar	
Feasts of Israel	Passover Nisan 14 Unleavened Bread Nisan 15-21 First Fruits Starts 1st Sunday in Unleavened Bread (50 days)		Pentecost 50th day after Firstfruits Starts				Trumpets Tishri 1 Tishri 10 Yom Kippur (Atonement) Tishri 15-21 Tabernacles Tishri 22 Last Great Day of Tabernacles						
Crops Rains Sheep	Barley Latter Rains Flocks moved to Field	Wheat	Figs	Grapes	Fruits	Dates Grapes Figs	Ploughing Planting Early Rains	Olives	Flocks to Winter quarters	Wild and Domestic Crops Grow	Almonds	Citrus Fruits	

To keep the lunar and solar calendars synchronized, an extra 13th month was periodically added to make a 13 month year. This extra month is always added just before the month of Nisan and just after the month of Adar. It is called *Adar II* and usually consisted of 29 days. Before the Nation of Israel fell to the Babylonian empire in 605 BC, the Levitical priesthood decided when to insert an extra month by observing when wheat and barley would not come to maturity soon enough to support the Feast of Firstfruits which begins on Nisan 15. The wheat and barley was observed just prior to Nisan 1, and if the corn and wheat had not begun to mature in the stalk an extra month was added. It was a simple system, based upon observation of the moon and crop maturity. However, this system was probably not used after the return from the Babylonian exile of 70 years around 538 BC. The Babylonians had long determined the cycles of the sun and moon very accurately. The original Hebrew calendar started a new year on *Tishri 1* (September/October), but when the exodus from Egypt occurred in 1457 BC, God declared that the yearly Hebrew calendar would start with the first day of the old 7th month called *Nisan*. The old Hebrew calendar was a lunar-based calendar of length 354 days, while a solar year was 365.2422 days. It is clear that the old Roman calendar would lose about 11.25 days a year against the solar year. It had to be adjusted by adding 7 extra months of 29 days every 19 years, which we will discuss later.

ANATOMY OF THE JEWISH CALENDAR

THE JEWISH DAY

A Jewish day is 24 hours long, but each day starts at 6:00pm and ends at 6:00pm; contrasted to the modern Gregorian calendar and the ancient Julian calendar days which start at midnight and end at midnight. Hence, one Jewish calendar day spans two Gregorian calendar days.

Sunday	Monday	Tuesday	Wednesday	Thursday	Friday	Saturday
יוֹם רִאשׁוֹן	יוֹם שֵׁנִי	יוֹם שְׁלִישִׁי	יוֹם רְבִיעִי	יוֹם חֲמִישִׁי	יוֹם שִׁשִּׁי	יוֹם שַׁבָּת
Yom Rishon	Yom Sheni	Yom Sh'lishi	Yom Revi'i	Yom Chamishi	Yom Shishi	Yom Shabbat

A JEWISH WEEK

A Jewish week is composed of 7 days. Each week starts on Sunday at 6:00 PM and ends at 6:00 PM (Gregorian calendar Sunday). The seventh day of the week is a day of no work and rest called a *shavu'a*, and it is the Jewish Sabbath day. This was because God rested on the 7th day. This day was set apart by God to remember His creative work.

Hebrew Day...	First Day of The Week
Gregorian Day...	Sunday: 6:00PM - Monday: 6:00PM
Hebrew Day...	Second Day of The Week
Gregorian Day...	Monday: 6:00PM - Tuesday: 6:00PM
Hebrew Day...	Third Day of The Week
Gregorian Day...	Sunday: 6:00PM - Monday: 6:00PM
Hebrew Day...	Fourth Day of The Week
Gregorian Day...	Sunday: 6:00PM - Monday: 6:00PM
Hebrew Day...	Fifth Day of The Week
Gregorian Day...	Sunday: 6:00PM - Monday: 6:00PM
Hebrew Day...	Sixth Day of The Week
Gregorian Day...	Sunday: 6:00PM - Monday: 6:00PM
Hebrew Day...	Seventh Day of The Week
Gregorian Day...	Sunday: 6:00PM - Monday: 6:00PM

A JEWISH MONTH

The Jewish month is composed of either 29 or 30 days, with an occasional day added to the months of Kislev and Heshvan; and the addition of 7 extra months called Adar II (following the 12th month of Adar). Adar Ii is added during the 3, 6, 8, 10, 11, 14 and 17 year in each 19 year Metonic cycle. Using a set of complicated rules of when to insert additional days, the lunar based Jewish calendar almost exactly balances a solar based year every 19 years.

Hebrew	English	Number	Length	Civil Equivalent
נִיסָן	Nissan	1	30 days	March-April
אִיָּיר	Iyar	2	29 days	April-May
סִיוָן	Sivan	3	30 days	May-June
תָּמוּז	Tammuz	4	29 days	June-July
אָב	Av	5	30 days	July-August
אֱלוּל	Elul	6	29 days	August-September
תִּשְׁרֵי	Tishri	7	30 days	September-October
חֶשְׁוָן	Cheshvan	8	29 or 30 days	October-November
כִּסְלֵו	Kislev	9	30 or 29 days	November-December
טֵבֵת	Tevet	10	29 days	December-January
שְׁבָט	Shevat	11	30 days	January-February
אֲדָר א	Adar I (leap years only)	12	30 days	February-March
אֲדָר אֲדָר ב	Adar (called Adar Beit in leap years)	12 (13 in leap years)	29 days	February-March

A Jewish month always consists of alternating 29 or 30 days, except Kislev and Cheshvan, which are periodically adjusted by one day. Months 7-12 (Nisan - Elul) never change.

THE JEWISH YEAR

A Jewish Civil year will consist of 12 months, starting with the month of Nisan and ending with the new moon of Tishri; except when an extra month (Adar II) is added after the 12th month of Adar. Adar II is added in 7 times in a 19 year Metonic cycle; in years 3, 6, 8, 10, 11, 14 and 17. A Jewish calendar which shows crop harvests in parallel with the 12 Jewish months is shown on the previous page. Note that the 13th month is shown as Vedar, which was later called Adar II. Understanding how the Jewish calendar operated is crucial to understanding when events occurred in ancient Israel and in the time of Christ.

HISTORICAL DEVELOPMENT OF THE JEWISH LUNAR CALENDAR

A *new moon* starts to form after the moon is completely dark, and a *full moon* occurs when it is fully visible. For discussion purposes, we will call the point at which the moon as viewed from earth is in perfect alignment with the sun a *molad*. In a perfect world, the subsequent time at which a small sliver of the moon could be observed as it passes through the *Waxing Crescent* would be a constant, but due to the orbit of the earth around the sun and the tilting of the earth's axis; it can take anywhere between 13 to 20 hours for a sliver of light to be seen from any one molad. Each Hebrew calendar month started with a new moon and it took about 15 days for a full moon to occur. Although not quite correct, a full molad to molad cycle was 29.5 days. The approximate time that the moon takes to start from one molad and move to the next was known from ancient times. However, the high priest would declare any one month to begin by a report from two reliable witnesses that the new crescent had been seen. Although this could never happen within 13 to 20 hours from when the actual molad occurred, this was a fairly good system. It is obvious to me, that after some point in time the varying time between any one monthly molad and when the first crescent of a new moon was seen could be fairly accurately predicted during any one month of the year. At some point in time, the priesthood was able to start each month by calculation and not observation. When this occurred is unknown, but we do know that the Babylonian empire was using accurate calculations to start each month by the time that Israel was released from exile around 539 BC. It is almost certain that when most of the Babylonian calendar was adopted after the exile ended that the rules were adopted also. The modern Jewish calendar is based entirely upon a rule based system to balance the solar year against the lunar year.

A new moon occurs when the moon is completely dark, and a full moon is when it is fully visible. This is called a *New Moon* and a *Full Moon*, respectively. For discussion purposes, we will call the point at which the moon as viewed from earth is in *perfect alignment* with the sun a *molad*. In a perfect world, the subsequent time at which a small sliver of the moon could be observed as it starts to pass through the *Waxing Crescent* would be a constant, but due to the orbit of the earth around the sun; it can take anywhere between 13 to 20 hours for this to be seen from any one molad. Each Hebrew calendar month started with a new moon and it took about 15 days for a full moon to occur.

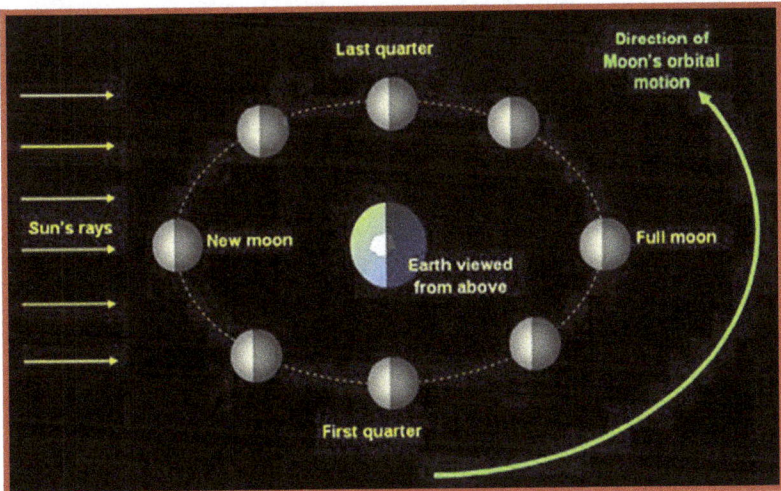

Although not quite correct, a full molad to molad cycle was about 29.5 days. The approximate time that the moon takes to start from one molad and move to the next was known from ancient times. However, the high priest would declare any one month to begin by a report from two reliable witnesses that the new crescent had been seen. Although off by 13 to 20 hours from when the actual molad occurred, this was a fairly good system. It is obvious to me, that after some point in time, the maximum and minimum amount of time between any one monthly *molad* and when the *first crescent* of a new moon was seen could be fairly accurately predicted.

At some point in time, the priesthood was able to start each month by calculation and not observation. When this occurred is unknown, but we do know that the Babylonian empire was using accurate calculations to start each month by the time that Israel was released from exile around 539 BC. It is almost certain that when most of the Babylonian calendar was adopted after the exile ended that the rules were adopted also. The modern Jewish calendar is based entirely upon a rule based system to balance the solar year against the lunar year. An ancient Greek astronomer named Meton of Athens, Greece discovered around 432 BC that 19 solar years was almost exactly equal to 6,940 days. He proposed that this relationship could be achieved by using 125 months of 30 days and 110 months of 29 days over a 19 year period of time. The 19 year base period of time became known as the **Metonic cycle.** The difference between these 235 months and a 19 solar years was only a few hours. By 380 BC, this cycle was adopted and used in the ancient Babylonian calendar. After the 70 year Babylonian exile of Israel ended in 539 BC, a Jewish calendar was created based almost entirely upon the Babylonian calendar. By 400 BC, the Levitical priesthood and the High priest had stabilized the calendar so that a basic calendar year consisted of 6 -30 day months and 6-29 day months. Over a period of 19 years it was found that if 7 extra months of 29 days were added then the Metonic cycle could be almost achieved. Notice that using this scheme; over a 19 year period of time there would be 114 months of 30 days and 121 months of 29 days.

This period of time is 6,929 days. Since a Metonic cycle was 125 months of 30 days and 110 months of 29 days this is a total of 6,940 days: Hence, the Jewish calendar would be 11 days short of a Metonic cycle. In order to match the Metonic cycle they then added 11 days over a 19 year period by periodically adding one day to either the month of Kislev or Cheshvan as shown by the Hebrew calendar which was shown previously in our discussion of a calendar month. . The sum of things is that every 19 years every date/day on the Hebrew calendar will reoccur on exactly the same day. It is not known (at least by me) how long they did this, but it turns out that in using this scheme, two Sabbath days (holy high days or regular Sabbath days) periodically occurred back to back. Since this placed a great burden on the Jewish people, some complicated rules called *postponements* were added to prevent this from happening. These rules were known only by known only by the high priest. The modern Jewish calendar uses these rules today.

The point of all this is to establish using known historical records the Jews had a sophisticated and very accurate calendar in place at least 300 years before the Reign of King Herod the great and the birth of Jesus Christ. We will prove that this is true when we establish the regnal years of King Herod in Chapter 5. For now, notice what Jonathan told David in I Samuel 20:18: *Tomorrow is the New Moon, and you will be missed because your seat is empty.* If the new moon was strictly determined by the observation of two reliable witnesses, how could Jonathan (and King David) know that the New moon was to arrive tomorrow? The answer is, of course, they could not! ... unless it had already been predicted to be tomorrow. It should be clear that the ancients knew about the movements of the moon and sun, and the almost exact length of a lunar month and a solar year. This is well attested to by the design of the Egyptian pyramids, the Mayan Temples and Stonehenge. Since the lunar and solar cycles have not changed since the Jewish calendar was accurately implemented, any Jewish date in antiquity can be determined for thousands of years back in time. There are several calendar conversion programs which can be used free on the internet. One we

9

particularly recommended for its accuracy and completeness is *Abdicate* at the *Shepherd's Website* (http://www.abdicate.net/cal.aspx).

SUMMARY

Sometime after the Jews returned from a 70 year deportation to Babylon, they formally adopted the Babylonian calendar, and it is my belief that they very accurately knew the duration of both a solar and lunar year (it was certainly known by the Egyptians and Babylonians). A new moon determines the first day of every Jewish month. As previously stated, in ancient times the beginning of each month was by observation and each month began on a command from the High Priest based upon when two reliable witnesses saw the first sliver of a new moon. Every year when the month of Adar ended, a decision was made on whether or not to insert an extra month (Adar II) between Adar and Nisan. This decision was based upon whether or not the corn and wheat had matured enough to support the Feast of Unleavened Bread, which started on Nisan 15. Well before 300-400 BC, it appears that observation gave way to a complicated set of rules known only to the Levitical priesthood and the High Priest. The basic rule is based upon the following observation. Every 19 years there are $(365.2422)(19)=6939.6$ days. Over that same period of time, the basic Jewish calendar would result in $(354)(19)=6726$ days. Left unadjusted, the Jewish lunar calendar would fall back against the solar calendar 213.6 days over this same period of time. This is almost exactly 7 lunar months of 30 days. Hence, it should be obvious that if 7 extra months of 30 days were inserted as Adar II months every 19 years, the Lunar Jewish calendar would return to the solar calendar every 19 years. In other words, if a 19 year cycle started on Nisan 1 and 7 extra months were added over the next 19 years, Nisan 1 exactly 19 Jewish years later would be on the same day on the Julian solar calendar. It was decided to add Adar II months in the 3rd, 6th, 8th, 11th, 14th, 17th and 19th years of the cycle. The mathematically inclined can verify that even when this is done, the Jewish calendar will lose only about 3 days every 19 years.

This scheme is still used today, with minor adjustments periodically to make the cycle exact.

It was necessary to discuss the Jewish calendar used during the lifetime of Christ, since it must be used when we show the month and year that Christ was born. In summary, during the 33.5 years that Christ lived there were two calendars in common use: The Jewish Lunar based calendar and the Julian solar based calendar. We will shortly prove with certainty that both had become synchronized as early as 63 BC.

Finally, many biblical researchers project the modern Gregorian calendar back through time, and then cross-reference it to the Jewish calendar. Since the modern Gregorian calendar was not implemented until 1582 BC, all projections further back in time simply relate what the Gregorian date would have been if the calendar existed. These artificial dates are called *Proleptic* dates. Between 45 BC and 1582 BC the calendar used in the Roman Empire, which included Israel, was the 365.25 day Julian solar calendar. Since our entire scope of interest is between 7 BC and 70 BC, we will use the Julian calendar when quoting monthly (January-December) and day dates (1-31). These will always be given with the Jewish calendar monthly designation for the same date (Nisan-Adar II) and the day of the week (Sunday-Saturday).

NOTES AND THINGS TO REMEMBER:

CHAPTER 2

THE SEVEN FEASTS OF ISRAEL

If the correct birth and death date of Jesus Christ is to be determined, it is necessary to understand the historical and prophetic meanings of the *Seven Feasts of Israel*. The seven feasts of Israel were ordained by God shortly after the law was given at Mt. Sinai following the exodus from Egypt. They were given for two reasons. The *first* was to commemorate the deliverance of Israel from Egyptian bondage and oppression. The *second* was to prophesy of seven events which will herald the first and second coming of Jesus Christ. We are particularly concerned with how the Seven Feasts of Israel were harbingers of both the birth and death of Jesus Christ.

The seven feasts and their appointed time on the ancient Hebrew calendar are shown in the following table.

	Feast	Hebrew Calendar Date
1	Passover (Pesah)	Nisan 14
2	Unleavened Bread	Nisan 15-21
3	Firstfruits (Weeks)	Lasts 50 days, starting on first Sunday during Feast of Unleavened Bread
4	Pentecost	50th day of Feast of Firstfruits
5	Trumpets (Rosh Hashanna)	Tishri 1
6	Yom Kippur (Atonement)	Tishri 10
7	Tabernacles (Booths)	Tishri 15-22 Tishri 22 is "Last Great day"

The *Seven Feasts of Israel* are divided into two separate seasons of the year. The Feasts of Passover, Firstfruits, Unleavened Bread and Pentecost all take place in the spring. The last three Feasts of Rosh Hashanah, Yom Kippur, and Tabernacles take place in the fall. The Feast of Unleavened Bread is a 7 day feast, and the Feast of Tabernacles is an 8 day feast. The feasts have a dual meaning; they commemorate the deliverance of the Hebrew nation from

Egyptian bondage, and they also prophesy of the first and second coming of Jesus Christ. The Hebrew word for feast is *moed* which means a *set time* or an *appointed time*. God has not only set an appointed time for each feast, he has also commanded that every male in Israel must be at the place of his choice (Jerusalem) for the Feasts of Passover, Unleavened Bread, Pentecost and Tabernacles. The feasts are also called a *holy convocation*. The Hebrew word for convocation means *rehearsal*. The implication is that God has commanded the Children of Israel to observe each feast at the *appointed time* as *a rehearsal* for seven things which will happen to Israel on those days. Looking back, it is now obvious that Jesus Christ fulfilled the first four feasts at His crucifixion between when He died on the cross of Calvary and when He sent the Holy Spirit to dwell in man on the Feast of Passover. The last three feasts will be fulfilled at the second advent of Christ. All seven feasts were divinely ordained by God and given to the nation of Israel for a perpetual observance. The historical and physical aspects of each feast will now be briefly discussed.

THE SPRING FEASTS OF ISRAEL

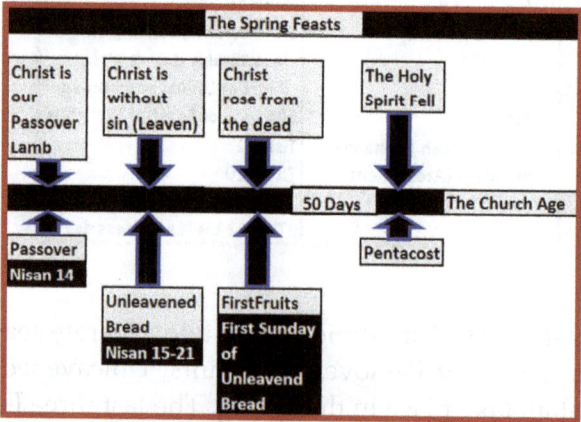

FEAST OF PASSOVER (NISAN 14)
The Feast of Passover is in remembrance of the night that the Hebrew nation left Egypt on Nisan 15 (Exodus 12:2-11). On

Nisan 10, God instructed the Children of Israel to select an unblemished lamb one year old and bring it into each house for four days. Each day the lamb was examined to make sure that it was still unblemished. On *Nisan 14* at 3:00 pm, they were instructed to slaughter the lamb and prepare it for the evening meal. The blood was to be caught in a bowl, and smeared over the lintel or over the door of each Hebrew house. The lamb was to be eaten that evening, which was the first few hours of Nisan 15. At midnight, the *Avenging Angel* of the Lord would pass over every house in Egypt. The firstborn male in any house without blood over the door would be killed, and the firstborn of all livestock outside the house would be killed (Gen 12:29). This was the event that caused the Pharaoh of Egypt to *let the people go* after his firstborn son was slain. The Feast of Passover was to commemorate and recall remembrance of this event for perpetual generations.

Spiritual Application

Jesus Christ arrived in Jerusalem on the afternoon of Nisan 8. Nisan 10 arrives after 6:00 pm, and He stays at the house of Mary, Martha and Lazarus exactly four days before He was to be crucified on Nisan 14. He was examined and scrutinized by the Sadducees and Pharisees who sought to discredit Him. He was found to be without spot or blemish. Pilate even declared: **Then said Pilate to the chief priests and to the people, I find no fault in this man** (Luke 23:4). Christ completely fulfilled the Feast of Passover when He was crucified on the cross of Calvary.

For even Christ our Passover is sacrificed for us.
I Corinthians 5:7

The next day John seeth Jesus coming unto him, and saith, Behold the Lamb of God, which taketh away the sin of the world.
John 1:29

The word *Passover* is literally translated *Lamb* and Christ is God's perfect Passover sacrificial lamb. He was both the sacrifice and the one who offered the sacrifice.

> *For even Christ our Passover is sacrificed for us.*
>
> I Corinthians 5:7

Our Lord Jesus Christ died for our sins at 3:00 pm on Nisan 14, at exactly the same time that the High Priest was killing the Passover Lamb in the temple. At that time the veil that separated the Holy Place from the Holy of Holies was *rent in two* from top to bottom, signifying that the Levitical sacrificial system had ended. The old covenant had passed away; the new covenant had come.

FEAST OF UNLEAVENED BREAD (NISAN 15-21)

The Feast of Unleavened Bread is a memorial to when the Children of Israel left Egypt in haste on the evening of Nisan 14, which was the night portion of Nisan 15. The Feast of Unleavened Bread started at 6:00 pm on Wednesday and continued for seven full days until 6:00 pm on Nisan 21. It is important to note that both Nisan 15 and Nisan 21 were designated as a *High Sabbath*. On these days there was to be no unleavened bread in any household. No servile work was to be done on these days, and if food is to be consumed it must be prepared by the family in their house. The Exodus from Egypt was sudden. In Exodus 12 we are told: **So the people took their dough before it was leavened, having their kneading bowls bound and in their clothes on their shoulders** (Exodus 12:34). When the Feast of Unleavened Bread was observed in subsequent years, starting with Nisan 15 there was to be no leavened bread at all in any household for seven days. All leaven was to be removed on or before Nisan 14. This was serious business.

> *For seven days no leaven shall be found in your houses, since whoever eats what is leavened, that same person shall be cut off from the congregation of Israel, whether he is a stranger or a native of the land.*
>
> Exodus 12:19

16

In Exodus 16:2, the Israelites complained that they had no food, so God miraculously provided *manna* to them every day. The manna was picked in the morning on Sunday-Friday. It only lasted one day; the manna picked on Friday morning lasted two days and then spoiled on the third day to honor the Jewish Sabbath (Saturday). Moses put a *pot of manna* into the Ark of the Covenant; it *never* spoiled.

Spiritual Application

In the scriptures, *leaven* is representative of *sin*. Our Lord Jesus Christ fulfilled all of the law. His life was perfect in every way. He was the unleavened, sinless bread from heaven. Since He was sinless, He was without *spot or blemish*. He was resurrected and lifted up to God, and He was an acceptable and perfect sacrifice to God.

> *Your glorying is not good. Know ye not that a little leaven leaveneth the whole lump? Purge out therefore the old leaven, that ye may be a new lump, as ye are unleavened. For even Christ our Passover is sacrificed for us.*
> I Corinthians 5:6-7

Our Lord Jesus Christ said that He was the Unleavened Bread which fulfilled the feast at the Lord's Last Supper.

> *And as they did eat, Jesus took bread, and blessed, and brake it, and gave to them, and said, Take, eat: this is my body.*
> Mark 14:22

> *And Jesus said unto them, I am the bread of life: he that cometh to me shall never hunger; and he that believeth on me shall never thirst.*
> John 6:35

He was also the *manna that never spoiled*, eternally perfect.

17

I am the living bread which came down from heaven: if any man eat of this bread, he shall live forever: and the bread that I will give is my flesh, which I will give for the life of the world.

This is that bread which came down from heaven: not as your fathers did eat manna, and are dead: he that eateth of this bread shall live forever.

John 6: 51,58

Christ was crucified on Nisan 14. He said *It is finished*, and died at 3:00 pm, at exactly the same time that the High Priest in Herod's Temple slaughtered the Passover lamb. Jesus was placed in the tomb just before the *Feast of Unleavened Bread* started at 6:00 pm on Wednesday night. Jesus was our perfect Passover Lamb, without spot or blemish. He was also the perfect *Bread of Life*, without leaven (sin).

FEAST OF FIRSTFRUITS

The Feast of Firstfruits is also called the *Feast of Weeks*. Unlike the Feast of Passover and the Feast of Unleavened Bread, it has a specific time when it is observed, but not a specific day of the month.

Speak unto the Children of Israel, and say unto them, When ye be come into the land which I give unto you, and shall reap the harvest thereof, then ye shall bring a sheaf of the firstfruits of your harvest unto the priest: And he shall wave the sheaf before the LORD, to be accepted for you: on the morrow after the Sabbath the priest shall wave it. And ye shall offer that day when ye wave the sheaf and the lamb without blemish of the first year for a burnt offering unto the LORD. And the meat offering thereof shall be two tenth deals of fine flour mingled with oil, an offering made by fire unto the LORD for a sweet savour: and the drink offering thereof shall be of wine, the fourth part of an hin. And ye shall eat neither bread, nor parched corn, nor green ears, until the selfsame day that ye have brought an offering unto your God: it shall be a statute forever throughout your generations in all your dwellings. And ye shall count unto you from the morrow after the sabbath, from the day that ye brought the sheaf of the wave offering; seven sabbaths shall be complete: Even unto the morrow after the seventh sabbath shall ye number fifty days; and ye shall offer a new meat offering unto the Lord.

Leviticus 23:10-16

The Feast of Firstfruits starts on the *morrow after the first normal Jewish Sabbath* which occurred during the Feast of Unleavened Bread. There was a raging battle between the Pharisees and the Sadducees as to what this means. The first day of the Feast of Unleavened Bread was a *Sabbaton*, a *High Sabbath*. The Pharisees held that the Feast of Firstfruits started on Nisan 16 every year, while the Sadducees maintained that it started on the day after the *weekly Sabbath* (Saturday).The above passage says that *seven Sabbaths must be complete* in the 50-day period. This seems to refer to seven complete weeks. This will happen every year if the feast starts on the Sunday following the only Sabbath (Saturday) of Unleavened Bread. Eventually the Sadducees prevailed but the controversy remained. The real key is in the spiritual fulfillment of this feast by Jesus Christ. Christ rose just as Saturday turned into Sunday at exactly 6:00 PM, and he is the *firstfruits* of the church, so the feast must also begin on a Sunday to satisfy typology. In the time of Jesus, the Feasts of Passover, Unleavened Bread and Firstfruits were considered to be one long feast season which was generally referred to as the *Passover Season*. It was not uncommon to refer to Passover and Unleavened Bread as simply *Passover*. The Feast of Firstfruits lasted 50 days and is observed in the spring. It signified the early maturation of the barley crop. The Feast of Firstfruits was ritually observed by all Jews throughout the temple eras. The *Firstfruit Offerings* were to both please God and to support the Levitical priesthood (Lev 23:10-17, Exodus 23:19, Deut 26:1-11). On the first day of the feast, a *sheaf of barley*, which was an omer (about 2 quarts), was to be picked from the fields and offered up to God as a wave offering. It was *waved before the Lord* in a sheaf.

Spiritual Application

The firstfruits sheaf was symbolic of the greater harvest to come, if it pleased the Lord. If the firstfruit was holy, then the entire harvest would be holy unto the Lord. Paul confirmed the spiritual intent of the firstfruit offering, and directly related it to the *root* (Israel) and the *branches* (the body of Christ).

> *For if the firstfruit be holy, the lump is also holy: and if the root be holy, so are the branches.*

> Romans 11:16

The first day firstfruit offering consecrated the entire harvest to the Lord. It was an *earnest offering* or a *pledge* of the full harvest which was yet to come. It was very important, because no barley from the field could be picked or eaten until the ceremony was completed. In fact, ancient tradition held that on Nisan 1 the High Priest would inspect the *barley in the ear*. The word Nisan actually means *green ear*. If the crop had not matured enough by Nisan 1 to pick a *wavesheaf* on Nisan 15, then an extra month of 29/30 days called *Adar II* would be immediately added to the year. While not exact, this was elegant in its simplicity. Periodic insertion of an extra month kept the Jewish lunar-based calendar from getting very far *out of sync* with the solar calendar and the agricultural seasons. It is not known when the *Metonic cycle* was discovered, and exact insertion rules were put into place, but a sophisticated system appeared to be in operation shortly after the Babylonian exile had ended (See Chapter 1)

> *The first of the firstfruits of thy land thou shalt bring unto the house of the LORD thy God.*

> Ex 34:26

How beautiful and prophetic was the firstfruit offering! Christ is everywhere present in the typology. The offering was to be made of *green ears* of corn that would be dried in the fire. Was not our Lord Jesus Christ *tried as if in the fire* by the Pharisees and Sadducees? Was He not tempted at every turn just as we are today? After being offered to the Lord, the dried corn was then to be *beaten* out of the ear for food for the Levites. Was not our Lord Jesus Christ *beaten and bruised* for our sins, and then accepted by God as the firstfruit offering? *Oil* was also to be poured over the firstfruits offering; did Jesus not pour out the *oil* of the Holy Spirit on the day of Pentecost? Today the Feast of Firstfruits is observed by Christians for one day only and is called *Easter*. It is appropriate that Christians observe the resurrection of our risen Savior, but the modern observance called *Easter* has been corrupted. The modern observance of Easter was initiated by the Roman Catholic Church, and received its name from the Babylonian goddess, *Ishtar*. Ishtar is the pagan god of fertility, love, and sex; and that is why eggs are a part of the modern Easter celebration. The same thing is true as to why rabbits are part of the pageantry. Although children use rabbits, colored eggs and green grass to celebrate Easter, adult Christians observe Easter as the day of our Lord's resurrection from the dead. Instead of calling this celebration *Easter*, we should call it *Firstfruits*. The festival is also called the *Feast of Weeks*, since it lasts exactly seven weeks (49 days) and one day. The 50th and final day is called *Shavuot* by the Jews. In 1491 BC the Children of Israel left Egypt during the night of Nisan 15 (Wednesday evening; Thursday on the Jewish calendar). Three days later they crossed the *Sea of Reeds*. They emerged on the other side a free nation, miraculously saved from the armies of the Pharaoh when God drowned all of the pursuers in the Red Sea. Fifty days later, they were given the law by God at Mt. Sinai. On the first day of the Feast of Firstfruits a remarkable thing happened. On that day, our Lord Jesus Christ rose from the grave: Three days and three nights after He was placed in the grave. Christ arose just as Sunday was *dawning* or about to start just at 6:00 pm. There is no proof in the scriptures that Christ rose from the grave just before daylight on Sunday morning. This is another story that the Catholic Church instituted. To be clear, there is no problem in celebrating Christ's resurrection at a *sunrise service* on Sunday morning, it is holy that we should do so. The point is that Christ rose early that previous evening, just as Sunday began Nisan 18, and not just before sunrise 12 hours later.

> *But now is Christ risen from the dead, and become the firstfruits of them that slept.*
>
> I Corinthians 15:20

21

Christ was the *First of the Firstfruits*. He was not the only person that had been resurrected from the dead; but he was the first to ascend to heaven, receive His glorified body, and not taste death again.

> *For if the firstfruit be holy, the lump is also holy: and if the root be holy, so are the branches.*
>
> Romans 11:16

Christ is the vine and we are the branches. Christ spoke of this during his earthly ministry.

> *And Jesus answered them, saying, the hour is come, that the Son of man should be glorified. Verily, verily, I say unto you, except a corn of wheat fall into the ground and die, it abideth alone: but if it die, it bringeth forth much fruit. He that loveth his life shall lose it; and he that hateth his life in this world shall keep it unto life eternal. If any man serve me, let him follow me; and where I am, there shall also my servant be: if any man serve me, him will my Father honour.*
>
> John 12:23-26

The Apostle Paul made an astonishing statement in his first letter to Corinth.

> *But now is Christ risen from the dead, and become the firstfruits of them that slept. For since by man came death, by man came also the resurrection of the dead. For as in Adam all die, even so in Christ shall all be made alive. But every man in his own order: Christ the firstfruits; afterward they that are Christ's at his coming. Then cometh the end, when he shall have delivered up the kingdom to God, even the Father; when he shall have put down all rule and all authority and power.*
>
> I Corinthians 15:20-24

Christ is clearly called the *firstfruits* of all that *slept* (died). He then goes on to say that following Christ there will one day be a resurrection of the dead. After that, the end (of the age) will come and all *powers, authorities and rulers* will be put under His feet. There is no indication whatsoever that there will be a seven-*year* period of time between when the resurrection of the dead will occur and the *end*.

PENTECOST

The last day of the Feast of Firstfruits is called *Shavuot*, which we call *Pentecost*. Jewish tradition teaches that on the day of Pentecost the law was given to Israel on Mt. Sinai. There were 50 days that elapsed between when the Children of Israel emerged a new nation out of the Sea of Reeds, and when the law was given on Mt. Sinai. The word *Pentecost* is derived from the Greek word *Penta*, which means fifty. Israel departed Egypt on Nisan 15, and emerged from the Sea of Reeds three days later. This is exactly the same day that Jesus Christ emerged from the grave. In typology, a Friday crucifixion declared by the Roman Catholic Church and the subsequent resurrection from the grave on Sunday is impossible. The Israelites had to move quickly and take a full three days between when they left Egypt and when they arrived at the Red Sea. There is simply no getting around a *full* three-day journey. In order to satisfy type, Christ was in the grave for a *full* three days and three nights. The Children of Israel then traveled 47 days until they finally reached Mt. Sinai. The Lord told the people to sanctify themselves for two days (Gen 19:10), and on the *third* day He would come down to them in a cloud. On the *50th day* after emerging from the Red Sea the Lord kept his promise and appeared to the people. A *Shofar* (trumpet made of the rams horn) was loudly sounded: louder, and louder, and louder until *fire* was seen on the mountain. A mighty wind blew and the ground shook as if an earthquake was going to occur. At that point God began to deliver the law to Moses and the nation of Israel. It is taught that every nation and every tongue heard the Lord in their own language. According to tradition, there was the Hebrew language and 69 other languages spoken throughout the world. In a miraculous and divine act, the voice of God was divided into *70 different tongues*. It is also taught by the Rabbis that as God spoke, the Children of Israel not only heard the words but actually saw each word emerging from the cloud as *tongues of fire*. The words encircled the camp and then entered each person individually. After each commandment was given, God asked: **Do you accept upon yourself this commandment?** and everyone present answered *yes*. The tongues of fire then fell upon stone tablets and the words of the law were recorded. The Jewish Feast of Shavuot on the 50th day commemorates these events (Joseph Good)

Spiritual Application
When Christ ascended from the grave he commanded his disciples to *go unto Jerusalem* and wait for Him to come to them.

> *And when the day of Pentecost was fully come, they were all with one accord in one place. And suddenly there came a sound from heaven as of a rushing mighty wind, and it filled all the house where they were sitting. And there appeared unto them cloven tongues like as of fire, and it sat upon each of them. And they were all filled with the Holy Ghost, and began to speak with other tongues, as the Spirit gave them utterance. And there were dwelling at Jerusalem Jews, devout men, out of every nation under heaven. Now when this was noised abroad, the multitude came together, and were confounded, because that every man heard them speak in his own language.*
>
> Acts 2:1-6

What an amazing event!! On the very day that God gave the law to the people on Mt. Sinai, Jesus Christ gave the Holy Spirit to his chosen people. The falling of the Holy Spirit at Pentecost in 30 AD almost exactly paralleled the giving of the law 1500 years earlier. The law was written on tablets of stone. The *old covenant* was based upon man fulfilling the law, which was impossible. The *new covenant* was based upon grace, and written on the heart of man. The impossible task of living a perfect life under the law was fulfilled in every way by our Lord Jesus Christ, who then imputed His righteousness to all who believed in His name. Only Jesus Christ fulfilled every *"jot and tidle"* of the law. He was our *perfect Passover sacrifice for sin*, the Lamb of God. He was the *Firstfruits* offering waved before the Lord by Christ himself. He was both the *offerer* and the *offering*, our eternal High Priest. The old covenant that God had established with His people required obedience to the Old Testament Mosaic law. Because the wages of sin is death (Romans 6:23), the law required that people perform rituals and sacrifices in order to please God and temporarily cover their sins. The prophet Jeremiah predicted that there would be a time when God would make a new covenant with the nation of Israel.

> *The day will come* said the Lord, *when I will make a new covenant with the people of Israel and Judah... But this is the new covenant I will make with the people of Israel on that day, says the Lord. I will put my law in their minds, and I will write them on their hearts. I will be their God, and they will be my people.*
>
> Jeremiah 31:31, 33.

Jesus Christ came to fulfill all of the Law of Moses (Matt 5:17) and create a new covenant between God and His people. He is now our High Priest who sits on the throne of God and continually intercedes for us.

> *This is the covenant that I will make with them after those days, saith the Lord, I will put my laws into their hearts, and in their minds will I write them.*
>
> Hebrews 10:16

The old covenant was written in stone, but the new covenant is written on our hearts, made possible only by faith in Christ, who shed His own blood to atone for the sins of the world.

> *And he took bread, and gave thanks, and brake it, and gave unto them, saying, This is my body which is given for you: this do in remembrance of me. Likewise also the cup after supper,*

saying, this cup is the new testament in my blood, which is shed for you.

Luke 22:19-20

Now that we are under the new covenant, we are not under the penalty and curse of the law. We are now given the opportunity to receive salvation as a free gift (Eph 2:8-9) by grace and not by works. Through the life-giving Holy Spirit who lives in all believers (Romans 8:9-11), we can now share in the inheritance of Christ.

> *For this reason Christ is the mediator of a new covenant, that those who are called may receive the promised eternal inheritance — now that He has died as a ransom to set them free from the sins committed under the first covenant.*

Hebrews 9:15

SUMMARY OF THE FOUR (SPRING) FEASTS OF ISRAEL

The spring feasts of Israel are (1) Passover, (2) Unleavened Bread, (3) First Fruits and (4) Pentecost. Each of these feasts was to provide historical and prophetic truth to the Children of Israel. Christ fulfilled each of these first four feasts at the end of his 3.5 year earthly ministry. *Passover*: Christ was the perfect Passover Lamb, slain from the foundation of the world. *Unleavened Bread*: Christ was without sin (leaven). He fulfilled the laws given to Moses by God in every way. He is our *bread of life*, and whosoever will eat of His bread will never hunger. *Firstfruits*: Christ was the perfect firstfruits offering waved before the Lord and fully accepted. He was the *first* to be raised from the grave never to die again. *Pentecost*: Christ ratified the *new covenant* on the Feast of Pentecost 50 days after he arose from the grave, He offered the Holy Spirit as our comforter and guarantee. Salvation is now offered free to all who believe that Jesus Christ is the only Son of God. The curse of the law has been replaced by amazing grace. We who are now called *Christians* can live life *more abundantly*. Every feast was a *moed*, a *set time* or an *appointed time*. The feasts are also called a *holy convocation*. The Hebrew word for convocation means *rehearsal*. Paul referred to this:

> Let no one judge you in food or in drink, or regarding a festival or a new moon or Sabbaths, which are a shadow of things to come, but the substance is of Christ.
>
> Col 2:16-17

It is more than interesting that God commanded that every Jewish male appear in Jerusalem at the Feasts of Unleavened Bread; the Feast of Pentecost; and the Feast of Tabernacles (Ex 23:14, Deut 16:6). God was not only calling Israel to a time of remembrance, but he was preparing Israel for the appearance of their long-awaited Messiah in the person of Jesus Christ. All males were to witness the crucifixion of Christ (Passover) in 30 AD which was the day before the Feast of Unleavened Bread Started at 6:00 PM). The *Parakletos* (Holy Spirit) fell on the Feast of Shavuot (Pentecost); All Jewish males (and their families) who will accept Christ as their savior will be required to participate in the last Feast of Tabernacles to celebrate Christ's victory at Armageddon (Zach 14:16-19). It is strange that after all that was prophesied in the Old Testament, and all that was written by the prophets of His ministry here on earth, that the Children of Israel failed to recognize or accept Christ as their long awaited Messiah. We have shown how Christ satisfied and fulfilled each of the four spring Feasts of Israel at exactly the appointed times and on exactly the appointed days. This fulfillment of prophecy cannot be misunderstood by either Jew or Gentile if carefully studied.

We will now briefly review the last three annual feasts of Israel (1) *The Feast of Rosh Hashanah (Feast of Trumpets)*; (2) *The Feast of Yom Kippur (Feast of Yom Teruah)* and (3) *The Feast of Tabernacles (Feast of Booths)*.

Date	Feast	Typology	Fulfillment
Nisan 10	The Passover Lamb is Selected. *"Bring an unblemished Lamb into the house on Nisan 10, Four days before it is to be slain And inspect it for spot or blemish"*	God commands Israel in Egypt to select a Passover Lamb for slaughter on Nisan 14.	Jesus, the perfect Lamb of God, arrives in Bethany four days Before his crucifixion. He stood In the temple each day and was questioned by the Pharisees and Sadducees to find fault in him.
Nisan 15	First day of the Feast of Unleavened bread. A loaf of bread is baked from the Firstfruits of Barley (Old Testament Saints); prepared with no leaven, and offered to the Lord *"with fire."*	The Pharaoh let *"the Children of Israel go"* after his firstborn son was slain. The departure is in haste. The bread they took with them was unleavened.	Christ lay in the grave the first day. He is the *"loaf without leaven"*. He said *"I am the bread of life"*. He is the *"first"* and only to live a sinless life under the law. John said he will *"baptize you with water and fire."*
Nisan 15-21	The Feast of Unleavened Bread lasted 7 days. Both the first and last day of the feast were *"high holy days"*	The Children of Israel ate unleavened bread until God gave them *"manna"* from heaven.	Christ said "I am the Bread of Life". He was the true bread without leaven. He was sinless and blameless.
First Sunday in the Feast of Firstfruits (Feast of Weeks)	Feast of Firstfruits starts on this day…always a Sunday. The Feast lasts 50 days. Every day a sheath of the emerging wheat crop is *"waved"* before the Lord.	On this day the Children of Israel crossed over the Red Sea, and was saved from death at the Pharaoh's hand. They emerged a new Nation under God.	Christ arose from the dead on this day. He was the *"Firstfruit"* unto God of all who will someday also rise from the grave by believing upon His name.

Last Sunday of the Feast of Firstfruit	The Feast of Pentecost or Shavuot. "Penta" means fifty. Pentecost occurs 50 days after the first Sabbath (Saturday) in the Feast of Unleavened bread.	The Nation of Israel received the law from God at Mt. Sinai. The law was written on tablets of stone. The Levitical Priesthood was established. The High Priest was anointed to serve as the intercessor between man and God	On the Day of Pentecost Christ fulfilled his promise to leave with us the Holy Spirit. On Pentecost the Holy Spirit fell on the disciples and 5,000 people were saved. The new covenant based upon grace replaced the old covenant based upon the law. This new law of grace is written in the heart and not in stone

THE FALL FEASTS OF ISRAEL

We have seen how Christ fulfilled each of the four spring feasts of Israel at his first coming. It is not difficult to believe that He will also fulfill each of the last three feasts of Israel at his second coming. It remains to be seen exactly when this will be accomplished, but the prophetic fulfillment and relevance of each feast can be determined. The last three feasts are partly concealed. Since all of the feasts are Jewish in nature, we would be wise to examine what Jewish tradition has to say about the last three feasts. In doing so, we will unveil a better understanding of how we might expect the age of grace to come to an end. If Christ is going to satisfy the last three feasts at his *Second Advent*, we can say with certainty that this will come to pass at the end of Daniel's last and 70th week. The prophetic fulfillment of the last three feasts can only occur as Christ returns to the earth to initiate His eternal kingdom; set up His throne in Jerusalem; and purge all evil from the nations. The three fall feasts are:

(1) *The Feast of Rosh Hashanah* (Feast of Trumpets);
(2) *The Feast of Yom Kippur* (Feast of Yom Teruah)
(3) *The Feast of Tabernacles* (Feast of Booths).

The three fall feasts all occur in the Jewish month of *Tishri*. Tishri is the first month of the *Jewish Civil Calendar* and the seventh month of the Jewish religious calendar. All three feasts will occur in a 22-day period of time in one of the Gregorian calendar months of September or October. Like the spring festivals, they are closely aligned and associated with the agricultural cycle. The month of *Nisan* brings forth the new crops of barley (Jews) and wheat (Gentiles). The month of Tishri ushers in the final harvest of wheat, corn, grapes and figs. Both the spring and fall festivals require rain to bring the precious fruit of the earth into full maturity.

> *Therefore be patient, brethren, until the coming of the Lord. See how the farmer waits for the precious fruit of the earth, waiting patiently for it until it receives the early and the latter rain.*
>
> James 5:7

The early rains fell on the newborn body of Christ on the day of Pentecost in 30 AD. We have been patiently waiting for the *latter rains* to fall when Christ returns for His second advent. As

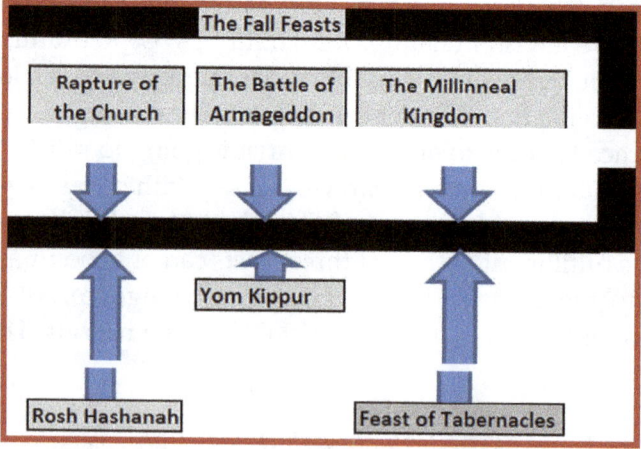

The Fall Feasts

Rapture of the Church | The Battle of Armageddon | The Millinneal Kingdom

Yom Kippur

Rosh Hashanah | Feast of Tabernacles

previously noted, the feasts represent both historical and spiritual significance. Historically they represent significant events that occurred when God chose Moses to lead His people

30

out of Egyptian bondage. Spiritually, each feast is a rehearsal or an appointment that God has made for Jesus Christ at His second advent.

There is an interesting correlation between the civil and the religious calendar. The civil calendar starts in September or October on Tishri 1. This is said to be the birthday of the creation of the world and the day on which Abraham was born. It is also when the wheat crop came to fullness and was harvested. The religious calendar begins in the month of March/April on Nisan 1. Nisan 1 is when the barley crop was coming into maturity and the wheat crop was starting to really grow. For those who have accepted the vicarious sacrifice of Jesus Christ on Nisan 14, the promise of resurrection from the dead and the gift of the Holy Spirit to every believer, the month of Nisan represents new beginnings in their spiritual relationship with Jesus Christ.

As we have already observed, there are almost 120 days between the Feast of *Pentecost* and the Feast of *Rosh Hashanah*. This is the long growing season for the precious crop of wheat. The wheat maturing and growing to the harvest is a shadow and type of the church age. The body of Christ is growing and one day God will declare that the harvest season is near. We will not be surprised when the *war in the heavenlies* is seen (Rev 12) and Satan is cast down to the earth. At that time we will know that the tribulation period has begun. It is a fallacy that believers will not know when the end is approaching. There will be plenty of heavenly and earthly signs for those who are watching. It is certainly true that only God will know when the tribulation period will begin and on what calendar day the church age will end, but Paul in his first letter to the Thessalonians assured them that while the end will come suddenly, they were not to be unaware of what is about to happen. If this was true then, it is true now.

But concerning the times and the seasons, brethren, you have no need that I should write to you. For you yourselves know perfectly that the Day of the Lord so comes as a thief in the night. For when they say "peace and safety" then sudden destruction comes upon

31

them, as labor pains upon a pregnant woman. And they shall not escape. But you, brethren, are not in darkness, so that this day should overtake you as a thief.

I Thessalonians 5:1-4

Notice that the apostle Paul is not denying that destruction and the Day of the Lord will come suddenly, but he emphatically and clearly assures them that they will not be surprised. Why would Paul assure them (and us) of this if it is not true? One thing should be pointed out which is highly relevant to our study. In the Jewish mind, the Feasts of Rosh Hashanah, Yom Kippur and Tabernacles are separate feasts, but the Jews consider this time of year to form one season containing the three feasts, just as the first four feasts were generally called Passover.

THE FEAST OF TRUMPETS (ROSH HASHANAH)

The next feast of Israel that Christ is appointed to fulfill is commonly known as the *Feast of Trumpets*. What will this feast ultimately accomplish according to Jewish teaching? The answer might surprise most Christian readers. Sometime in the future, the Feast of Trumpets will be a time of great joy. The following events are taught to occur on the last Feast of Trumpets.

> ➤ The long-awaited Messiah of Israel will finally come on that day,
> ➤ The dead will be raised and given a body just like that of Adam and Eve before the fall,
> ➤ The earth will be restored to its former Edenic state,
> ➤ All men will be judged at this time,
> ➤ The Wedding Feast of the Messiah will take place,
> ➤ God's covenant with Israel concerning inheriting the land of promise will finally come to pass.

According to Jewish tradition, this *final Feast of Trumpets* will be initiated by the blast of a *shofar*. The *shofar* is not a normal horn, but is said to have been reserved for this special occasion since the *binding of Isaac*. Recall that God commanded Abraham to

32

sacrifice his only son of promise, Isaac. As Abraham raised his knife to kill his son, God stayed his hand and delivered a ram as the substitute sacrifice. The ram was to be burned completely as a *burnt offering*. The only thing left was the two ram's horns. The *first horn* was said to have been blown on Mt. Sinai when the law was given; the *second horn* is reserved for the *last trump* at the last Feast of Rosh Hashanah (Trumpets). A special season which includes the Feast of Trumpets is called *Teshuvah*. It begins on the first day of the month of *Elul*, which immediately precedes the month of *Tishri*. Teshuvah lasts 40 days, and ends on the Feast of Yom *Kippur* (Tishri 10). The Feast of Trumpets starts 30 days into the season of *Teshuvah* on Tishri 1. It is relevant that every morning during the month of Elul, a trumpet is sounded to warn all the people that the time has come to repent of their sins and return to God. Ask any orthodox Jew what the *last trump* means in relation to the ancient feasts of Israel and the period of Teshuvah, and he will immediately respond the last trump is the *shofar*, which will be blown at the last Feast of Rosh Hashanah. *On the last Feast of Trumpets,* it is taught that there are several books which will be opened. The first is the *Book of Remembrance*.

> *Then they that fear the Lord spake often to one another: and the Lord hearkened, and heard it, and a Book of Remembrance was written before him for them that feared the Lord, and that thought upon his name.*
>
> Malachi 3:16

The second is actually *three sets of books*. Those who have committed to God and turned to righteousness are written in the *Book of the Righteous* or the *Book of Life* for the coming year. All other people living and dead are then divided into two groups. The first group is written into a book called the *Book of Rashim*, or the *Book of the Totally Wicked*. These are those who have totally rejected God and would not turn away from unrighteousness. The third or *last book* contains the names of those still alive who are not yet judged to be totally wicked, but have not yet fully repented and returned to God. Those people will have *ten more days* before their fate is sealed. These 10 days are called the *Days of Awe* and are the days between Nisan 1 and Nisan 10. The *Feast of Yom Kippur* occurs on only one day: Nisan 10. For this reason, the Feast of Yom Kippur is called the *Day of Judgment*. If these *gleanings* left in the *field* do not repent and turn away from sin by Tishri 10, their names will not be inscribed in the **Book of Life** for the coming year.

THE FEAST OF YOM KIPPUR (ATONEMENT)

The Feast of Yom Kippur is on Tishri 10, which is also known as the *Feast of Atonement*. This day was a *holy convocation* and it was also a day of *fasting*. It was being observed when Nadab and Abihu, the two sons of Aaron, filled a censor with *profane fire* and used it to offer up incense in the Holy Place. Fire (coals) was not to be used at the Altar of Incense unless it came from the Brazen Altar. After their death, Aaron the high priest was told that he could not come before the Lord in the Holy of Holies without observing strict laws put down by God (Lev 16). The only day of the year that the high priest could come before God was on the *Day of Atonement*. On that day he would make a sacrifice for his sins, and then for the sins of the people. It was also on this day that two goats were chosen for a special offering to the Lord. One goat was for a sin offering unto the Lord, the other was to be led away into the wilderness and pushed over a high cliff outside of Jerusalem. This was called the *scapegoat*. The high priest would choose which goat would be the scapegoat by using the *Urim* and the *Thummin*. Once the scapegoat was chosen, a red scarlet cloth was tied around his horns, and the high priest would place his hands on the scapegoat, symbolically transferring the sins of the people to that goat. The scapegoat was then led away to a high cliff outside of the city and pushed to its death, symbolically representing the *removal of sin from the people*. The other goat was then sacrificed and his blood caught in a bowl. After cleansing himself again, the high priest would sprinkle the blood on the *Altar of Incense*, and then enter into the *Holy of Holies* behind the veil which separated the Holy Place from the Holy of Holies, where the Ark of the Covenant stood. The High Priest would come before the Ark and sprinkle the blood *seven times* on the *mercy seat*. The High Priest would then plead the sins of the people to God, who would come and dwell above the mercy seat in a cloud (Gaster). This is clearly a picture of Jesus Christ. He was *the scapegoat* who was led outside the city and put to death. Like the scapegoat, He took the sins of the world upon himself. *He who knew no sin became sin for us.* He was also the *sin offering* represented by the second goat. His precious blood was shed for us; it was sprinkled on everyone from Adam to the millennial kingdom, and He sprinkled it Himself before the throne of God for the sins of all mankind. Jesus was *both* the sacrifice and the one who offered the sacrifice. He is now our High Priest who continuously intercedes for us as He sits on the right hand side of God the Father on His throne. At his sacrificial death, the veil in the temple which separated man from God was rent in two, from top to bottom. This represented that there was no longer a separation of the people from God, but now by the blood of Jesus Christ we can boldly go before the Throne of God in the presence of Jesus Christ who intercedes for us. He is both our *redeemer* and our *High Priest.* In one person at one cross, Christ was both the scapegoat for all our sins, and the blood offering to God. The writer of Hebrews spoke of the necessity for a blood sacrifice.

> *And almost all things are by the law purged with blood; and without shedding of blood is no remission.*
>
> Hebrews 9:22

> *Now where remission of these is, there is no more offering for sin.*
>
> Hebrews 10:18

The Feast of Yom Kippur terminates a 40-day period called *Teshuvah.* It begins on the first day of the 12th Jewish month of the civil calendar called *Elul.* The 30 days in Elul which precedes the Feast of Trumpets is a time when all Jews are to repent of their sins so that their name will be inscribed in the *Book of the Righteous.* As previously mentioned, the 10 days between the Feat of Trumpets on Tishri 1 and Tishri 10 are known as the *Days of Repentance* or the *Days of Awe.* This 10 day period is the last chance that a person has to humble himself before God and repent of their sins for the previous year. On Yom Kippur, an individual's fate is sealed. At the last Feast of Yom Kippur, this will be a permanent and eternal fate. Jewish tradition teaches that at this time all persons will be held accountable for his/her sins. Perhaps of more significance to this study is the belief that on Yom Kippur the long-awaited Messiah of the Jews is expected to establish his earthly kingdom in Jerusalem. Jewish tradition holds that the Feast of Trumpets will begin the 1000-year millennial kingdom of Christ.

THE FEAST OF TABERNACLES (BOOTHS)

The Feast of Tabernacles is an eight-day feast. It occurs between Nisan 15-Nisan 22. King Solomon dedicated his new temple on the feast of Tabernacles. The temple of David was constructed for the Lord to come and *tabernacle* or dwell for a short time with man. It is the last of the three fall feasts, and it follows the Feast of Yom Kippur. The historical significance of the feast is well understood. It commemorates the Exodus from Egypt, and the 40 years of wandering in the wilderness, in which the Hebrew nation dwelled in temporary tents called *booths*. The feast is sometimes called the *Feast of Booths*. The English equivalent of the Latin word for tabernacle is *hut*. A third name for the full eight-day feast is the *Feast of Ingathering* (Exodus 23:16). Harvest of the fall crops of wheat, figs and grapes are all completed at this time. The Feast of Tabernacles is one of the three annual feasts at which every male Hebrew is commanded to attend in Jerusalem. The other two were the Feast of Passover and the Feast of Weeks (Exodus 23:17, 34:22, Deut 16:16). The feast is marked by celebration and praise to the Lord for both providing the crop just harvested, and for His provisions of quail, manna, and fresh water throughout the 40-year sojourn of the Exodus in the wilderness. During the seven days between Nisan 15 and Nisan 21, the people live in temporary dwellings typically constructed of palm leaves and willow branches. This is a time of great celebration and introspection of God's goodness.

During the seven days beginning on Tishri 15, there were typically three daily acts of praise; (1) the people were to wave

36

branches before the Lord (Lev 23); (2) there were daily sacrificial offerings (Num 29); and, (3) the entire law was to be read in public gatherings. The entire 24 courses of priests were all put into service during this week. The last day of the feast is called *Shemini Atzeret*, referred to in the scriptures as simply the *eighth day of assembly* (Num 29:35). The term Shemini Atzaret is historically interpreted as *tarry or stay another day*. However, the Jewish emphasis on staying one more day as a request is not scripturally correct. The eighth day is ordained by God, and to stay is not an option but a command. The eighth day is primarily directed to the *Tefillat Geshem* or the *prayer for rain*. The months following Tishri are particularly critical to a successful planting season and a successful growing season. The *early rains* came during this time and nourished the emerging crops. According to Jewish tradition, God decides at the Feast of Tabernacles on the eighth day whether He will provide abundant rain or little rain in the coming months. The *latter rains,* which occurred just before the month of Nisan, enabled the crops to mature to fullness. The first and second coming of our Lord Jesus Christ was equated to the early and latter rains, which clearly reflected the Holy Spirit falling during his *first advent* and the pouring out of the Spirit of the Lord in the latter days at His *second advent.*

> *Be patient therefore, brethren, unto the coming of the Lord. Behold, the husbandman waiteth for the precious fruit of the earth, and hath long patience for it, until he receive the early and latter rain.*
>
> James 5:7

> *And it shall come to pass afterward, that I will pour out my spirit upon all flesh; and your sons and your daughters shall prophesy, your old men shall dream dreams, your young men shall see visions. And also upon the servants and upon the handmaids in those days will I pour out my spirit.*
>
> Joel 2:28-29

The requirement for the Lord to be satisfied and produce an abundance of the early and latter rains dominated the temple services each day. Every morning in the temple the High Priest would go to the Pool of Siloam and fill a pitcher full of water. He would return to the temple among the people waving palm branches and reciting Isaiah 12:3: *With joy shall ye draw water out of the wells of salvation.* He would then enter the temple and pour the water out on the Altar of Sacrifice as all the people waved palm branches in the air as an offering to the Lord for His favor. It was during this sacred ceremony on the last day of the feast that Christ arose, stood in front of all the people and shocked them all by loudly proclaiming: *If any man thirst let him come unto me, and drink. He that believeth on me, as the Scripture hath said, out of his belly shall flow rivers of living water.* Christ boldly spoke of when after his resurrection that the Holy Spirit would fall on all believers. This was the water that would continuously provide sustenance and never dry up.

A special season which ends on Yom Kippur is called *Teshuvah.* It begins on the first day of the month of *Elul,* which immediately precedes the month of *Tishri.* Teshuvah lasts 40 days, and ends on the Feast of Yom Kippur (Nisan 10). The Feast of Trumpets starts 30 days into the season of Teshuvah. It is relevant that every morning during the month of Elul, a trumpet is sounded to warn all the people that the time has come to repent of their sins and return to God. The first day of the feast (Tishri 15) and the last day of the feast (Tishri 22) are both *High Sabbaths.* There could be no work done on these days, and travel was limited to a Sabbath-day's journey. The cool evenings during this time were spent in a festive celebration. Every night there were torches lit everywhere to provide light. Dancing, rejoicing and banquets were enjoyed every evening into the wee hours of the morning. It was a time of pure joy. Tradition has it that no celebration in all of ancient Israel could compare to that which took place during the Feast of Tabernacles, and no single day could compare to the last day. The rabbis wrote: *He that hath not beheld the joy of this celebration had never experienced real joy in his life* (Joseph Good).

Jesus was undoubtedly referring to this joy when He spoke of the light that He can bring to all people.

> *Then spake Jesus again unto them, saying, I am the light of the world: he that followeth me shall not walk in darkness, but shall have the light of life.*
>
> John 8:12

A detailed study of the Feast of Tabernacles is both an enlightening and rewarding study. There are many shadows and types of Jesus Christ in this eight-day feast. The Feast of Tabernacles has significant application to the second coming of Jesus Christ and His initiation of the millennial kingdom. After His second advent and the battle of Armageddon, the 144,000 Hebrews who have been sealed to enter the millennial kingdom; the remnant who have survived the seven bowl judgments; survivors of the sheep and goat judgment; the Bride of Christ and all glorified believers will rest at a great Feast of Tabernacles. It is also interesting that of all the seven feasts, only the Feast of Tabernacles is mentioned as continuing over the 1000 year Millennial Kingdom.

> *And it shall come to pass, that every one that is left of all the nations which came against Jerusalem shall even go up from year to year to worship the King, the LORD of hosts, and to keep the Feast of tabernacle.*
>
> Zech. 14:16

For a detailed study of how the last 3 feasts are satisfied in the last 3.5 years of the church age, which is called the *Great Tribulation* see Phillips, *The Book of Revelation: Mysteries Revealed*.

SUMMARY OF THE SEVEN FEASTS OF ISRAEL

We have given a brief overview of the 7 Feasts of Israel. For the 4 spring feasts, we have offered a discussion of both the physical and spiritual meanings of each feast since each was satisfied at the first coming of Christ. All seven feasts are *rehearsals* for seven

39

appointments that have been ordained since time began for our Lord Jesus Christ. The first four (spring) feasts were fulfilled at the first advent of Christ, and the last three (fall) feasts will be fulfilled at the rapture of the church and at the second advent of Christ. Collectively, all seven feasts provide a *blueprint* for the work that Christ will accomplish. During the 3.5 year ministry of Christ, many important events occurred on the feast days. We will shortly see that Christ was born and died on a feast day.

The three tables on the next page provide a concise overview of both the spring and fall feasts, along with their Christian meanings.

The Seven Feasts of Israel

The Spring Feasts

Feast	Date	Prophetic Significance
Passover	Nisan 14	Redemption and Salvation. Christ is our perfect Passover Lamb. The new Covenant replaces the Old Covenant
Unleavened Bread	Nisan 15-Nisan 21	Sanctification. Christ was without sin. He is the Bread of Life
Firstfruits	First Sunday of Unleavened Bread	Resurrection and eternal life. Christ rose from the grave and conquered death
Weeks (Pentecost)	Lasts 50 days. Starts on Firstfruit. Pentecost is 50th Day (Always a Sunday)	Spiritual maturity. Power and the Holy Spirit

The Fall Feasts

Feast	Date	Prophetic Significance
Trumpets	Tishri 1	Rapture of the saints and Resurrection of the Dead. Wedding of the Lamb. Bema Seat Judgement
Yom Kippur	Tishri 10	Second Coming of Christ. Armageddon. Defeat of Satan, the Antichrist & False Prophet. Judgement of the nations
Tabernacles	Tishri 15- Tishri 21	Millenial Kingdom. Temple is Cleansed. Tribulation Martyers Raised
	Tishri 22	Sabbath and the "Great Day"

Christian Meaning : *Feasts of Israel*

Feast	Christian Meaning	Key Concept
Passover	Justification	Crucifixion
Firstfruits	Sanctification	Victory over Death
Unleavened Bread	Glorification	Sinless, Perfect Sacrifice
Pentecost	Power	Holy Spirit Fell
Trumpets	Transformation & Resurrection	Rapture of Church
Yom Kippur	Battle of Armageddon	Vctory over Satan
Tabernacles	Rule and Reign with Christ	1000 Year Millennial Kingdom

CHAPTER 3

THE STAR OF BETHLEHEM

From ancient times, man has been studying the planets and the stars as part of almost every culture. The monoliths that still exist as part of the Stonehenge ruins have been decoded to reveal that they were built to predict the changing of seasons; particular the summer and winter solstices. The pyramids in Egypt serve similar purposes, and are perfectly aligned with significant heavenly constellations and stars. The Mayans of Central America and the Yucatan Peninsula built magnificent temples to predict the planting seasons and to worship imaginary gods in the heavens. To modern man, the stars and planets are simply romantic settings to enjoy with someone special. However, ancient cultures spent an enormous amount of time and energy studying the stars and planets. To ancient cultures, the stars held the key to predicting and heralding significant events; both prophetic and emerging. It was in this setting that the Magi arose as powerful and respected soothsayers in Babylonia, China and Persia during the time of Christ birth. To Kings and Princes, these people were religious leaders, interpreters of dreams and sophisticated astronomers. The movements of the stars, planets, moon and sun were used to set the time of celebrations, festivals, sowing and reaping, and important religious ceremonies. When unusual or spectacular events occurred in the heavenlies, they always caused great excitement and commanded great attention.

To modern Christians, the mention of a biblical *star* has always been identified with one heavenly and historical event: the *Birth of Jesus Christ*. The Birth of Jesus Christ is in turn closely linked to the *Star of Bethlehem*. Each is closely entwined with the other, and to identify when the Star of Bethlehem arose is to identify when Christ was born. The Star of Bethlehem heralded the birth of Christ, an event so important that time is divided into two fundamental epochs; *Anno Domini* (**AD** or **A.D.**) and **Before**

41

Christ (BC or B.C.) The term *Anno Domini* is translated as *In the year of our Lord* Jesus Christ. The modern era (AD) is based on the traditionally reckoned year of the conception or birth of Jesus of Nazareth, with *AD* counting years from the start of this epoch, and *BC* denoting years before the start of the era. There is no year zero separating BC from AD, so the year AD 1 AD immediately follows the year 1 BC. The designation of when 1 AD occurred was devised by the Christian monk Dionysius Exiguous in the year 525. It is commonly understood that he made a mistake of 3-4 years in determining when AD started, and that Christ was actually born some years before BC turned to AD.

What do we know about the Star of Bethlehem from the Holy Scriptures? We know that some celestial phenomena called a *star* appeared that could be seen from much of the eastern world. According to the scriptures, it appeared at the birth of Jesus Christ and led a group called the *wise men* to see the Christ-child. Whatever was the Star of Bethlehem, it appeared and led the wise men to Jerusalem. It was a harbinger that a prophesied king and a Jewish Messiah had been born. This *star* which was a *heavenly sign* had several important characteristics.

1. It signified the birth of the Messiah; Jesus Christ
2. It represented kingship
3. It had prophetic significance to astrologers north and west of Jerusalem
4. It arose in the east as viewed from Babylon or Persia, and appeared to move through the eastern sky until it became stationary to the visible eye over the vicinity of Jerusalem.
5. It appeared at a specific time
6. It was not noticed by King Herod
7. It lasted for a considerable amount of time
8. It appeared to remain ahead of the Magi as they traveled south of Jerusalem to Bethlehem
9. It continued to lead the wise men until they found Jesus and Mary

It is important to ask what might be this Star of Bethlehem? There are several possibilities. (1) A real star (2) A nova (3) A meteor (3) A comet (4) A conjunction (5) An occultation

A STAR

A Star is a large, gaseous, self-illuminating celestial body that was widely considered to be God's handiwork, and therefore, a source of divine guidance. The sun in our galaxy is a star. No one would ever seriously believe that the Star of Bethlehem was a real star. Stars are massive in size, and could not possibly lead anyone on a 500 mile journey. Stars do not move, although as the earth rotates and moves through its orbit, stars might appear to change position. We must dismiss the possibility that the *sign* was actually a real star.

A NOVA

A nova is a star which explodes at the end of its life cycle. A nova could possibly arise suddenly in the east and appear as a brilliant, bright light...much brighter than other heavenly objects. An explosion would only last for a relatively short period of time, and like a star it would emanate from millions of light years away. However, it would not appear to move. A nova would be spectacular and noticeable, but is not the Star of Bethlehem that we seek.

A COMET

A comet is a celestial object which has a large, re-occurring orbit that will repeat itself over long periods of time. Halley's Comet... whose tail is composed of ice particles.... is one of the most famous comets known to man. It orbits the sun in a 75.5 year circuit. Comets suddenly

appear, and they are able to endure over long periods of time. Comets were regarded as harbingers of both good and bad omens. To ancient cultures, their action of breaking through the sky was often interpreted as a sign of defiance. When Christ came, He challenged the entire Jewish system of worship. A comet with its bright tail moving through the sky would seem to *point the way*. A spectacular comet divinely appointed by God to herald the birth of His Son would be a definite possibility.

A CONJUNCTION

Seen from millions of miles away, a conjunction of two or more *planets* as viewed from the earth would appear as one very bright light in the sky. As planets progress through their orbital motion, there are times when one or more planets line up from a particular point of observation. When this is observed from the Earth, it seems as if it were one luminous body. It is not likely that a conjunction would be a sign which would lead the Magi south and east, but a spectacular conjunction would certainly be noticed and regarded as a special sign or harbinger of a special event.

AN OCCULTATION

In the era of Jesus Christ birth, there were also a few occurrences of occultation. An occultation occurs when a celestial object passes in front of another celestial object, obscuring one from the other. A good example to illustrate this fact occurs when our moon passes in front of the light from a distant star. If the Moon passes in front of light from a star within line of sight, light from the background star is prevented from reaching the Earth. A shadow of the Moon is cast by the star onto the Earth, and this shadow sweeps across the Earth at roughly the same speed as the Moon is moving. An occultation probably was not the Star we seek, but it would also be rare and noticed.

REVIEW OF ASTRONOMICAL EVENTS BETWEEN 7 BC AND 4 BC

We have described a number of astronomical events that could have signaled that Christ had been born, but taken as individual occurrences they likely would be viewed as just another periodic celestial event, or a minor sign. Novas can be ruled out as *the star* that *led* the Magi to Jerusalem since it does not last long enough. A conjunction or an occultation would have caused widespread interest and qualify as a harbinger of some important event, but neither qualify as the star. A divinely inspired comet might qualify. So what celestial events did occur between 7 BC and 4 BC that have been documented?

A TRIPLE CONJUNCTION IN 7 B.C.

In the year 7 BC a very rare event occurred not once but three times! A conjunction involving Jupiter and Saturn in the constellation of Pices dazzled the universe on three different occasions, making it the perfect sign to signify the birth of the Jewish Messiah, but its prominence in the sky is not the only characteristic which would call attention to the Magi. The planet Saturn represented the divine Father and Jupiter represented his son. The constellation Pisces was astrologically associated with Israel. Thus, it is suggested that the heavenly message conveyed by the conjunction of Saturn and Jupiter in Pisces in 7 BC was that a son of a divine Father will be born in Israel.

The fact that the conjunction happened *three times* in 7 BC (May 29, September 30 and December 5) served to reinforce this message. Thus, it is suggested that the 7 BC triple conjunction alerted the Magi to the coming of the Messiah. We know that this 7 BC triple conjunction was important to Babylonian astronomers since an ancient clay tablet, the *Star Almanac of Sippar*, was found about 30 miles north of Babylon; and it refers in detail to this triple conjunction. The tablet has been positively dated to 7 BC.

THREE PLANETS MOVING IN CONJUNCTION IN 6 BC

Shortly after the triple conjunction of Saturn and Jupiter in 7 BC, *Mars* joined Jupiter and Saturn in the sky so that on February 25, 6 BC the three planets (still in Pisces) were separated by only about eight degrees. To the naked eye, they would appear as one bright light... brighter than any other star in the sky. There is a tradition handed down that the massing of these three planets would precede the birth of Christ. In 1465, Jakob von Speyer, who was the Court Astronomer for Prince Frederic d'Urbino, asked the following question to Regiomontanus :*Given that the appearance of Christ is regarded as a consequence of the Grand Conjunction of the three superior planets, find the year of his birth'; a question that Regiomontanus was unable to answer*. Regiomontanus was an ancient astronomer who proposed that a massing of the three planets of Mars, Saturn and Jupiter preceded the birth of Christ. We will shortly show that he was correct !

A similar conjunction was observed by the famous astronomer Kepler in 1504 AD, and he calculated that such a massing of Jupiter, Saturn and Mars occurred only every 805 years. Kepler also suggested that this triple conjunction was by divine origin, and coincided with great events in history (Moses in 1617 BC, Isaiah in 812 BC, Christ in 6/7 BC, Charlemagne in AD 799 and the Reformation in AD 1604). He was not far off in his conjecture of when Christ was born. To the trained eye of the Magi, the conjunction of three planets in 6 BC and the triple conjunction of two planets in 7 BC would command much attention, and they would likely see these events as a harbinger that a Messiah-king would shortly be born in Israel. Kepler was almost right when he predicted that a triple conjunction would signal the birth of Chris. This conjunction was not indicating that Christ had been born, but that His birth was to shortly take place. The scene was now set: Expectations were aroused for another, final sign which would indicate that Christ had been born. It was not long in coming. The final sign was in 5 BC.

THE CONFIRMING SIGN

In the spring of 5 BC a *comet* blazed forth in the constellation of Capricorn, moving toward the east of Babylon and Persia. This would have been extremely significant to the Magi following the spectacular events of 7 BC and 6 BC. The significance of the Magi seeing *His star in the east* (Matthew 2:2) was that Jerusalem and Bethlehem was east of Babylon, in which it was prophesied where Christ was to be born. The comet of 5 BC clearly provided the final sign that the birth of a king was imminent or had just occurred. The writings of the Old Testament prophet Daniel were known to the Magi, since he was chief of the soothsayers and astrologers while in exile (Daniel 1:1). He frequently met and talked to the Babylonian astrologers (Daniel 1:19; 2:2; 4:5; 5:7). It is suggested here that the remarkable sequence of the triple conjunction in 7 BC; the massing of the three planets in 6 BC; and the comet which streaked across Capricorn in 5 BC provided a clear message to the Magi that a very great king was shortly to be born in Israel. In fact, Christ had already been born as we will shortly show to be true.

The first sign was a *triple conjunction of Jupiter and Saturn, in 7 BC.* On **May 29,** 7 BC the two planets passed a degree apart in the constellation of Pisces the Magi held that Jupiter was a royal planet, and Pisces was a constellation associated with the Jews. On **September 29,** the two planets came together again in Pisces and on **December 4** the planets converged a third time, separated by barely one degree. So three times in eight months, the royal planet of Jupiter and Saturn had met in the Jew's constellation. This would have implied that a king was arising from the Jews. (Jesus is a King, but not in this world).

The second sign was a *conjunction of Jupiter, Saturn and Mars in Pisces in February, 6 B.C.* As Jupiter and Saturn conjuncted, the Magi would have also noticed **Mars** entering the constellation of Pisces and coming toward *Jupiter and Saturn,* until they were separated by only 8 degrees in the sky. Since Mars represented conquest, the skies now suggested that a great Jewish ruler would arise on a mission of conquest. (That conquest would be over Satan and sin).

47

The third sign was **two retrograde conjunctions of Jupiter and the Moon in Pisces on February 20, 5 BC.** On the evening of February 20, the two-day-old new Moon passed very close to Jupiter so that astrologers saw a *pairing of Jupiter and the Moon,* and slightly to the east a *pairing of Mars and Saturn was taking place.* From all the signs they had seen, the Magi could have reasoned that a great ruler (Jupiter) was soon to arise from Judea (Pisces), to challenge another ruler (Saturn) by either physical or spiritual conquest (Mars). Perhaps they remembered Balaam's Messianic prophecy: *"I see him, but not now; I behold him, but not near – a star shall come forth out of Jacob, and a scepter shall rise out of Israel; it shall crush the borderlands of Moab, and the territory of all the Shethites"* (Num 24:17).

The fourth and final sign *suddenly appeared in the southeastern sky, and was visible for 70 days during March-April, 5 BC.* This startling "new light in the heavens" blazed between the constellations of Capricorn and Aquila. Chinese records record that it was quite bright; even very bright. This spectacular heavenly sign must have convinced the Magi that a royal birth had occurred. The entire sequence of related astronomical events that we have recounted here could only happen about every 2,000 years. The Magi would now be convinced that this new King must be the prophesied Messiah of Israel, and that they would find him in Bethlehem; the prophesied place of His birth.

THE BIRTH OF CHRIST

The Chinese kept accurate and complete records of all comets, believing that they were divine signs. *Chinese records* note that a spectacular event occurred in the second month of the second year of the reign of Chien-p'ing; which was March 9 - April 6, 5 BC. The exact date was not recorded. The written records further state that it remained visible for over 70 days; adequate time to *follow* this *star.* Thus, the earliest date for the Magi to have seen the *star* at Bethlehem was March 9, and the latest was April 6. A remarkable fact can be found regarding what happened during this same period of time.

By using digital computer calculations, one can confirm that Nisan 15 in 5 BC fell on March 23! Nisan 15 is the first day of the Feast of Unleavened Bread!! This day would have been an extremely good choice for the birth date of Christ. Christ made a remarkable statement during His 3.5 year ministry on another Feast of Unleavened Bread 32 years later.

> *Then Jesus said unto them, Verily, verily, I say unto you, Moses gave you not that **bread** from heaven; but my Father giveth you the true **bread** from heaven. For the **bread** of God is he which cometh down from heaven, and giveth life unto the world. Then said they unto him, Lord, evermore give us this **bread**. And Jesus said unto them, I am the **bread** of life: he that cometh to me shall never hunger; and he that believeth on me shall never thirst. The Jews then murmured at him, because he said, I am the **bread** which came down from heaven.*
>
> John 6: 32-35, 41

If this evidence is accepted, Jesus was born on Nian 15, March 23 in 5 BC when the comet first appeared. This is the *SIGN* we seek!!! If Christ was born on the first day of The Feast of Unleavened Bread, which starts on the evening of Nisan 14 after 6:00 PM and lasts 7 days. Christ would then be circumcised on the 8th day according to the Law. This explains why this Feast is 7 days long. Note that a March birth is also perfectly in line with the Sheppard's abiding in the field at this time. If this analysis is true, and evidence supports the conclusion; a December birth date for Christ is completely dismantled. It is worth noting that many theologians claim that the birth narratives in Matthew and Luke are inconsistent. This is incorrect. The birth narratives now become complementary and easily reconcilable.

Having shown that Christ was born on Nisan 15, March 23 in 5 BC... We now turn to how this correlates with the reign of King Herod. We will see that everything fits perfectly.

NOTES AND THINGS TO REMEMBER:

CHAPTER 4

THE MYSTERIOUS MAGI
AND THE BIRTH OF CHRIST

There have been thousands of sermons preached; hundreds of articles published; and enough paintings of the magi and the nativity of Christ to fill galleries all over the world. Bards and poets have sung songs that warm our hearts every Christmas season. Unfortunately, almost everything institutionalized by poets and painters is wrong in both its message and meaning. In this section, we will try to tell the real story of the nativity and the magi which came to worship the Christ.

Around the world, the birth of Christ is celebrated on December 25, but there are several strong reasons to believe that Christ could not have been born on December 25. The date of December 25 that is currently celebrated as the month and day that Christ was born is a relatively new date. This date does not appear in the Holy Scriptures, and seems to have never been mentioned for over 300 years after Christ was born. By the early fourth century, Church leaders decided they needed a Christian alternative to rival popular pagan celebrations. They chose December 25th as the date of Christ's birth, and held the first recorded *Feast of the Nativity* in Rome in A.D. 336. Whether they did so intentionally or not, church leaders placed the nativity on December 25th; which was also when the Cult of Mithras celebrated the birth of their infant god of light.

- This date seems to have first occurred in 336 AD on the Roman calendar *Chronograpacus Anni CCCLIXII*. The reason was to attract pagan worshippers to a Christian celebration and convert them to Christianity.
- The date of December 25 is not even universally accepted by the Roman Catholic Church. The European western Roman Catholic Church holds to a January 9 birth date.

- The period between Dec 25 and Jan 9 became the holiday season known as the 12 days of Christmas.
- In about 200 BC, Clement of Alexandria wrote that several different days had been proposed by various Christian groups for the birth of Christ. Surprising as it may seem, Clement doesn't mention January 9 at all.

    By the fourth century we find references to two dates that were widely recognized – and now also celebrated – as Jesus' birthday: December 25 in the Western Roman Empire and January 6 in the East (especially in Egypt and Asia Minor). The modern Armenian church continues to celebrate Christmas on January 6; for most Christians, however, December 25 would prevail, while January 6 eventually came to be known as the Feast of the Epiphany, commemorating the arrival of the magi in Bethlehem (Clement in *Stromata* 1:21).

- Using biblical narratives, it is difficult to accept that either December 25 or January 9 was the birth date of Christ. In Luke 2:8 we are told that: *there were in the same country shepherds abiding in the field, keeping watch over their flock by night.* In ancient Israel, sheep and goats were extremely important to both provide food and wool to individual families, and to supply the great quantities of sacrificial goats and lambs required for temple sacrifices. It was common practice to keep flocks in the field during the summer, spring and early fall; but the flocks were brought into a protected manger during the winter months. These were generally the months of Nov-Dec-Jan-Feb and part of March. There were almost no flocks in the field between late November and late February… it was too cold and rainy. In this book we propose an early spring birth of Jesus Christ; perfectly supporting the presence of flocks and Sheppard's in the field.

Whatever good men might believe, we can be sure that in the fullness of time, our Lord and Savior Jesus Christ was born into a sinful world; His birth date being preordained from the beginning of time. The arrival of a long promised Messiah was predicted in over 300 places in the Old Testament.

THE BIRTH OF CHRIST

Messianic expectations were running high about the same time that Herod was nearing the end of his reign as King of the Jews. We will later show that Herod died in the early spring of 4 BC. About 500 years had passed since the Nation of Israel returned from their 70 year exile in Babylonia. During this exile, a prophecy had been given to Daniel (Daniel 9:27) that a Messiah would arise that would establish an earthly kingdom that would never end and restore the Throne of David. This prophecy predicted that 70-7's or 490 years would elapse from when the prophecy would begin until righteousness would be restored and that *all Israel would be saved*. It was not known exactly when this prophecy would begin and end, but since about 500 years had passed since the prophecy went forth, people were anxiously awaiting the Messiah's appearance. We are told that a man named Joseph lived in a town called Nazareth, and that he was betrothed to a virgin called Mary. The apostle Matthew recorded that the angel Gabriel appeared to Mary and announced that even though she was a virgin, she would conceive of a Child who would be called Jesus.

Now the birth of Jesus Christ was on this wise: When as his mother Mary was espoused to Joseph, before they came together, she was found with child of the Holy Ghost. Then Joseph her husband, being a just man, and not willing to make her a publick example, was minded to put her away privily. But while he thought on these things, behold, the angel of the Lord appeared unto him in a dream, saying, Joseph, thou son of David, fear not to take unto thee Mary thy wife: for that which is conceived in her is of the Holy Ghost. And she shall bring forth a son, and thou shalt call his name JESUS: for he shall save his people from their sins. Now all this was done, that it might be fulfilled which was spoken of the Lord by the prophet, saying, Behold, a virgin shall be with child, and shall bring forth a son, and they shall call his name Emmanuel, which being interpreted is, God with us

Matthew 1:18-23

Luke 2:1-4 adds to this story. He plainly states that Joseph and Mary did not live in Jerusalem, but in the town of Nazareth, which was about 20-30 miles north of Jerusalem. So why were Mary and Joseph in Jerusalem when Mary had the Christ Child?

> *And it came to pass in those days, that there went out a decree from Caesar Augustus, that all the world should be taxed. (And this taxing was first made when Cyrenius was governor of Syria.) And all went to be taxed, every one into his own city. And Joseph also went up from Galilee, out of the city of Nazareth, into Judaea, unto the city of David, which is called Bethlehem; (because he was of the house and lineage of David: To be taxed with Mary his espoused wife, being great with child. And so it was, that, while they were there, the days were accomplished that **she should be delivered**. And she brought forth her firstborn son, and wrapped him in swaddling clothes, and laid him in a **manger**; because **there was no room for them in the inn**.*

Luke 2:1-7

In those days was the time that Christ was born. Joseph had no choice in going to Jerusalem. He had two compelling reasons: (1) We have shown that Christ was likely born on the first day of the Feast of Firstfruits; Nisan 15 in 5 BC. This was a Feast at which all Jewish males were required to attend. Hence, Joseph would have traveled to Jerusalem to attend this Feast under the Law of Moses. At this same time: (2) Caesar Augustus called for everyone under the Iron Boot of Rome to register for a taxation census *in his own city*. Joseph was of the line of David, and *his city* was Jerusalem. These two concurrent events would have combined to fill the town with visitors, all of whom would be seeking a place to stay. But why would Mary...*being great with Child...* make this long journey over difficult terrain? Perhaps she did not want to leave Joseph. Perhaps wives might also be expected to register. The correct reason is undoubtedly to satisfy the prophecy that Jesus would be born in a place called Bethlehem, which was no more than 3 miles from the city of Jerusalem

> *But thou, **Bethlehem** Ephratah, though thou be little among the thousands of Judah, yet out of thee shall he come forth unto me that*

is to be ruler in Israel; whose goings forth have been from of old, from everlasting.

Micah 5:2

So Mary and Joseph left for Jerusalem. Being in the last weeks of her pregnancy, we can imagine the difficulty that Mary experienced as she journeyed.

The birth of Jesus Christ is recorded in the English translation of the Greek and Hebrew Holy Scriptures as occurring in a *manger*. We will discuss this shortly in some detail, but for now we simply ask *"why was there no room in the inn"*? The answer is that as we have noted; Cesar Augustus declared that all males must return to their own place of ancestral origin to register for a *census*. This might have caused a problem in finding a room, but we suggest that it was also because this was when the Feast of Passover (Nisan 14) and the Feast of Firstfruits (Nisan 15- Nisan 21) were being held in Jerusalem at that time. Jerusalem would have been clogged with Jewish worshippers. It is likely that Joseph and Mary actually retreated to Bethlehem, which was only about 6 miles away. Of course, this was primarily to fulfill the prophetic scripture of Micah 5:2.

We have two mysteries which must be addressed. The first is to explain why Mary gave birth to the Christ in a *manger*. The scriptures say that there was no room at the *inn*. When Mary and Joseph went up to Jerusalem they probably intended to stay with one of the families in Jerusalem. This was common practice.... There were no Holiday Inns or Hilton Hotels in those days. Often total strangers would knock on the door and be welcome for the night..... very similar to our old western settlers in the pioneer days. An inn (εν τωι καταλυματι – *en toi katalumati*) was in the Greek a house or a dwelling place. This is where a family lived, and for all but the very poor the typical Jewish *house* was attached to a stable area called a *manger* (εν πατνηι – *en phatneī*), in which the sheep and goats were housed during the winter months of November to March. The winter months in Israel can be very cold, and sheep must be protected from the cold and freezing weather (1 Kings 1:13). There would usually be a rectangular or square inner court with an open gallery, and around the four sides there would be stables for the animals: The stable area would almost be empty when the animals were in the field, and this is where visitors might stay if the guest room was taken. Because of the required census and the Feast that was going on, there was no room in the house itself. Second, we always associate the appearance of three *wise men* in Jerusalem, who had journeyed from afar to worship the Christ. The correct identification for these wise men is that they were *Magi*. Who were these Magi? Where did they come from? How did they know that the child had been born? These questions have lingered for over 200 years. Let us see if we can answer these questions.

WHO WERE THE MAGI ?

We always depict the wise men worshipping the child in a manger. In fact, when the Magi arrived, Mary and Joseph were not even in Jerusalem. Here is the way things actually happened at that time. The Magi have been widely depicted as in the above graphic. Almost everything in this picture is attributed to imagination. What we know about the visitors is recorded in the gospel of Matthew.

> *"Now when Jesus was born in Bethlehem of Judaea in the days of Herod the king, behold, there came wise men from the east to Jerusalem, Saying, Where is he that is born King of the Jews? For we have seen his star in the east, and are come to worship him."*
>
> Matthew 2:1-2

- The term *wise men* is a translation of the word Magi. The *mágos*, Magi, or Magian is the root word for magician. The Magi was a practitioner of magic, astrology, alchemy and the interpretation of dreams. We see three men on their journey. Nowhere in scripture or any other ancient writing is it said that there were three men. There might have been two, three or more.

- We sing of; *we three Kings of Orient are, bearing gifts we traverse afar.* There is no record of these visitors being kings. The Magi were probably identified as kings because of Psalms 72:11. In fact, they were likely not Kings or Princes but astrologers or soothsayers.

- The *wise men* are shown riding camels. Camels were widely used in Arabia, Babylon and some parts of Persia. However, there is no biblical record of the Magi riding any animal. It is likely that the visitors walked to Jerusalem.

- The scriptures indicate that the wise men *followed a star*. As we have already discussed, it is impossible to follow a star. We will present evidence that the object called a *star* was likely a *comet*: Moving from west to east as viewed from Babylon or Persia, and finally appearing to move down and stationary over Jerusalem.

Continuing with our inquiry, we know that the Magi did not immediately seek to find the Christ Child, but first went to see King Herod.

> Now when Jesus was born in Bethlehem of Judaea in the days of Herod the king, behold, there came wise men from the east to Jerusalem, Saying, Where is he that is born King of the Jews? For we have seen his star in the east, and are come to worship him.
>
> Matthew 2:1-2)

This was undoubtedly due to two things. First, it would have certainly been politically correct to first pay homage to the king. Herod was a very dangerous man. The second was a partial verification that the natural phenomenon of a comet *pointing* or *indicating* the way to Jerusalem / Bethlehem is correct. Any natural celestial object would not be capable of standing directly over Bethlehem, much less the exact place of birth. The Magi would not have needed a great deal of help; they would have known that Christ was to be born in Bethlehem because of scripture. But, Jerusalem was already a large, thriving city and Bethlehem was likely a joining suburb of Jerusalem. Because of this, the Magi inquired of Herod as to where the child might be found: *Where is he that is born King of the Jews? For we have seen his star in the east, and are come to worship him?* (Matthew 2:2). Herod had no idea of where Jesus might be found, and he was obviously disturbed at this news, because he commanded the Magi as follows.

When Herod the king had heard these things, he was troubled, and all Jerusalem with him. And when he had gathered all the chief priests and scribes of the people together, he demanded of them where Christ should be born. And they said unto him, In Bethlehem of Judaea: for thus it is written by the prophet, And thou Bethlehem, in the land of Juda, art not the least among the princes of Juda: for out of thee shall come a Governor, that shall rule my people Israel. Then Herod, when he had privily called the wise men, inquired of them diligently what time the star appeared. And he sent them to Bethlehem, and said, Go and search diligently for the young child; and when ye have found him, bring me word again, that I may come and worship him also.

Matthew 2:3-8

So the Magi departed to find the child. But what compelled them to leave Babylon and make a difficult 500 mile journey in the first place? How did they know to come at this time? There is no hint in the scriptures that an angel or a dream told them to do so. We must look elsewhere to find the answer.

THE SIGNS

The Magi were convinced that a Jewish Messiah had been born by a series of heavenly signs that suddenly appeared between 7 BC and 5 BC. The following remarkable events occurred within a relatively short period of time.

- In 7 BC there were *three conjunctions* of the planets Saturn and Jupiter in the constellation Pisces. Each conjunction could be seen by the naked eye, and would have been observed with great interest; but *three* conjunctions in one year would have really caught the attention of ancient astronomers. These astronomers were the Magi. A conjunction of the planets Jupiter and Saturn was of importance to the astrological Magi since Jupiter was known as the *planet of Kings* and Saturn as the *Protector of the Jews* (Carroll). Further, all three conjunctions occurred in the constellation *Pisces,* which has long been associated with the *Hebrew nation.* Not once, but three times, a heavenly message was conveyed that a new King of the Jews was about to arise.

- Shortly after the triple conjunctions of Saturn and Jupiter in 7 BC, Mars joined Jupiter and Saturn so that on February 6, 6 BC they were separated by no more than 8 degrees; appearing to the naked eye as one bright heavenly light. There was an ancient tradition that three planets massing would precede the birth of a Jewish Messiah. In addition to the presence of Jupiter (Planet of the Kings) and Saturn (Protector of the Jews), we now have Mars which is associated with a conqueror and a victor; often in the context of war. Kepler suggested that this massing occurred only about every 800 years, and preceded several important biblical events. In any case, these celestial events caused great excitement and expectations; a final, significant sign was about to appear in 5 BC.

- The last sign was on Nisan 15, March 12, 5 BC. Having seen the last of three celestial signs, the Magi prepared to leave and worship the new born King. If they were in either Babylon or in Persia as some have proposed, the preparations would take about two weeks and the journey about two months. Recall that March 12 was the exact day that the first day of the seven day Feast of Firstfruits in 5 BC.

In the spring of 5 BC a comet blazed across the south and eastern sky in the constellation of Capricorn, which was clearly visible from Babylon and Persia. The ancient Chinese viewed the appearance of a comet as a harbinger of significant events. Chinese records record this event as occurring in the second month of the second year of the reign of Chien-p'ing; which was March 9-April 6, 5 BC. This was a major celestial event in which the comet slowly moved east to southeast toward Jerusalem. The Chinese recorded that this comet was clearly visible for about 70 days; about the period of time required to pack up and make the journey to Jerusalem.

- This third and final heavenly display would have convinced the Magi that the long awaited Messiah had finally been born.
- It is more than coincidental that the Jewish Feast of Unleavened Bread started on Nisan 15, March 23, in 5 BC. Since the spectacular comet of 5 BC was recorded by the Chinese as appearing between March 9 - April 6, 5 BC. There is a perfect match between these two events. This is an extremely unlikely and unusual occurrence which to the best of our knowledge has not been noticed before this study. We accept March 23 as a most appropriate date for the birth of Christ; and we will have much more to say about this, with more justification, in subsequent discussions related to the Reign of Josephus.
- The Magi would have spent about 2-3 weeks preparing for their trip to Jerusalem, and depending upon the weather, availability of water and the strength of their entourage; they would have arrived in Jerusalem about two months later near early June, 5 BC in the month of Tammuz. They would follow after the *star* which we have assumed was the comet of 5 BC; visible for about 70 days which is very consistent with our timetable.
- The Magi would immediately visit King Herod, who would send them on their way to find the Christ so that he might kill the babe.

- The Magi would have normally gone directly to Bethlehem, but the *star* miraculous reappears (this is not a celestial star but an angelic light that appeared to be a star) to lead them to the Christ-child. This was necessary, because the Magi were not aware that Joseph and Mary had returned to their own house in Nazareth (Luke 2:39), which was about 50 miles away. We believe that this star was probably a mighty angel leading the way in a bright light, which was similar in appearance to the celestial comet of 5 BC that led the Magi to Jerusalem. Please note that the Magi would only need the series of heavenly signs to convince them that this great event had happened, and that the comet would only need to point them towards Jerusalem as it crossed the sky. They already knew that Christ was to be born in Bethlehem from the scriptures. There is no way that they could have known that Christ was in Nazareth when they arrived.

What has been happening to Mary, Joseph and the Child during the time that the Magi left Babylon and arrived in Herod's palace?

AFTER THE BIRTH OF CHRIST

The Feast of Unleavened Bread is a 7 day feast. In addition, the first and last days of this feast are special Jewish Sabbath days. Why are the first and last days uniquely special? Now it is clear; according to Jewish custom a newly born male Child remains in seclusion with his mother and is then circumcised on the 8th day. This 8 day period is part of a larger 40 day period that begins with the male child's birth, and ends with the child's redemption and dedication 40 days later. During this period of time, Mary would have been ritually unclean and would not receive visitors. Forty days after the birth of Christ, Mary and Joseph brought Jesus to the temple (Luke 2:21-39) to be dedicated.

*And when the days of her purification **according to the law of Moses** were accomplished, they brought him to Jerusalem, to* *present him to the Lord; (As it is written in the law of the Lord, Every male that openeth the womb shall be called holy to the Lord;) And to offer a sacrifice according to that which is said in the law of the Lord, A pair of turtledoves, or two young pigeons.*

Luke 2:22-24

After that time, Joseph and Mary had no reason to stay in Jerusalem. After all, they were only visiting there and had a house in Nazareth. So, Mary and Joseph returned to their *house* (Matthew 2:11). The journey home would have taken no more than one week, and would have occurred almost immediately after the 40 day purification period of Mary and the dedication of Jesus in the temple. The Magi would arrive about one month later.

THE ADORATION OF THE MAGI

We will now carefully examine what happened after the Magi after they departed from King Herod.

 It is plainly stated that the Magi departed from the King and again saw a *star*…. the *same star* that they had seen in the east. Of course, this only looked like the same star. This star was said to *go before them*. Divine guidance was necessary because Mary, Joseph and the babe were no longer in Jerusalem. They had by now returned to Nazareth, which is about 50 miles north of Jerusalem; not south or east. Here we have two possibilities: (1) the comet had once again began to move to lead them to the Christ. This is highly unlikely if not impossible. (2) This **star** was not natural at all, but a supernatural phenomenon caused by the will of God. This would not have been unique in scriptures: A bright light led the children of Israel through the wilderness in the exodus. The light probably *appeared* as if it was a star.

We are here caught in a scriptural paradox: Matthew recorded that it was *the same star* they had seen (previously) *in the east*. Here we have a real mystery. How could it have been the same star now leading them back north? The most logical explanation, which has been previously suggested, is that there were real celestial signs which heralded the birth of Christ and pointed the way to Jerusalem; but the *star* which now led them to Nazareth looked in appearance to be the previous star, but was in fact supernatural. Here the appearance of that *star/comet* was visually duplicated in a supernatural way... possibly by the brightness of a mighty angel who led the way.

We will now uncover a fact that will likely surprise most Christians. The Magi left after their meeting with King Herod, but they never visited Mary and the baby Jesus in a manger. In fact, the Magi did not go to Bethlehem at all, but to a town called Nazareth where Joseph lived. This is plainly stated by Matthew.

> *And when they (the Magi) were come into the **house** (of Mary and Joseph), they saw the **young child** (Christ Jesus) with Mary his mother, and (they) fell down, and worshipped him: and when they had opened their treasures, they presented unto him gifts; gold, and frankincense, and myrrh.*
>
> Matthew 2:11

Notice carefully how Matthew describes the visit of the Magi. The Magi are not in a manger, they are in a **house**. This is the

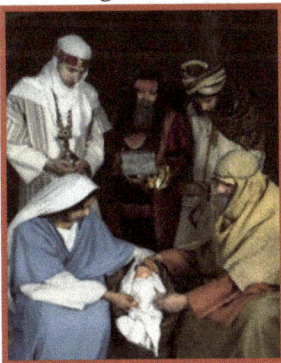

house of Joseph and Mary in Nazareth, over 50 miles north of Jerusalem. Why are they there? After registering for the taxation census in Jerusalem, birthing Jesus, circumcising the Child and then dedicating the child after a 40 day period of purification: Why would they stay? Joseph was a poor carpenter with a new wife and a new child. He would have left to resume his normal life as soon as possible. If Christ was born on March 12 and the Magi departed Babylon after a short period of preparation, they would have visited Herod sometime in late April/early May, and after being led to Nazareth by a Star they would arrive no more than one week later. Hence, if this timetable is fairly accurate Christ would be about 3 months old.

- In any event, the Magi arrive at the house of Joseph where they worship Him, and they present Him gifts of gold, frankincense and myrrh. Why such extravagant gifts? The obvious answer is that our Messiah is Lord of Lords and King of Kings and He is worthy. This is true, but I suggest that these gifts have a more practical meaning.

And when they were departed, behold, the angel of the Lord appeareth to Joseph in a dream, saying, Arise, and take the young child and his mother, and flee into Egypt, and be thou there until I bring thee word: for Herod will seek the young child to destroy him. When he arose, he took the young child and his mother by night, and departed into Egypt: And was there until the death of Herod: that it might be fulfilled which was spoken of the Lord by the prophet, saying, Out of Egypt have I called my son.

Matthew 2:13-15

We know that Joseph was a poor man, because Christ was redeemed in the temple with an offering of *a pair of turtledoves, or two young pigeons*: This is an offering that only a poor family would give. After being warned by the Magi, the family immediately fled to Egypt, where they stayed until King Herod was dead. This was a long journey to a strange land, with a young child. It would take a lot of money to stay in a strange land with a new child. How could Joseph afford an extended stay in Egypt? The answer is now clear: This is why the Magi brought gifts of gold, frankincense and myrrh. Isn't it marvelous how God prepares for our needs? So the wise men returned home, not returning to King Herod as commanded; and Mary and Joseph went to Egypt. This sequence of events is verified by carefully examining the scriptural accounts, and can be believed. It is not difficult to imagine how King Herod reacted when the Magi failed to return and reveal the location of the Christ.

When Herod realized that he had been outwitted by the Magi, he was furious, and he gave orders to kill all the boys in Bethlehem and its vicinity who were two years old and under, in accordance with the time he had learned from the Magi. Then what was said through the prophet Jeremiah was fulfilled: *A voice is heard in Ramah, weeping and great mourning, Rachel weeping for her children and refusing to be comforted, because they are no more.* (Jeremiah 31:15)

The infants are known in Jewish historical accounts as the *Holy Innocents*. Traditional accounts number them at more than ten thousand, but it is more likely that they were no more than 15-24 children. Some even doubt that this ever occurred, but it is recorded in the Holy Scriptures and most definitely did occur. We will now return to King Herod and how he spent the last few months of his life. Many terrible things will happen between when he realizes that he was deceived by the wise men, and when he died. In the timetable that has been presented, he will have only about 9 more months to live. This is more than enough time for the events recorded by the Jewish historian Josephus to occur.

We will now turn our attention to the reign of King Herod. We will see that all the facts and scenarios fit together hand in glove.

NOTES AND THINGS TO REMEMBER:

CHAPTER 5

THE REIGN OF HEROD

In the gospel of Matthew the tax collector, we find the following passage.

> *Now when Jesus was born in Bethlehem of Judaea in the days of Herod the King*
>
> Matthew 2:1-2

This passage of scripture informs us of two significant things: (1) Jesus Christ was born in Bethlehem and (2) Christ was born when Herod was King of Judea. This Herod was Herod the great, who reigned as King of the Jews. If we are to confirm when Jesus Christ was born, it is necessary to find out when Herod reigned. The years in which Herod reigned have been a subject of much scholarly investigation and debate for over 800 years. Since so many noble and dedicated scholars have come and gone, why would it be presumed that the truth has now been found? There are at least three good reasons: *First,* the very fact that so many biblical scholars have studied the reign of King Herod gives a wealth of opinions and facts which can be examined. *Second,* the ancient scholars obviously had other written records to assist their research, but they were scattered and existed in remote places. Today, we are blessed to have the internet and the World Wide Web to gather information and facts from thousands of sources. *Third,* and perhaps the most important reason is modern laptop computers. Biblical scholars for the first time in history have personal access to millions of biblical documents. It is now possible to investigate thousands of written records in a short period of time. A tremendous investigative tool has been the use of computers to go back thousands of year referencing the Hebrew calendar and cross referencing the old Julian calendar. We will do this extensively in this book. Finally, we need to make two other key observations:

Much of what we know about King Herod is found in the monumental records of Josephus, a first century Jewish historian who wrote two historical accounts of the Jewish people; *Antiquities* and *Wars*. Josephus was born a Jew in 37 AD, probably only about 40 years from when Herod died. He was part of the Roman army under Titus who completely destroyed Herod's Temple in 70 AD and ended the Jewish religious system which had existed for over 2600 years. The point is that Josephus is a well-respected historian who had obviously heard reliable accounts of Herod's reign, but he often creates problems which cannot be resolved in some of his historical accounts. Nevertheless, his compilation of *Wars and Antiquities* stands as a significant historical record of the Jewish nation. In spite of frequent and sometimes justified criticisms, the historical records and history of King Herod's reign cannot be far from the truth. Josephus was in the broader scope of history a near-contemporary of King Herod. He undoubtedly heard eye witness accounts that had been passed down from father to son, and without a doubt he heard accurate stories from his immediate family. In summary, while some of Josephus' accounts which were over 1000 years old might be questioned; those of King Herod and his exploits should be accepted as accurate. Second, the Roman Empire was in full power during the reign of Herod, and they kept accurate and extensive records of key events. In particular, the consular records and the reign of Roman Caesars were also available.

THE REGNAL YEARS OF HEROD THE GREAT

Almost all biblical scholars agree that King Herod started his reign no earlier than 40 BC by Roman decree, and died no later than 1 AD. Is it possible to authoritatively state when Herod became King of the Jews and when he died? We believe the answer is *yes*. We begin in what seems to be a reasonable place; the year and month that Herod became King by edict of the

Roman consulate. Before we do that, it will first be necessary to summarize the events which led up to this point in time.

The Jewish people had been under the reign of the Asamoneans (Hasmonians) for over 100 years, which began with the Maccabean revolt. The last King of the Hasmonian Dynasty was Antigonus, the son of Aristobulus. Josephus records that:

> .....and when he (Antigonus) had reigned three years and three months, Sossius and Herod besieged him, and took him. Then Antony had him (Antagonus) brought to Antioch and slain there. Herod was then made King by the Romans.
>
> Antiquities 10: 1

The events leading up to the overthrow of Antigonus are well accounted for by Josephus. Antigonus was made King of the Jews after the previous king... Hyranicus.. was overthrown. Now Antagonis was of Jewish descent, but Herod was not... so Herod was rejected by the people and by Jewish tradition; but during the years preceding the rise of Antagonis to King, Herod had made friends with Antony who was then in Rome. Herod left Jerusalem and went to Rome…a trip we will examine later in some detail. Upon arriving in Rome, Antony greeted him and the next day presented Herod to the counselors of Rome as the most logical and politically correct choice to become king (Wars 1: 14 4). The senate immediately named Herod King of Judea at the insistence of Antony. Herod returned to Jerusalem within 7 days, and in the summer months during the third year after he left Rome he began a siege on Herod's Temple where Antagonis and his armies had gathered. After a long 5 month battle (Wars 1:18:2) Antagonis was defeated. Herod immediately sent Antagonis to Antony in Rome; where he was sent to Italy and executed. At this time, Herod became the defacto *King of the Jews* (Wars 1:14:4). With this short narrative, we are ready to ask: When did all of this happen? We must now ask two important questions:

(1)   When was Herod named King of the Jews by the Roman Senate?

(2)   When did the Battle at Jerusalem begin and end?

In Antiq. 14:14:5 Josephus tells us that Antony took Herod to the Roman consuls, and after an eloquent speech by Antony Herod was named King by the Roman senate. Either that night or the next day, Antony held a great feast in his honor. Josephus is quite specific on when this happened.

> *Antony also* (after presenting Herod to the Senate) *feasted Herod the first day of his reign. And thus did this man* (Herod) *receive the Kingdom* (Israel)*, having obtained it on the hundred and eighty fourth Olympiad, when Caius Domithis Calvanus was consul the second time, and Caius Asinius Pollio the first time.*

The Olympiads referenced here are the *Greek Olympic cycles*. The Greek Olympic cycles lasted 4 years, and the first Greek Olympiad was held from the summer of 776 BC to the summer of 772 BC. Olympic years started on July 1 and ended on June 30. Ancient historians and kingly records often referenced major events by citing the Olympiad number. It is easy to verify that the 184th Olympiad ran from July 1, 44 BC to June 30, 40 BC.

Roman consuls are elected for one year terms starting on January 1 each year. However, their term of office began on either March 1 or March 15, depending upon what authority is referenced. Consuls could be appointed to serve more than one term, but this was not common practice. Important events are often marked by a statement such as *when Pollio and Calvinus were consulars in the Roman senate*. In referencing the Roman Consular records, both Pollio and Calvinus are listed as consulars who served between Jan 1 - Dec 31 in 40 BC. This is also in complete agreement

40	Cn. Domitius M.f. Calvinus II C. Asinius Cn.f. Pollio *Suff.*:L. Cornelius L.f. Balbus P. Canidius P.f. Crassus

with Josephus' statement that it happened late in the 4th year of the 184th Olympiad. By the testimony of two witnesses, we can deduce that Herod was named King by the Roman Senate no later than March 15, in 40 BC.

Josephus provides great detail about what happened next. Eager to claim his throne in Jerusalem, Herod left immediately within 7 days of his arrival. (Antiq. 14:14:5). This would make his departure no later than March 21, 40 BC. Herod crossed the Mediterranean Sea in a winter trip that is known to have taken about 55 days. Herod set sail from Italy to the southern port of Ptolemais and recruited a small army. Hence, Herod would have reached Ptolemais around late May, 40 BC. Antony commanded Two Roman legions to join Herod; one led by Silo and one by Ventidius (Antiq. 14:15:1). Herod now had a strong army which grew every day, and as he crossed Israel he defeated resistance forces that were following Antagonis. These battles went on for some time, but how long?

> ...when the rigors of winter was over, Herod removed his army, and came near to Jerusalem, and pitched his camp hard by the city. Now **this was the third year** since he had been made King by Rome.
>
> Antiquities 14:14:16

The scenario so far is summarized as follows: Herod was named King....Likely on March 15, 40 BC in Rome. He left within 7 days, and after about 55 days he crossed the Mediterranean Sea. Crossing Israel he encountered continual resistance. After several major battles, he reached Jerusalem with a large army. We must be careful to not misinterpret the words of Josephus.... He clearly states that Herod arrived at Jerusalem *in the third year since leaving Rome*. This would be no earlier than late spring of 38 BC, or no later than the winter months of 37 BC, according to Antiq.14:14:16. We believe that Herod actually arrived in the late winter months of 37 BC. The three years referenced by Josephus are therefore as follows.

Year 1: March, 40 BC-March, 39 BC
Year 2: March, 39 BC-March, 38 BC
Year 3: March, 38 BC-March, 37 BC

71

Based upon the subsequent series of events described by Josephus, we believe that Herod camped outside of Jerusalem in the early winter of 37 BC. This observation will provide the key to showing that Herod died just before the Jewish Feast of Passover in 4 BC. Herod did not immediately launch his siege. He began constructing war machines for the upcoming conflict. Preparations continued from when he arrived to midsummer.

> *Now the three bulwarks were easily erected, because so many hands were continually at work on it; for it was summertime.*
>
> Antiquities 1:14:2

He first built towers and siege machines (Antiq. 1:14:2). We are also told that while preparations for the siege were taking place, Herod... to strengthen his political position.... went to Samaria and married a Jewish woman (Herod was not a legitimate King by lineage, for he was not of Jewish Descent). The forces of Antagonis were surrounded by Herod's army, with limited food and water (Antiq. 14:16). The battle raged on for 5 months (Footnote, Antiq 16, Page 397 and Wars 1:18:2). Josephus also recorded how the city fell: *the first wall fell in 40 days and the second (wall) took 15 (days) more* (Antiq. 14:16:2). Piecing things together, Herod would have arrived in Jerusalem, likely in the early winter months of 37 BC. Herod subsequently got married in the late spring, and construction of war machines continued into the summer months. (Antiq. 16:1:2) Adding it all up, we can now state that Herod began his assault in the summer months of 37 BC. Hence, Jerusalem and Antagonis fell in the early winter months of either 37 BC or early in 36 BC. Can we determine the exact month and date when the temple walls were breached and Antagonis was defeated? ...the answer is *Yes!*

> *This destruction befell the city of Jerusalem when Marcos Agrippa and Caninius were consuls at Rome, on the hundred and eighty-fifth Olympiad, on the third month, on the solemnity of the fast, as if a periodical revolution of calamities had returned since that*

*which befell the Jews under Pompey; for the Jews were taken by him
(Pompey) on the same day, and this was after 27 years' time.*

Antiquities IV: 16.4

It is well known that Pompey, a Roman general, attacked
Jerusalem and destroyed the Holy Temple in 63 BC. The account
of the battle is given by Josephus in Wars 1:141. There are three
things which provide clues as to exactly when this event
occurred.

1.   *The destruction took place in the 185th Olympiad.*

     The Olympiads referenced here are again the 4 year
     Greek Olympic cycles. The Greek Olympics lasted 4
     years, and the first Greek Olympiad lasted from the
     summer of 776 BC to that of 772 BC. It is easy to verify
     that the 185th Olympiad ran from July 1, 40 BC to June 30,
     36 BC.

2.   *It occurred when Marcos Agrippa and Caninius were consuls
     at Rome.*

According to Roman consul lists, both Marcos Agrippa and
Caninius were consuls in 63 BC (Finnegan, Handbook of Biblical
Chronology and Wikipedia).

3.   *...as if a periodic revolution of calamities had returned since
     that which befell the Jews under Pompey; for the Jews were
     taken by him on the same day, and this was after 27 years'
     time.*

The statement of Josephus is astounding. He relates the fall of
Jerusalem (the Holy Temple) by Pompey in 63 BC to the fall of
Jerusalem (the Holy Temple) to Herod exactly 27 years later. But
what is more remarkable is that Josephus implies that it was not
only the same Jewish calendar day, but on the same day of the
week. As inferred from above, and attested to by many
historians, it is well known that Pompey conquered Jerusalem in
63 BC; and 27 years later would bring us to 36 BC. This seems to

settle the issue, but several well respected biblical researchers have asserted that Jerusalem fell in 37 BC. We could claim that Josephus was in error, but the language of Josephus is too strong and exact to ignore, so we must be sure. At this point we quote from the well-respected biblical scholar W.E. Filmer in a paper "*The Chronology of Herod the Great*", *Journal of Theological Studies*, Vol. 17, 1966.

> *Pompey captured Jerusalem in 63 BC, and 27 years later would bring us to 36 BC..... but Josephus states that on both occasions Jerusalem was taken, not only on the same Jewish calendar day but also on the same day of the week. Now 27 years is almost exactly 334 lunar months, and 334 lunations require 9,836 days, 5.5 hours. Since 9,863 is evenly divided by 7, every date on the Jewish calendar in BC would fall on the same day of the week as it did in 63 BC.*

This statement by Filmer was checked for accuracy and was found to be absolutely correct. It should also be noted that this sort of calindrical behavior could never be true during this time period in reference to the Julian solar calendar: It can only be true using the Jewish lunar calendar. The problem again is that if the solution posed by Filmer is correct, Jerusalem would have fallen in 36 BC; while most biblical scholars have identified 37 BC as the fall of Jerusalem.

We know that one end of the 27 year time line will be on a day in 63 BC, and the other end of the timeline on the exact same day in either 36 BC or 37 BC. It will be shown that the correct *terminus quo* is 36 BC. Josephus has provided information which will lead us to the correct day in 36 BC. Josephus said that this occurred "*in the 3rd month, on the solemnity of the fast*". Two questions arise.

What 3rd month? What Fast?

As discussed in Chapter 1, the Jewish calendar actually had two months that might be considered as month one. Before the exodus from Egypt, the first month on the Jewish calendar was the month of Tishri: Sept/ Oct on the Julian calendar. After the exodus from Egypt, God instructed the people to use the month of Nisan: March/April as the first month of the year. After the exodus, the Jewish year that began on Tishri 1 was called the Jewish *Civil Year*, and the Jewish year that began on Nisan 1 was called the Jewish *Religious Year*. By late 1st century BC, the Jewish New Year had been firmly established as officially starting on Nisan 1. The practice of having two New Year days in two different months should not be strange to the American people. We use the modern Gregorian calendar, which evolved from the less accurate Julian calendar and New Year's Day is January 1. However, the federal government's New Year begins on October 1. Most University and high school years begin on September 1. So the practice of multiple New Year days is actually quite common. Without further information, the 3rd month indicated

1. **Ta'anit Bechorim** - The Fast of the Firstborn is a fast observed only by firstborn males, commemorating the fact that they were saved from the plague of the firstborn in Egypt. It is observed on the day before Pesach (Nisan 14).

2. **Tzom Tammuz** - Fast of the 17th of Tammuz. Fast day commemorating the breaking down of the wall of Jerusalem by Nebuchadnezzar and the cessation of Temple worship during the siege of Titus (Jun/Jul). In the Bible, this is referred to as the Fast of the 4th month.

3. **Tishah B'Av** - The Ninth of Av, a fast day remembering the tragedies of the Jewish people (July/Aug). In the Bible, this is referred to as the Fast of the 5th month. Note that many people also fast on the first of Av, since this is the *yahrzeit* of Aaron the High Priest. The Fast of Tishah B'Av is the second most important fast in Judaism (next to Yom Kippur, which is the most important fast day). On the eve of the Tishah B'Av fast, it is customary to eat a boiled egg sprinkled with ashes...

4. **Tzom Gedaliah** - The fast right after Rosh Hashanah (on Tishri 3) commemorating the murder of the Judean governor Gedaliah by misguided zealots (Sept/Oct). In the Bible, this is referred to as the Fast of the 7th month.

5. **Yom Kippur** - The Day of Atonement (Tishri 10) is the most holy day of the Jewish year. This a fast day where no work of any kind is permitted. Note that Yom Kippur is the only fast day mentioned in the Scriptures for the purpose of teshuvah (repentance). So important is this fast that it is permitted even when it falls on a Shabbat (unlike other fast days that are postponed if they fall on the Sabbath).

6. **Asarah B'Tevet** - The 10th of Tevet, a fast day commemorating the fall of the Jerusalem. In the State of Israel, Kaddish (the Jewish prayer for the deceased) is recited on this day for people whose date or place of death is unknown (Dec/Jan). In the Bible, this is referred to as the Fast of the 10th month.

7. **Ta'anit Esther** - The Fast of Ester is observed on the day before Purim, on Adar 13 (In Feb/Mar).

by Josephus could have been either Sivan (May/June) or Kislev (Nov/Dec). Finally, Josephus could have been referring to the Julian month of March. In carefully studying the account of Josephus, it is almost certain that Josephus was referring to the Jewish calendar and not the Julian calendar. Following our previous chronology, the month of Sivan on the religious calendar is much too early (May/June) to be considered. Hence, we are quite certain that Josephus was referring to the third month of the Jewish Civil calendar; Kislev in Nov/Dec. This conjecture will shortly be near certainty with further investigation. In order to establish that Jerusalem fell to Herod in the early months of 36 BC, it will be necessary to find out what *fast day* is being referenced to the fall of Jerusalem. A table on the next page shows the *fast days* which were observed every Jewish year. All Jewish calendar month/day dates are from the Jewish lunar calendar: All contemporary dates are from the Julian calendar in use at that time. Let us examine each fast day.

- *Fast of the Firstborn:* Nisan 13 is one day before the Feast of Passover. It is a minor fast observed by only the firstborn. In 36 BC it fell on April 4; much too late to match previous known facts.

- *Fast of Tammuz* : 17th of Tammuz: Fell on July 5.....disqualified

- *Tisha B'Av* : 9th of Av : Fell on July 26... disqualified

- *Tzom Gedeliah:* Fell on Tishri 3..... Fell on Sept 28 in 37 BC and on Sept 17 in 36 BC.... disqualified

- *Yom Kippur:* Always on Tishri 10: Fell on Sept 24 in 36 BC and on Oct 5 in 37 BC... a weak candidate but cannot be completely disqualified.

- *Asarah B'Tevet:* Always on Tevet 10: Fell on Jan 2 in 36 BC... a candidate

- *Taanit Esther:* Fast of Esther: Always fell on Adar 13: Fell on March 5, 36 BC... a candidate.

Looking at the Jewish fast days, the best choice which agrees with all previous findings is either the *Feast of Esther or the Feast of Asarah B'Tevet.* To determine which is the fast of Josephus; let us again closely examine the known sequence of events which occurred between when Herod was declared King in Rome, and when he arrived at Jerusalem, and what events took place before the Temple fell. Using a 40 BC departure date from Rome:

- Herod named King by the Roman consulate on or near March 15, 40 BC (Antiq. 14:14:4) and previous analysis.

- Herod leaves no later than 7 days later (Antiq. 14:14:5)..... Say March 21.

- Herod crosses the Mediterranean Sea and arrives at the port of Ptolemais (Antiq. 14:15:1) about 55-60 days later.... Say May 21.

- Herod and a strong army fight their way to Jerusalem. The conflicts covered 3 years (Antiq.14:15:14)... Herod arrives in Jerusalem late winter (Antiq. 14:15:14).

When the rigors of winter was over, Herod removed his army, and came near to Jerusalem, and pitched his camp hard by the city. Now this was the third year since he had been made King by Rome.
Antiq. 14:15:14, Wars 1:17:8

March, 40 BC – March, 39 BC - Year 1
March, 39 BC – March, 38 BC - Year 2
March 38, BC – March, 37 BC – Year 3

- Herod prepares weapons of war for a long, difficult siege. This continues until the summer of 37 BC...... Say mid-July of 37 BC

*Now the three bulwarks were easily erected, because so many hands were continually at work on it; for it was **summertime**.*

Antiquities 14:16:2

During this period of time, Herod marries Mariamne; the daughter of a Jewish man named Alexander in order to strengthen his claim to be king (Wars: 1:17:9). He returns after the marriage and the siege begins in midsummer… say July 15, 37 BC.

- The siege lasts 5 months until the outside wall was breached…. Say July 15 to Dec 15.

*Indeed, since they (Antagonis) had so great an army lying about them, they bore a siege of 5 **months**, till some of Herod's chosen men ventured to get upon the wall, and fell into the city.*

Wars 1:18:2

However, the city did not immediately fall. The first (outer) wall was breached in about **55 days** and the second (inner wall) took another **15** days to cross (Antiq. 14:16:2). This will take the siege of Herod to about February 25.

- Josephus now records that the forces of Antagonis then prepared for their last-ditch battle. They retreated into the *inner temple and the upper city* (Antiq.14:16:2). We can be sure that every male Jew fervently pledged to fight to the death to defend their sacred temple of worship. While not specifically stated, they probably thought that God would dramatically and miraculously rescue them as he did King Hezekiah when Nebuchadnezzar sieged Jerusalem hundreds of years before. It would not be farfetched to imagine that they held out for another week. This would take us to early March 4 of 36 BC.

We should not be too far off in this reconstruction of events. This would indicate the Feast of Atonement in Sept/Oct is much too early. That leaves *Asarah B'Tevet or Taanit Esther* (Feast of Esther). To determine which Fast day is the one cited by Josephus, we have taken the time and effort to see when each Fast day fell in both 36 BC and 23 BC.

Fast	Date of Occurrence 63 BC	Date of Occurrence 36 BC
Fast of Taanit Esther	Adar 13, March 5 Wednesday	Adar 13, March 5 Wednesday
Fast of Asarah B'Tevet	Tevet 10, Dec 22 Tuesday	Tevet 10, Jan 2 Thursday

The verdict is undeniable if the facts presented by Josephus are to be believed. The Fast on which Jerusalem fell in both 63 BC and 36 BC is the Fast of *Taanit Esther*. What is even more remarkable is that both events fell not only on the same Jewish calendar date (Adar 13) and on the same day of the week (Wednesday), but incredibly on the same day of the Julian Calendar (March 5) !!!! ... just as Josephus said. We should also note that the very fact that Josephus could make this statement proves beyond a shadow of a doubt that a highly sophisticated calendar system with accurate knowledge of both lunar and solar cycles existed well before 63 BC. This analysis makes conjecture a near certainty: Herod the Great conquered Jerusalem and deposed Antigonus on March 5, 36 BC. Antigonus the Hasmonian was captured and taken to Antony in Rome, who subsequently had him executed: And so the Hasmonian dynasty came to an end after 163 years. So, Herod the great *procured Antigonus to be slain* on March 5, 36 BC.

> ....he (Herod) *died... having reigned since he had **procured Antigonus to be slain**, 34 years; but since he had been **declared King by the Romans**, 37 (years)*.
>
> Antiquities 17:8:1

The following diagram summarizes the entire sequence of events from when Herod arrived in Jerusalem and the Temple/Antigonus fell.

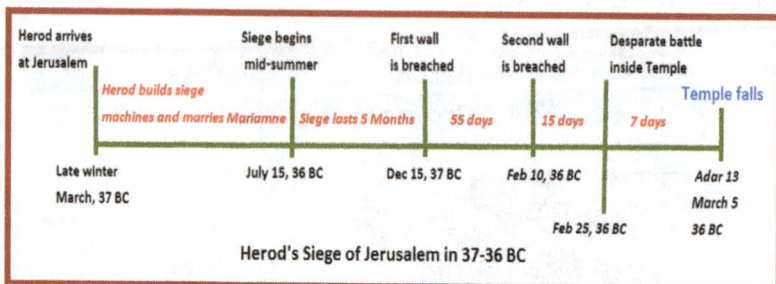

Herod arrives at Jerusalem		Siege begins mid-summer	First wall is breached	Second wall is breached	Desparate battle inside Temple	
	Herod builds siege machines and marries Mariamne	*Siege lasts 5 Months*	*55 days*	*15 days*	*7 days*	*Temple falls*
Late winter March, 37 BC		July 15, 36 BC	Dec 15, 37 BC	Feb 10, 36 BC	Feb 25, 36 BC	Adar 13 March 5 36 BC

Herod's Siege of Jerusalem in 37-36 BC

THE REIGN OF HEROD THE GREAT

We can now determine with near certainty the regnal years of Herod the Great. Josephus fully and frequently assures us that there passed three years between when Herod was named King by the Roman Senate in Rome and when he obtained the kingdom by conquest at Jerusalem and Antigonus was deposed of his Kingship. We have carefully traced the series of events between these two points in time in the previous section.

The 27 regnal years of Herod, which were initiated by appointment at Rome; and the 34 years of reign by procurement of Antagonis at Jerusalem, would normally terminate at the same point in time.... at the Death of King Herod. However, the *credited years* of reign depend upon when Herod actually died and the system used to credit years of reign: *actual, accession or non-accession*. We have established with a high degree of certainty that Herod's years by Roman appointment began on or very near to March 15, 40 BC. We have shown beyond reasonable doubt that Herod's reign by conquest began on the day that Antagonis and Jerusalem fell on March 5 in 36 BC.

Herod the Great became King of the Jews by Roman Appointment
in early 40 BC.... No later that March 15, 40 BC

Herod became King of the Jews by conquest when he defeated
Antigonus at Jerusalem on March 5, 36 BC

Year of Reign Dates: *37 years* By Roman Appointment		Year of Reign Dates: *34 years* By Conquest of Artabanus	
1	March, 40 BC - March, 39 BC	1	March 5, 36 BC (Adar 13) - March 22, 36 BC (Nisan1)
2	March, 39 BC - March, 38 BC	2	Nisan 1, 36 BC - Nisan 1, 35 BC
3	March, 38 BC - March, 37 BC	3	Nisan 1, 35 BC - Nisan 1, 34 BC
4	March, 37 BC - March, 36 BC	4	Nisan 1, 34 BC - Nisan 1, 33 BC
5	March, 36 BC - March, 35 BC	5	Nisan 1, 33 BC - Nisan 1, 32 BC
6	March, 35 BC - March, 34 BC	6	Nisan 1, 32 BC - Nisan 1, 31 BC
7	March, 34 BC - March, 33 BC	7	Nisan 1, 31 BC - Nisan 1, 30 BC
8	March, 33 BC - March, 32 BC	8	Nisan 1, 30 BC - Nisan 1, 29 BC
9	March, 32 BC - March, 31 BC	9	Nisan 1, 29 BC - Nisan 1, 28 BC
10	March, 31 BC - March, 30 BC	10	Nisan 1, 28 BC - Nisan 1, 27 BC
11	March, 30 BC - March, 29 BC	11	Nisan 1, 27 BC - Nisan 1, 26 BC
12	March, 29 BC - March, 28 BC	12	Nisan 1, 26 BC - Nisan 1, 25 BC
13	March, 28 BC - March, 27 BC	13	Nisan 1, 25 BC - Nisan 1, 24 BC
14	March, 27 BC - March, 26 BC	14	Nisan 1, 24 BC - Nisan 1, 23 BC
15	March, 26 BC - March, 25 BC	15	Nisan 1, 23 BC - Nisan 1, 22 BC
16	March, 25 BC - March, 24 BC	16	Nisan 1, 22 BC - Nisan 1, 21 BC
17	March, 24 BC - March, 23 BC	17	Nisan 1, 21 BC - Nisan 1, 20 BC
18	March, 23 BC - March, 22 BC	18	Nisan 1, 20 BC - Nisan 1, 19 BC
19	March, 22 BC - March, 21 BC	19	Nisan 1, 19 BC - Nisan 1, 18 BC
20	March, 21 BC - March, 20 BC	20	Nisan 1, 18 BC - Nisan 1, 17 BC
21	March, 20 BC - March, 19 BC	21	Nisan 1, 17 BC - Nisan 1, 16 BC
22	March, 19 BC - March, 18 BC	22	Nisan 1, 16 BC - Nisan 1, 15 BC
23	March, 18 BC - March, 17 BC	23	Nisan 1, 15 BC - Nisan 1, 14 BC
24	March, 17 BC - March, 16 BC	24	Nisan 1, 14 BC - Nisan 1, 13 BC
25	March, 16 BC - March, 15 BC	25	Nisan 1, 13 BC - Nisan 1, 12 BC
26	March, 15 BC - March, 14 BC	26	Nisan 1, 12 BC - Nisan 1, 11 BC
27	March, 14 BC - March, 13 BC	27	Nisan 1, 11 BC - Nisan 1, 10 BC
28	March, 13 BC - March, 12 BC	28	Nisan 1, 10 BC - Nisan 1, 9 BC
29	March, 12 BC - March, 11 BC	29	Nisan 1, 9 BC - Nisan 1, 8 BC
30	March, 11 BC - March, 10 BC	30	Nisan 1, 8 BC - Nisan 1, 7 BC
31	March, 10 BC - March, 9 BC	31	Nisan 1, 7 BC - Nisan 1, 6 BC
32	March, 9 BC - March, 8 BC	32	Nisan 1, 6 BC - Nisan 1, 5 BC
33	March, 8 BC - March, 7 BC	33	Nisan 1, 5 BC - Nisan 1, 4 BC
34	March, 7 BC - March, 6 BC	34	Nisan 1, 4 BC - Nisan 1, 3 BC
35	March, 6 BC - March, 5 BC		
36	March, 5 BC - March, 4 BC		
37	March, 4 BC - March, 3 BC		

This table requires some further explanation.

In looking at the previous table, the first year of reign credited to
King Herod by conquest began March 5, 36 BC and ended on
March 22 on Nisan 1. The years shown are *regnal* years..... the
years that Herod would claim as King of the Jews. So how are

regnal years calculated? The answer requires knowledge of what time of year the reigning king took office. We quote from a Jewish rabbinical writing which interprets the *Gemara*. The Gemara is the component of the *Talmud* comprising rabbinical analysis of and commentary on the *Mishnah*. After the Mishnah was published by Judah HaNasi this work was used to interpret scriptures by generation after generation of rabbis in Babylonia and the Land of Israel. Their discussions were written down in a series of books that became the *Gemara*, which when combined with the *Mishnah* constituted the *Talmud*. Consider the following ruling.

> *If a King ascends the throne on the twenty-ninth of Adar, as soon as the first of Nisan arrives he is reckoned to have reigned one year. This teaches us that Nisan 1 is the New Year for kings, and that one day served as king in a year is counted as a full year.*

This ruling and interpretation by the Jewish Rabbi was in force during King Herod's reign, and it implies that regnal years attributed to King Herod were reckoned from Nisan 1 to Nisan 1 and that the regnal years attributed to a king followed what is known as an *accession year system*. In an accession year system, if a king comes to the throne any length of time before Nisan 1 (even 1 day!); that period of time is counted as one full year. In a *non-accession*-year system, a king's reign is counted strictly from Nisan 1 to Nisan 1, with partial years credited to the king who had not died and not to the succeeding king. It should be noted that if a non- accession year system is in use, and the years given to successive kings are simply added up; the calendar year duration is one year too long for each king involved. In an accession year system, the calendar year count would be correct. This must be taken into account when adding up the number of years attributed to successive kings in historical records. Both systems were in use after the death of King Solomon and during the divided kingdom, and from that point on the system used to record the length of reign for each king has not consistently followed one scheme or another. In fact, during the divided kingdom following King Solomon's reign it can be shown that the Southern Kingdom of Judah used a non-accession year system and the Northern Kingdom led by Ephraim used an accession year system. Things are further complicated by the fact that some king's began their reign on Nisan 1, and others on Tishri 1. It takes a LOT of investigation and serious biblical research to decide what combination of systems was in use during any one period of time. It will be stated now that multiple researchers have determined that King Herod started his regnal years on Nisan 1 (March/April) and used an accession year system.

Based upon the above discussion and a previous review of the Jewish calendar, the recognized Jewish New Year for the reign of Kings starts on Nisan 1, which on the old Julian and the modern Gregorian calendar falls in March or April. As already established by previous researchers, the reign of Herod under Jewish rules also began on Nisan 1. To accurately determine how King Herod was credited with both his first and last year of reign, we have to look carefully at when King Herod assumed the throne of Judea by conquest, and when he died to determine how the years of his reign were counted. We have established that Herod became King of the Jews on March 5, 36 BC. Nisan 1 in 36 BC fell on Saturday, March 22. Recall that the Jewish rabbinical position on how regnal years were determined as follows.

> If a king ascends the throne on the 29th of Adar, as soon as the first of Nisan arrives he is reckoned to have reigned a year. This teaches us that Nisan is the New Year for Kings, and that one day in a (reigning) year is reckoned as a (whole) year. But, if he ascends the throne on (or after) the first of Nisan he is reckoned to have reigned a year till (when) the next first of Nisan comes around.
> Jack Finnegan, Handbook of Biblical Chronology

It should now be clear that the first year of Herod's reign was counted to him as Nisan 1, 37 BC to Nisan 1, 36 BC; since he reigned without controversy between March 5, 36 BC and March 22, Nisan 1, 36 BC. Using the same rules, we will now show that

Nisan 1, 4 BC to Nisan 1, 3 BC was credited to Herod as his last year of reign.

THE DEATH OF HEROD THE GREAT

Josephus records that as Herod's death approached, he was about 70 years of age (Antiq. 17:6:1). Just before Herod died, a significant series of events occurred. King Herod had erected a large golden eagle over the gate of the temple. The Jewish people were greatly disturbed, because the law strictly forbids erecting any graven images. A report came to the Jewish men that Herod had gotten sick and died. They immediately marched to the temple and tore down the golden eagle. They were led by Judas and Matthias, who was a high priest. However, the report was not true and Herod in a rage arrested 40 young Jewish men, together with Judas and Matthias. After pleas from the people, Herod released the 40 men but kept Judas and Matthias. He deprived Matthias of the priesthood, and appointed another Jew to officiate in the temple. This occasion was on the *Feast of Atonement*, which always falls on Tishri 10 in September or October. On the night before the Feast, the high priest is not allowed to sleep or have intercourse. However, this *second Matthias* did go to sleep and became unclean when he had what is commonly called a wet dream. Herod was so mad that he burned the Matthias who had defiled himself and forbid the real high priest to serve. Josephus then records:

> *"On that very night there was an eclipse of the moon."*
>
> Antiquities 17: 6: 4

The precise time of lunar eclipse' over the past 2500 years can be accurately determined using a modern digital computer. Here is a listing of lunar eclipses that occurred between 7 BC and 2 BC.

7 BC...	No eclipses
6 BC....	No eclipses
5 BC....	A total eclipse on March 23 at 8:30 pm
5 BC....	A total eclipses on Sept 15 at 10:30 pm
4 BC....	A partial eclipse on March 13 at 2:30 pm
3 BC...	No eclipse
2 BC...	No eclipses

On the surface, there appear to be no legitimate candidates... but is there one? Note that the most important Jewish Feast day of the year is the Feast of Atonement, which always falls on the Jewish Lunar calendar day of Tishri 10.

The Feast of Atonement in 5 BC occurred on September 11. Not even Herod would dare desecrate the Day of Atonement, and Josephus simply states that *"he burned the Matthias who had raised the sedition"*. It would make perfect sense if Herod executed Matthias 4 days later on September 15. If this conjecture is true, then the problem is solved. The only other candidate is the partial eclipse of 4 BC. This has long been accepted as the eclipse that preceded Herod's death. It is well documented that Herod died just before the Feast of Passover came around on Nisan 14 in 4 BC. Nisan 14 in 4 BC fell on April 11. This is less than one month after the eclipse of March 13. Several biblical scholars have pointed out that this is too short a time to contain all of the events recorded by Josephus between when Matthias was executed and Herod died. The following key events happened between when Herod executed Matthias (March 13, using the partial eclipse of March 13, 4 BC) and when he died; which was before the Feast of Passover (April 11). The following events had to have occurred in 29 days or less.

- Herod's health suddenly got very bad (Wars 1:33:5)
  o He developed an enlarged colon
  o His feet became diseased
  o His privates putrefied
  o He ate constantly and became bloated and fat
- Herod called physicians to him, but his health got progressively worse
- Herod decided to travel to just beyond the River Jordan to take "hot baths"
- He seemed to rally after hot spring baths and resting in "hot oil" (Wars 1:33:5)
- Feeling better, he went to Jericho where he contracted the cholera and "behaved like a madman" (Wars 1:33:6)

- o He issued a royal command that ALL Jewish males come to Jericho
- o Failure to comply was punishable by the death penalty
- o The men all gathered, and Herod "shut them all up in the Hippodrome"
- Herod then sends for his sister in Bethlehem (Wars 1:33:6)
- He orders that upon his death; all of the Jewish males in the Hippodrome be put to death. This was so that there would be no celebration by the Jews upon his death (Wars 1:33:6)
- Herod then proclaimed that one person in every family be slain upon his death
- Herod became so sick at this point, that while eating an apple he took the knife to kill himself, but a person called Achiabus stopped him from doing so (Wars 1:33:7)
- A report went out that Herod had died, and his son Antipater rejoiced…thinking that he might be the new king.
- When Herod hears of this, he orders his son Antipater be slain
- Antipater was executed as Herod commanded, and appointed Antipas to succeed him at his death (Wars 1:33:7)
- Five days after Antipater was slain, Herod dies (Wars 1:33:8)
- In an act of deliverance and common sense, all of the male Jews in the Hippodrome were set free and the order to kill one from each family rescinded (Wars 1:33:8)

Having reviewed the sequence of events which Josephus recorded; If the eclipse of March 13, 4 BC was the one that preceded the death of King Herod; Herod would have died about 30 days later. It is the opinion of this author that it would be very unlikely if not impossible for all of these things to transpire in that amount of time. This observation has confounded biblical scholars for years, because the only eclipse that was even considered was the one that fell on March 13, 4 BC. We have now identified another earlier eclipse which resolves many problems.

Considering all of the facts presented, it is my belief that the eclipse of the moon which occurred prior to the death of King Herod, and which was noted by Josephus, was NOT the partial eclipse of March1 13, 4 BC but was the full eclipse of September 15 in 5 BC. There is nothing in the account that Josephus wrote that *demands* a very short amount of time between the ellipse and Herod's death. The time which elapsed between September 15, 5 BC and the Death of Herod; which occurred no later than April 10, 4 BC; is a reasonable amount of time for all of the events listed by Josephus to transpire. To the best of my knowledge, this has not been proposed before this book was written.

The last few days of Herod were spent in intense agony. We have two critical pieces of information: (1) Herod lived only 5 days after he had his son Antipater slain (Wars 2:1:8) (2) Herod named his oldest son Archaleus his successor. After Herod died, Archaleus took the body of Herod 200 furlongs to Herodium to be buried and as was customary (Ecclesiastics 22:12) he mourned his death for 7 days (Wars 2:1:1). He then attended the Feast of Passover (Wars 2:1:3). Nisan 1 in 4 BC was on March 29 (Julian calendar) and the Feast of Passover was on April 11, 4 BC. Two highly respected biblical scholars, W.E. Filmer and E. Shurer place the death of Herod between Nisan 1 and Nisan 14. By the Jewish system being used to determine years of reign, Herod was credited with his last year of reign between Nisan 1, 4 BC and Nisan 1, 3 BC as previously shown.

We now know that Herod died in the spring of 4 BC, just before the Feast of Passover came around on Nisan 14. If Herod survived past Nisan 1, which seems to be the case, by using the Jewish non-accession system to determine Herod's regnal years the sequence of years shown in Table 1 now makes complete sense. From the detailed account of Josephus, Herod ruled for almost exactly 37 years after he was named King on March 15, 40

BC and 34 years after Jerusalem fell. Acting as King of the Jews, Herod died after the New Year for kings on Nisan 1 and before Passover on Nisan 14. By using the non-accession Jewish regnal year system, these few days were enough to credit the entire 4 BC – 3 BC regnal year to Herod.

For this author, the issue is settled…. or at least defensible. We now are ready to examine what happened in the last days of King Herod.

NOTES AND THINGS TO REMEMBER:

CHAPTER 6

THE LAST DAYS OF HEROD THE GREAT

We have previously shown that King Herod died just before the Feast of Passover in the spring of 4 BC. The closing events in King Herod's life can now be correlated to the heavenly signs which appeared between 7 BC - 5 BC, the birth of Christ in the spring of 5 BC, and the subsequent visit of the Magi.

- In 7 BC there were three conjunctions of the planets Saturn and Jupiter in the constellation Pices.
- Shortly after the triple conjunctions of Saturn and Jupiter in 7 BC, Mars joined Jupiter and Saturn so that on February 6, 6 BC they were separated by no more than 8 degrees; appearing to the naked eye as one bright heavenly light. There was an ancient tradition that three planets massing together to appear as one would precede the birth of a King. Kepler suggested that this massing occurred only about every 800 years, and preceded several important biblical events. In any case, these celestial events in 7 BC and 6 BC caused great excitement and expectations; shortly to be reinforced in 5 BC.
- In the spring of 5 BC a comet blazed across the south and eastern sky in the constellation of Capricorn, which was clearly visible from Babylon and Persia. Ancient civilizations viewed the appearance of a comet as a harbinger of significant events. Chinese records record this event as occurring in the second year of the Chien-p'ing era of reign, during his second month of reign, which was March 9-April 6, 5 BC. This was a major celestial event in which the comet slowly moved east to southeast toward Jerusalem. The comet was clearly visible for about 70 days.
- This third and final heavenly display would have convinced the Magi that the long awaited Messiah had finally been born.

- It is more than coincidental that the Jewish Feast of Unleavened Bread occurred on Nisan 15, March 23 in 5 BC. This coincides with the sudden appearance of the comet in 5 BC. We accept March 23, 5 BC as a most appropriate date for the birth of Christ.
- The Magi would have spent about 2-3 weeks preparing for their trip to Jerusalem, and depending upon the weather, availability of water and the strength of their entourage; they would have arrived in Jerusalem about two months later near early June, 5 BC in the month of Tammuz. They would follow after a *star* which we have assumed was the comet of 5 BC; visible for about 70 days and very consistent with our timetable. Please note that the Magi would only need the series of heavenly signs to convince them that this great event had happened, and that the comet would only need to point them towards Jerusalem as it crossed the sky. They already knew that Christ was to be born in Bethlehem from the scriptures.
- The Magi would immediately visit King Herod, who would send them on their way to find the Christ so that he might kill the babe.
- The Magi would have normally gone directly to Bethlehem, but the *star* miraculous reappears (this is not a celestial star but an angelic light) to lead them to the Christ-child. Notice that this was necessary, because the Magi were not aware that Joseph and Mary had returned to their own house in Nazareth. We believe that this *star* was a mighty angel leading the way in a bright light, which appeared similar to the celestial comet of 5 BC that led the Magi to Jerusalem. The distance from Jerusalem to Nazareth was about 50 miles, and would have taken only a few days... call it a week at most.
- The Magi arrive at Joseph's *house* in mid to late June of 5 BC. It is interesting that in Matthew 2:11 it is recorded that: *they* (the Magi) *saw the young child with Mary.* In the Greek language there are two words used to describe a young child". These two words are *paidion* and *brephos.*

Paidion: A young or little child, an infant; also a term of endearment.

Brephos: An *embryo*, or newly-born babe.

The word used in Matthew 2:11 is not *brephos* (a newly born babe) but *paidion* (a young child). In this determined chronology, Christ would have been a young child of 3 months, 4 at the most.

- Mary and Joseph would immediately depart for Egypt, after being warned that Herod sought to kill the child. The Magi then returned to their own home (Babylon or Persia), having fulfilled prophecy (Matthew 2:13)
- Herod would have waited impatiently for the Magi to return. He could have possibly waited 2 weeks before realizing that he had been deceived. This would have brought us to early July of 5 BC. This is when the *slaughter of the innocents* would have occurred. Herod would have remembered when the first sign occurred in the heavens: That was as early as the first conjunction of Jupiter and Saturn in May of 7 BC. From May, 7 BC to July of 5 BC is almost 2 years; which coincides nicely with Herod's decision to kill all male children 2 years and younger.

The events between the slaughter of the innocents and the death of King Herod will now be traced. Most of what we know about Herod's last days is from Josephus. As Herod began to approach the age of 70, his health began to deteriorate rapidly. Within 8-9 months of when he ordered the children to be killed, he would be dead.

A mystery that we will now unravel is found in Josephus, *Antiquities, Book 17: 6.* Herod had mounted a large golden eagle over the main gate to the temple. Jewish law (Laws of Moses) forbids any graven image to be cast or worshipped, and such a thing hanging in the temple was considered to be an abomination to God. There were two leaders of the Jews called

Judas and Matthias who decided to pull down the image. Word came that Herod had died, so in that very day they pulled the golden eagle down and cut it into pieces. The report was false, and in a rage Herod captured both Judas and Matthias along with 40 other young Jews. Herod had them taken to Jericho and spoke against them in front of all the people. For some unknown reason...perhaps he feared the people since the perpetrators were among the wisest and best... he held out mercy for the entire group. This would seem to be the end of the story, but something strange now happened. Josephus next records that Matthias was a priest of the Levitical priesthood, and Herod, acting against him, removed him from ever serving as a high priest and appointed another person named Joazar, who was Matthias's wife's brother, to take his (Matthias') place. The following narrative is written by Josephus (Antiq. 17:6:4).

> *Now it happened that when the time came for the deposed Matthias to serve as high priest, there was another person selected to serve as high priest. Josephus called this person the other Matthias That very day was called the great day of expiation and it was identified as a fast day.* **Expiation** *means* **atonement,** *This one feast day was also ordained as a* **fast day,** *so there is no doubt that this day is Tishri 10, the Jewish Feast of Atonement. Now, another very strange thing happened that pushed King Herod to the edge of madness.*

It happened that this *other Matthias* had a *seditious dream* the night before his assigned service and became defiled. Under Levitical law he could then not officiate. So Joseph, the son of Ellemus, was designated as the high priest and served during the Feast of Atonement. Herod fell into a state of madness, and he banned the original Matthias from ever serving in any capacity in the priesthood; burned alive the other Matthias who had experienced the sedition; and also burned *some of his companions alive* who were not further identified. That very night, there was an eclipse of the moon.

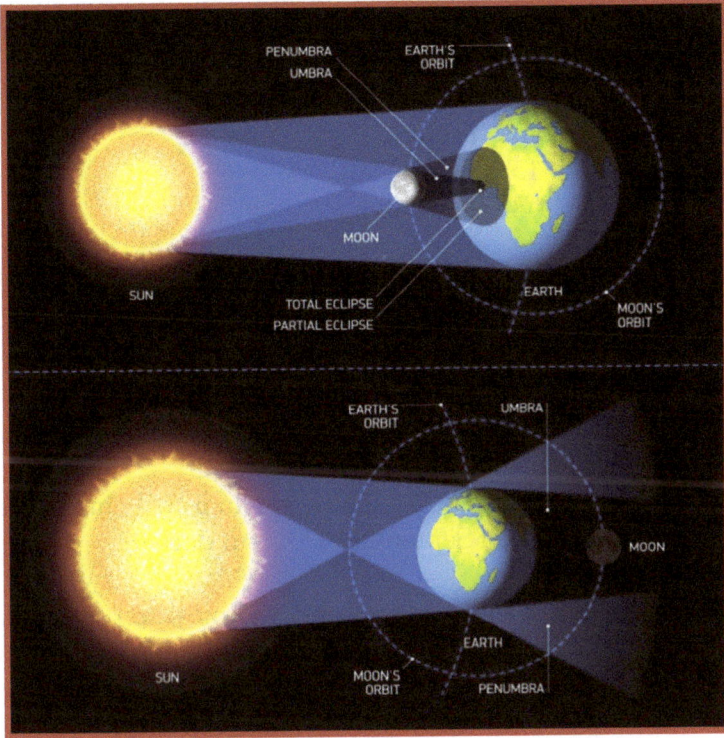

We have both a Day of Atonement and a solar eclipse pointing to when these atrocities took place. Obviously, if we could show that two such major events coincided in 5 BC; this would be strong proof that we have been correct so far. Lunar eclipses have been tabulated by NASA for the past 3000 years. Using modern digital computers, eclipses are very predictable as the sun and moon line up such that the earth is directly between them. When a lunar eclipse occurs, the earth blocks the rays of the sun from reaching the moon and darkness obscures the moon. An eclipse can be full or partial. In the entire, extensive body of Josephus' work he only records one eclipse; and that is one that preceded the death of Herod which marks the death of the *other Matthias* and several other young Jewish men. It can be assumed (although not certain) that this eclipse was full for such a unique identification. If one recovers the records of lunar eclipses that occurred within a reasonable amount of time prior to when Herod died, we find some interesting facts. The following eclipses were recorded.

- March 23, 5 BC (Total)
- September 15, 5 BC (Total)
- March 13, 4 BC (Partial)

The March 23 eclipse was the eclipse which convinced the Magi that Jesus had been born, and it occurred in the early spring of 5 BC. This cannot be the eclipse that Josephus records, because the eclipse that Josephus noted seemed to occur on the Feast of Atonement. However, there is another candidate... the total eclipse of September 15, 5 BC. But wait! ...The Feast of Atonement in 5 BC fell on September 11 in 5 BC. This seems to disqualify the eclipse of September 15... but does it?

The Feast of Atonement was arguably the most important Feast Day of the year for most Jews. It is the day on which the high priest enters the Holy of Holies and pleads for forgiveness of sins for the entire nation. It always occurs on Tishri 10, and is a *national* fast day. Even Herod, although deranged and furious, would not dare hold a massacre on the Day of Atonement. It is extremely likely that Herod delayed this mass execution for 3 days. If so, the execution would have taken place on the evening of Thursday, Tishri 13; which after 6:00 PM became Tishri 14, which was Friday, September 15 in 5 BC. That evening, the total solar eclipse took place. These dates were confirmed by three different Jewish calendar convertors. This scenario is plausible, defendable and unique to this study. Carefully reading the entire description of all these events by Josephus, there is not a single reason that Josephus demands that the slaughter of these Jews and an eclipse that very night had to coincide with the Feast of Atonement in 5 BC. In fact, there is a very good reason why Herod would never had killed the Jewish men on the holy Feast of Atonement. Here we see how totally cruel and deranged Herod could become over certain events, but how even in that state he would protect his kingship. In fact, Herod displays this behavior on several other occasions. We propose that he let the

Feast of Atonement be held as usual, and then he waited three days to execute the Jewish men (Antiquities 17: 6: 4).

All proposed scenarios are consistent with a 5 BC birth of Christ, a 4 BC death of King Herod., and the visit of the Magi. Why is this extremely important scenario? Note that a lunar eclipse (which was partial in Jerusalem and reported to be only partially visible) occurred on March 13, 4 BC. Almost all scholarly investigations accept this eclipse as the one mentioned by Josephus. There is, of course, no way to reconcile this eclipse with the Day of Atonement on Tishri 10 as we have just done. Josephus records in *Antiq. Book 17: Chapters 7-9* that Herod died just after Nisan 1 and before the Feast of Unleavened Bread. This is almost 6 full months after the Feast of Atonement. As to the partial lunar eclipse that did occur on March 13, 4 BC shortly before Herod's death: it was NOT the eclipse noted by Josephus and in fact played no role at all in any of Josephus' historical narratives.

Passover in 4 BC fell on Nisan 14, April 11; almost 6 months after Christ had been born and about 3 months after the Magi had deceived him. The Feast of Unleavened Bread in 4 BC occurred between April 12 and April 18. In Antiq. 2:1:1 the records of Josephus strongly indicate that Herod died on or near April 4. To this many researchers agree. This is attested by the fact that Herod's son Archaleus ascended to the throne immediately after his father's death. Josephus goes on to say that following Jewish custom, Archaleus mourned Herod's death for 7 days; ending before Passover which fell on Nisan 14, April 11 in 4 BC. At the latest, Archaleus would have begun mourning on April 4. Hence, Herod must have died between March 13 and April 4; a period of just over 3 weeks (22 days). According to Josephus, there are many events that took place in this short period of time. This includes the following events.

- *Part of Herod's body was putrefied and bred worms.*
- *He took a trip to warm baths 16 km away, and then returns after a few days.*

- *He ordered all important men in all villages to come to Jerusalem where he shut them up in the hippodrome*
- *Men begin to arrive*
- *His son Antipater is executed; Herod dies 5 days later.*
- *There is a magnificent funeral, and the body is carried 37 km (22 miles).*
- *Archaleus attends funeral, then returns to Jerusalem for Passover*
- *Archaleus conducts a seven-day period of mourning, followed by a funeral feast.*
- *Only then comes Passover.*

It has been pointed out by many biblical scholars that while not impossible, it is highly unlikely that all of these events could have occurred in a three week period of time. We agree. This has caused a host of researchers to challenge the traditional reign and death of King Herod in 4 BC.

To answer this problem, Filmer proposed that Herod died in 1 BC. This study has been widely accepted, mainly because it is supported by a total eclipse which occurred on January 10, 1 BC. This eclipse provides enough time for all of the events recorded by Josephus to take place between January 10 and the Feast of Passover. However, the chronology of King Herod which supports his death in 1 BC requires clever accounting of King Herod's regnal years. This study proposed an equally viable alternative which fully supports Herod's death in the spring of 4 BC. Nothing stretches the imagination, and it fully supports all known facts.

We propose that the eclipse that Josephus clearly referenced prior to Herod's death was the eclipse of March 23, 5 BC. The events recorded in Josephus then unfolded in a sequential manner over the next 7 months, including the progressive failure of Herod's health and subsequent attempts to recover. The eclipse of March 13, 4 BC certainly did occur; although partial and possibly partially obscured in Jerusalem. The misinterpretation of Josephus' account is quite understandable and believable. The commonly accepted theory that the March 13, 4 B.C. eclipse is the one recorded by Josephus must now be rejected in light of our findings. It is clear from historical evidence and our analysis that there was not enough time between a March 13 eclipse and the Nisan 14 Passover Feast of 4 BC on April 11 for all of these events to have transpired. The following observations are quoted from Ernest L. Martin in his book *The Star of Bethlehem*.

*Those theologians who adopted this astronomical principle (dates recorded for an eclipse) for solving chronological questions are absolutely correct. There is no arguing with eclipses. They are solid and unchallenged witnesses to support the truth of early historical records — **if the correct eclipse is considered**. But when astronomers in the last century told theologians that an eclipse of the Moon occurred during the evening of March 13, 4 B.C.E., this eclipse is the one that theologians accepted as the one referred to by Josephus. They particularly preferred this eclipse because Josephus also said Herod died before a springtime Passover. Since March 13, 4 B.C.E. was just one month before the Passover, they felt justified in placing all historical events associated with Herod's death and his funeral within that twenty-nine day period. The truth is, however, it is completely illogical to squeeze the events mentioned by Josephus into that short period of time. By selecting the wrong eclipse, modern scholars have been forced to tighten considerably the historical events into an abnormally compressed space of only twenty-nine days.*

Although we believe that the eclipse of March 13, 4 BC is not the one referenced by Josephus; our conclusion that Herod died shortly before the Feast of Passover in 4 BC is correct and is supported by many researchers.

Since we propose that Christ was *born* on the first day of the Feast of Unleavened Bread, Nisan 15, March 23 in 5 BC: It immediately follows that he turned 30 years old in 26 AD and that he was shortly baptized by John the Baptist. His death on the cross would have taken place on Nisan 14, 30 AD on the Feast of Passover. This sequence is *demanded* by the Holy

Scriptures if Christ was born in 5 BC. Can we show that Christ was crucified in 30 BC using other scriptures and historical events? The answer is: YES.

We will next look at the 490 year prophecy given to Daniel and show that: (1) This prophecy fully supports a 5 BC birth of Christ (2) Christ was crucified on Nisan 14 in 30 AD (3) Christ died on a Wednesday and that (4) Christ lay in the tomb for a 3 days and 3 nights... a full 72 hours... just as He said He would.

CHAPTER 7

DANIEL'S 70 WEEK PROPHECY AND THE CRUCIFIXION OF CHRIST

Daniel is one of the most remarkable persons in the entire Bible. He was never rebuked or criticized for departing from the word of the Lord. He was deported from Jerusalem by Nebuchadnezzar in the first group of exiles in 605 BC, along with Shadrach, Meshach and Abednego (Danial 1:6-7). God gave him the gift of interpreting visions and dreams, and he became the second most powerful man in Babylon. After the Persians conquered Babylon in 539 BC under Darius I, Daniel continued to serve in the King's palace. In the first year of Cyrus who was appointed king, he *understood by books* that the Jewish Babylonian exile would shortly come to an end (Dan 9:1-2). The *books* were the writings of the prophet Jeremiah. Jeremiah began prophesying at age 20 during the 13th year of the reign of King Josiah. At the age of 33 (23 years later), he predicted that the Southern Kingdom of Judah would be conquered, and that Israel would serve the king of Babylon for 70 years (Isa 25:11). As Daniel studied the books of Jeremiah (Jer 29:10-11), he realized that 70 years had almost passed since he was deported. Daniel began a remarkable prayer (Dan 9:1-18) in which he petitioned the Lord to end the captivity as prophesied, and *turn* (His) *fury from the Holy City of Jerusalem* (Dan 9:16). His prayer was answered by the Archangel Gabriel (Dan 9:20). The response from Gabriel should be carefully noted: *Oh Daniel, I am now come forth to give thee skill and understanding.* Gabriel clarified his mission: *I am come to show you; for thou art greatly loved: therefore understand the matter and consider the vision.* (Dan 9:23). Oh what a wonderful greeting! Daniel is said to be *greatly loved* by the Lord. The vision was then presented.

Seventy weeks are determined upon thy people and upon thy holy city, to finish the transgression, and to make an end of sins, and to make reconciliation for iniquity, and to bring in everlasting righteousness,

*and to seal up the vision and prophecy, and to anoint the most Holy.
Know therefore and understand, that from the going forth of the
commandment to restore and to build Jerusalem unto the Messiah the
Prince shall be seven weeks, and threescore and two weeks: the street
shall be built again, and the wall, even in troublous times.*

*And after threescore and two weeks shall Messiah be cut off, but not
for himself: and the people of the prince that shall come shall destroy
the city and the sanctuary; and the end thereof shall be with a flood,
and unto the end of the war desolations are determined.*

*And he shall confirm the covenant with many for one week: and in the
midst of the week he shall cause the sacrifice and the oblation to cease,
and for the overspreading of abominations he shall make it desolate,
even until the consummation, and that determined shall be poured
upon the desolate.*

Dan 9:24-27

This prophecy is considered to be one of the most important in
the entire Holy Bible. It spans a period of time from when it was
issued to the second coming of Jesus Christ. It also predicts
when the coming Messiah would be crucified. Note that this
prophecy begins with the *going forth of the commandment to restore
and to build (rebuild) Jerusalem.*

THE COMMANDMENT TO RESTORE THE TEMPLE AND REBUILD JERUSALEM

It is crucial that we determine exactly when this commandment
went forth. There are two basic things to consider. The *first* is
that we are able to look back in time and determine the most
likely time and place that this commandment occurred. *Second*,
the decree which will initiate the 70 week prophecy of Daniel
must lead to the *beginning* of the ministry of Christ when he
came to the River Jordan to be baptized by John at the end of 483
years. We have already established that Christ was born in 5 BC.
Can this date be confirmed by the Daniel prophecy?

THE DECREE OF CYRUS

In 539 BC, the Persian King Darius conquered Babylon and installed Cyrus (a Mede) to act as king. This happened after the prophet Daniel had almost completed his 70 years of exile, which had previously been prophesied by Jeremiah (Jeremiah 29:10). In Ezra 1:1 we read: *Now in the first year of Cyrus king of Persia, that the word of the Lord by the mouth of Jeremiah might be fulfilled, the Lord stirred up the spirit of Cyrus, king of Persia, that he made a royal proclamation.* This proclamation authorized the return of Israel to Jerusalem to *build (rebuild) the house (temple) of the Lord.* From 539 BC, a span of 483 years *unto the Messiah the Prince* (Jesus Christ), would take us to 56 BC. This is way too early, so we must look elsewhere.

THE DECREE OF DARIUS

The rebuilding of the temple authorized by Cyrus did not go well. The *people of the land* (Ezra 4:4) resisted the project, and it is recorded in Ezra 4:24 that the work *ceased until the second year of the reign of Darius, king of Persia.* Darius succeeded Cyrus in 518 BC. The work resumed in 520 BC under Haggai and Zechariah. The governor of the province surrounding Jerusalem came to the temple site and inquired: *Who hath commanded you to build this house?* (Ezra 5:3). They replied that King Cyrus had authorized the project. The governor then sent a letter to the king asking him to produce such a decree, if indeed one existed. A search was made and the original decree was found. Darius then reinforced this decree with one of his own. *Let the governor of the Jews and the elders of the Jews build this house of God in His place.* So Darius simply reissued the decree of Cyrus authorizing that the Temple of God be rebuilt. Based upon Ezra 4:24 and biblical/ archeological research, this event likely occurred in 520 BC. Again moving forward 483 years, we find an ending date of 37 BC. This was about when King Herod began to reign in Jerusalem, and is again much too early. We must search further.

THE FIRST DECREE OF ARTAXERXES

In Ezra 7:1-10, we read that Ezra the scribe, who was a descendent of Aaron, approached King Artaxerxes I and petitioned the king to allow him and a band of Israelites to return to Jerusalem. Biblical scholars are in almost universal agreement that this occurred in either 457 BC or 458 BC. We will later show that this occurred in the spring of 458 BC in the seventh year of Artaxerxes reign. Ezra wanted to *set magistrates and judges* in place, *teach the laws of God,* and *let judgment be executed speedily,* upon all who would not obey the laws of God (Ezra 7). The petition was granted, and Ezra left *on the first day of the first month of Artaxerxes Seventh year,* and arrived in Jerusalem *on the first day of the Fifth month.* We will later show that the departure from the city of Babylon was on Nisan 1 in 458 BC (Ezra 7:9). After a short delay to find some Levites to serve as priests, he arrived in Jerusalem after a journey of just less than five months; one month before Tishri 1, 458 BC (Ezra 7:8). Ezra assembled all of the people and read the proclamation and the law. The *decree went forth* at this time to all the people, and was put into effect. Synchronizing with Sabbatical years, the 70 weeks of Daniel would have started on *Tishri 1, 458 BC.* Subtracting 483 years from this date, we arrive at 26 AD. Please note that to arrive at 26 AD; we must subtract a total of 484 years because when one crosses from BC to AD, there is no year zero. 26 AD is considered by many to be the year in which Jesus Christ came to the river Jordan and started his ministry of 3.5 years. This would demand that Christ was crucified on Nisan 14 in 30 AD. This is a strong candidate, but we will consider the final possible decree.

THE SECOND DECREE OF ARTAXERXES

In the 20ᵗʰ year of King Artaxerxes (Neh. 1:1) word came to Nehemiah that things were not going so well in Jerusalem: *The remnant that are left of the captivity there in the province are in great affliction and reproach. The wall of Jerusalem also is broken down, and the gates thereof are burned with fire* (Neh. 1:3). Nehemiah wept, mourned, fasted and petitioned God to turn the heart of Artaxerxes to let him go to Jerusalem and rebuild, for he was the King's personal cupbearer (Neh. 1:11; 2:1). God moved Artaxerxes' heart, and he gave Nehemiah permission to return. He also sent a letter to *Asaph* informing him to supply timber to rebuild the gates, the walls and the temple (Neh. 2:6-8). This commission was issued to Nehemiah in the month of Nisan (Neh. 2:1). In 1882 Sir Robert Anderson published a book called *The Coming Prince*. In this book he determined that the month of Nisan in 445 BC must have been in the 20th year of Artaxerxes reign. Hence, Anderson declared that the decree was issued in the month of Nisan, 445 BC. After a five month trip to Jerusalem and installing a judiciary, Daniels 70th week would start on Tishri 1, 445 BC. If we subtract 484 years from this date we would arrive at September of 39 AD. The death of Christ would be on Nisan 14 in 43 AD. This is much too late for the death of Christ. At this point, Anderson made a rectifying assumption. Using the flood account of Gen 6-8, he determined based upon Gen 7:11, 7:24 and 8:4 that a *prophetic month* was only 30 days long, and a *prophetic year* was 360 days long. He supported this theory by referring to the Book of Revelation, which equates 1260 days to 42 months (Rev 11:2-3). Using a year as 360 days, he multiplied 360 days times 483 years. He then converted this number of prophetic days into a *Gregorian* calendar year, even though the Gregorian calendar had not even been implemented in Daniel's time. After adjusting for leap years, Newton arrived at Nisan 10, Psalm Sunday in 32 BC. The subsequent date for the crucifixion of Christ worked out to be on Thursday, Nisan 14, in 32 AD. The 7 years remaining in Daniel's 490-year prophecy were then given to the tribulation period of John's Revelation. However, the Roman Catholic Church has decreed for many centuries that Christ was crucified on a Friday in 33 AD. To accommodate this date, Hoehner assumed that the month of Nisan in 444 BC must have been in the 20th year of Artaxerxes reign. Hoehner then assumed that the 70 weeks of Daniel commenced on Nisan 1, 444 BC. Using an approach similar to Isaac Newton, Hoehner arrived at Psalm Sunday, Nisan 10 in 33 AD as his *terminus quo* of the first 483 years. It then followed that Friday, Nisan 14, 33 AD was the crucifixion date of Jesus Christ. Since the Roman Catholic Church dogmatically holds to a Friday crucifixion day, Hoehner's work has been widely accepted.

We can only applaud Sir Robert Anderson and Harold Hoehner for using such a clever approach to arrive at either 32 AD

(Newton) or 33 AD (Hoehner) as a crucifixion year. Both dates have been widely acclaimed as correct by two large groups of followers. However, the basic assumptions and methods used by both Anderson and Hoehner have been critically assailed and claimed in error by Pickle, Ice and Jones to name a few. *First*, the flood account in Genesis *does* state that over a period of 150 days, five months elapsed, but this does not guarantee that *each month* was 30 days in duration. In fact, if anyone wants to carefully study the narrative in Gen 7 & 8 they will find that from when Noah entered the ark until he left the ark was 365 days, and it could have been exactly one solar year of 365.2422 days which would imply a normal year. *Second*, the book of Revelation would not be written for about another 620 years, so Daniel would have no access to that text. *Third*, Daniel was nearing the end of the 70-year period of Babylonian exile when he received the prophecy. He was not experiencing 360-day prophetic years during his exile, but full solar years. He was also well aware that the 70 years of exile were almost over when he petitioned God in prayer and fasting. There would be no confusion whatsoever in associating full solar years with the 70 week prophecy given to Daniel (Dan 9:24). *Fourth*, if Daniel *understood* (Dan 9:23) that the 490-year prophecy was *not* based upon the Babylonian calendar year, which was very close to a modern solar year, there was certainly no indication of that in his response to Gabriel nor in the Biblical record. There is no proof or any revelation whatsoever that a 360-day year prophetic ever existed in the Holy Scriptures. In fact, to keep the Passover every year in the correct month at the correct time of year, a 360 year *could not* be in use. Of course, the 360 day year proponents never suggest that anything but a full solar year was in use following the exodus. They simply state with a great deal of confidence that the *360 year prophetic year* was a *mystery* hidden until Sir Isaac Newton discovered it! Finally, everyone today does have access to the book of Revelation, and there is no doubt that the last 3.5 years of the tribulation period is 1260 days, and this is equated to 42 months (Rev 11:2-3). Ah ha! They say, Daniel was told this by Gabriel and he knew it all along. After all, Gabriel told Daniel that he would *understand*. This is *high conjecture* at best. We will show in the next section that these 1260

104

days involving 42 months can and should refer to a 365.2425 solar year, and not a 360 day lunar year. In this author's opinion, the assumption of a 360-day *prophetic year* is simply unwarranted.

The conclusion of the matter is that the only decree which makes logical sense, and fits all the requirements of a normal 490-solar year prophecy, is the one issued by Artaxerxes in either 457 BC or 458 BC. We will now show that 458 BC is indeed the correct year.

THE SEVENTH YEAR OF ARTAXERXES

We believe that after examining the available options, the commandment to restore and to rebuild Jerusalem (Dan 9:25), which initiated the 70-week prophecy of Daniel is most likely the decree from Artaxerxes I to the scribe, Ezra. This decree *went forth* to the people of Israel when Ezra arrived in Jerusalem. Ezra left Babylon *on the first day of the first month* (Ezra 7:9). After gathering the people together and assembling a group of Levites to conduct temple services, he *departed from the River of A-Haya on the 12th day of the first month* (Ezra 8:31). He arrived in Jerusalem on the *first day of the 5th month*. Hence, the journey took almost four months. Ezra left in the first month and arrived in the fifth month of Artaxerxes seventh year. The key question is: *when was Artaxerxes seventh year? And when was the first month?* From the context of Ezra 7, the *first month* is undoubtedly the first month of the 7th year of Artaxerxes reign. To determine the seventh regnal year of Artaxerxes, we need to discuss two fundamental issues. Artaxerxes was a Persian king: (1) In what month of the year did Persian kings begin to count their regnal years? (2) How did Persian kings transition from the death of one king to the next?

THE BEGINNING OF REGNAL YEARS

We will briefly review calendar systems used to mark time. Each ancient kingdom had their own calendar system which was used to mark the beginning of a king's reign. Each ancient kingdom employed a slightly different calendar, but most had learned that the length of a solar year was determined by the sun; which we now know is exactly 365.2422 days. A modern solar calendar year was composed of 12 months and a week of seven, 24-hour days. Most ancient societies used a 12 month year, but the number of days in each month varied from kingdom to kingdom, as did the actual number of total days in each year. The length of a month in ancient times was usually set at either 29 or 30 days. This is because the actual length of a lunar month is determined by the rotation of the moon, and is 29.53059 days. Calendars are designed to mark time by the passage of months, with the number and initiation of each month designed so that a series of 12 or 13 months would coincide with the solar year. However, there is no combination of 30 and 29 day months that can equate to a solar year on a yearly basis. There were two common solutions to the problem: the first was to add days at the end of each year; the second is to periodically add an extra (13th) month to the normal 12-month year. For example, the Egyptians used a simple 12-month calendar consisting of 12 months of 30 days per year. This would total to 360 days per year. They then added 5 days at the end of the 12th month, so that their year was 365 days. This was close to the actual solar year, but fell short about 0.2422 days per year. Hence, the calendar *drifted backward* about one day every four years. It would continue to drift back through the solar year, so that after about 1460 years, the Egyptian year would move back in sync with a true solar year. For example, if today was Christmas using this calendar, in about 730 years Christmas would be in July!

The calendar used by the Jews was also a *lunar-Solar* calendar. It consisted of 12 alternating 30 and 29 day months. Simple math shows that a Hebrew year was only 354 days, which is about 11.25 days short of a solar year. About every three years, the calendar would drift back approximately 33.75 days. To keep the lunar-based 12-month year in sync with the solar year, it was discovered that by adding seven extra months over a 19-year period of time, 19 lunar calendar years of 12 (13) months would almost exactly equal the solar calendar over the same period of time. This 19-year period of time with seven inter-calculated months is called a *Metonic cycle*.

With some minor adjustments to prevent back-to-back Sabbaths and other anomalies, the same Jewish calendar with periodic inter-calculated months is in use today. The Babylonians seem to be the first to discover the *Metonic cycle* and put it into formal use. However, it must again be stressed that since the seven feasts of Israel were ordained by God, and were to be observed every year following agricultural cycles, the Hebrews after the exodus also *had* to keep their 12-month lunar calendar in sync with the solar year. Whether this was done by a formal method such as the one just described, or done by observation of crop maturity, is unknown. However, after the Babylonian exile, the Hebrews almost surely adopted and used a Metonic cycle. Each civilization had its own names for each month of the year, but after the 70-year Babylonian exile, the Hebrews adopted the Babylonian calendar names with only slight variations. The calendar we use today is called the *Gregorian calendar*. It was derived from the *Julian calendar*. The Gregorian calendar is very accurate, as is the modern Jewish calendar. The modern Jewish calendar was first implemented by the Patriarch Hillel II in 358 AD. The table on the next page is a summary of the Julian, Gregorian, Babylonian and Hebrew calendars.

After Medo-Persia overthrew the Babylonian empire in 539 BC, the Persian Empire also adopted the Babylonian calendar for their own use. The Babylonians, Hebrews, Egyptians and Persians all used a common method for determining when a king came to reign, and this was to use the first day of the first month in the civil year. The Babylonians and the Persians used Nisan 1 and the Egyptians used Thoth 1. The Hebrew Southern Kingdom of Judah used Tishri 1 until the Babylonian destruction and exile. This was proved and published by Edwin Thiele, and is now widely accepted.

	Julian	Gregorian	Hebrew	(Civil)	Babylonian	
Month	Name	Name	Name	Months	Name	Months
1	Januarius	Jan	Tishri	Sept/Oct	Nisanu	Mar/Apr
2	Februarius	Feb	Heshvan	Oct/Nov	Aiaru	Apr/May
3	Martius	Mar	Chislev	Non/Dec	Simanu	May/Jun
4	Aprilus	April	Tebeth	Dec/Jan	Duzu	Jun/July
5	Maius	May	Shevat	Jan/Feb	Abu	July/Aug
6	Junius	June	Adar	Feb/Mar	Ululu	Aug/Sept
7	Julius	July	Nisan	Mar/Apr	Tashritu	Sept/Oct
8	Augustus	Aug	Iyyar	Apr/May	Arahsamnu	Oct/Nov
9	Septembris	Sept	Sivan	May/Jun	Kislimu	Non/Dec
10	Octobris	Oct	Tammuz	Jun/July	Tebetu	Dec/Jan
11	Novembris	Nov	Ab/Av	July/Aug	Shabatu	Jan/Feb
12	Decembris	Dec	Elul	Aug/Sept	Addaru	Feb/Mar

*The Hebrew Civil year was used from antiquity to the Exodus. Month 1 was always Tishri. After the Exodus, God ordained that the Religious year would begin in Nisan. All festivals and "Month 1" in the scriptures always referred to the month of Nisan. Before the Exodus in scripture, all "Month 1" references referred to Tishri.

**Egyptian years always began on Thoth 1. The Julian date of Thoth 1 has to be calculated using modern computers. It "drifts" back across Julian months at a rate of about 1 day every 4 years.

DETERMINING THE SEVENTH YEAR OF ARTAXERXES REIGN

The Book of Ezra records that the decree which launched the 490-year prophecy of Daniel was given by King Artaxerxes I. Ezra left for Jerusalem in the 7th year of his reign.

> ...in the reign of Artaxerxes, King of Persia, the King granted him all his requests... This Ezra went up from Babylon.... for upon the first day of the first month began he to go up from Babylon... In the 7th year of Artaxerxes the King
>
> Ezra 7:1-10

From Ezra 7, we only know that Ezra left Babylon in the seventh year of Artaxerxes I reign, but the Biblical record is silent in recording any *calendar year* or the *name* of the *first month* for this event. Based upon a wide range of Biblical scholarly investigations, almost everyone agrees that *Persian kings used an accession year system and that Persian kings began their regnal years on Nisan 1.* It is also generally agreed that contemporary with Artaxerxes reign; *Hebrew Kings also used an accession-year system, but used a Tishri 1 regnal start date.* Ezra was a Hebrew writing for his Jewish people, but he was in Persian exile. So which system did Ezra use in the Biblical records? Ezra and Nehemiah were Hebrew contemporaries, and at least according to some sources the Biblical records of both Ezra and Nehemiah were originally one document and that both must have referenced Persian events using Hebrew dating schemes. Whether that is true or not, the book of Nehemiah as it now stands clearly indicates that Nehemiah cross referenced Persian events to a Hebrew Tishri 1-Tishri 1 regnal year system, and *NOT* the Nisan-Nisan Persian system (compare Neh. 1:1 to Neh. 2:1). If Nehemiah and Ezra were originally one document, the problem would be solved. However, no reliable data exists to prove or disprove this theory. Pragmatically, Ezra and Nehemiah were both serving in the King's court, and both were likely good friends; but this only suggests that both would use the same system to reference the reign of each king. Depending upon which system is being used by Ezra; the seventh year of Artaxerxes could be off by one year at Nisan 1. Hence, imminent scholars are divided upon exactly when Ezra left Babylon in the seventh year of Artaxerxes reign. Some defend a 458 BC date and some dogmatically defend a 457 BC date. So which is to be believed?

The most acceptable solution is to carefully examine historical and archeological records to determine when Ezra left in the seventh year of Artaxerxes. We are quite certain that a Persian King named Xerxes preceded Artaxerxes. It is also known that the Persian King Xerxes was assassinated in 465 BC. Scribes recorded Xerxes assassination date on a clay tablet known as the *Babylonian Astronomical Text.* Scholars have translated the text and determined that the murder of Xerxes occurred sometime between August 4 - August 18, 465 BC. Two other dates are recorded in the ancient literature, which indicate either late July or early August of 465 BC. By all historical accounts known to exist, Xerxes was murdered before Tishri 1, 465 BC. Xerxes was assassinated by a courtier of his court called Artabanus who wanted to usurp the king. He then had the brother of Artaxerxes assassinated, and also tried to assassinate Artaxerxes; but his plan was discovered and Artabanus was executed. No record has ever been found that credits Artabanus as a reigning king of Persia, but a second-century historian called Mantheo wrote that a power struggle did indeed take place between Artabanus and Artaxerxes. However, Mantheo wrote his comments more than 500 years after the fact. Turning to archeological records, in the 20th century evidence surfaced from a community of Jews living in Egypt on the upper Nile River. They were called the *Elephantine Community*, and records of financial and social transactions were found which provides important data for this investigation. Out of a number of documents found and restored, two are of great importance: They are known as *AP 6* and *AP 8*.

The Jewish document, called *AP 6* from the Elephantine community of Jews fails to resolve the issue. Scholars all agree that *AP 6* was written on Jan 2/3, 464 BC. Unfortunately, the document is severely damaged and a key phrase is partially missing. Paleographic science has been used to reconstruct the missing word(s), and it was found that it could be reconstructed in one of two ways. The first would indicate that Jan 2/3 is *in the first year* of Artaxerxes reign; the second is that it would read *in the acession year* of Artaxerxes. We now need to determine exactly when Artaxerxes assumed the throne and started his official reign. Clearly, if AP 6 was written in early January of 465 BC, and that date is in Artaxerxes *acession year*, the first year of Artaxerxes reign would either start on Nisan 1 (March/April) of 464 BC using Persian reckoning, or on Tishri 1(Sept/Oct) of 464 BC using Hebrew rekoning. If that date is in the *first year* of Artaxerxes, then Artaxeres would have *had* to assumed the throne on Tishri 1 (Sept/Oct) of 465 BC, and the document had to have used the Hebrew regnal years The following diagram graphically displays the relevant timeline.

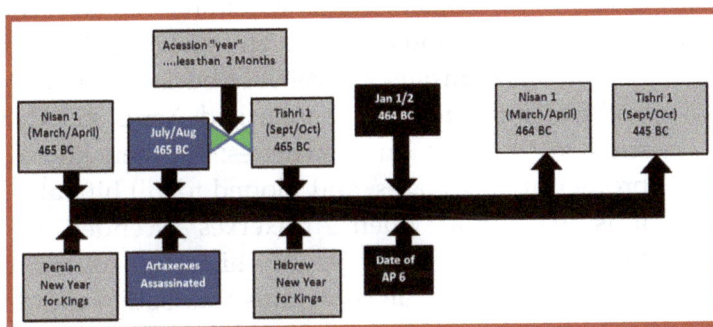

Recall that both the Persians and Hebrews used an acession year system: The Persians started their Kings reign on Nisan 1, and the Hebrews on Tishri 1. Also recall that AP 6 was written Jan 1 or Jan 2, 464 BC.

The conondrum can be stated as follows. If the throne became vacant with the assassination of Xerxes in July/August of 465 BC, regardless of the power struggle that ensued the following possibilities present themselves.

> If AP 6 recorded that Artaxerxes was in his *acession year* as of Jan 1 or Jan 2 of 464 BC, then using the *Hebrew acession year system*, something unusual would have had to occur between the death of Xerxes in July/Aug of 465 BC and Jan 2, 464 BC, such that Artaxerxes was not able to start his first year of reign until Tishri 1, 464 BC. If AP 6 is written using the Hebrew acession year viewpoint, this would create an unlikely situation of Artaxerxes not claiming a short acession year period between July/Aug of 465 BC and Sept/Oct of 465 BC, and then start his first credited year of reign on Tishri 1, 465 BC as was the normal custom. In addition, who would get credit for the full year of reign between Tishri 1, 465 BC and Tishri 1, 464 BC? Since all kings wanted to claim as many years in office as possible it is extremely likely

that Artaxerxes would want to claim this year. Xerxes would be credited with his last full year ending on Tishri 1, 465 BC, leaving no gap in the regnal records. Why did Artabanus never even appear in the official records? The answer is probably buried in a cloak of political intrigue. Artabanus had Xeres killed and tried to blame it on Artaxerxes: he then killed the brother of Artaxerxes, and plotted to kill him also. So it is likely that when Artaxerxes ascended to the throne, he would remove any historical reference of Artabanus....after all, Atabanus was both a murderer and a usurper. Artaxerxes could then claim that short period of political upheavel as his *accession year* under the acession year system. No record exists of any Persian King or Hebrew king using a non-acession system. The conclusion is that if AP 6 was written using an acession year system, and all traces of Artabanus were stricken from the King's records, it is logical (and likely) that Artaxerxes started his first year of reign on Tishri 1, 465 BC.

➢ If AP 6 recorded that Artaxerxes was in his *first year of reign*, then he would have *had* to start that first year on Tishri 1, 465 BC.

Both scenarios seem to indicate that the first year of Artaxeres began on Tishri 1, 465 BC. However, neither of these scanarios can be absolutely proved using only AP 6, although several researchers have tried to do so. In particular, Horn and Wood emphatically and mysteriously state that only the acession year reconstruction of AP 6 makes any sense They are equally emphatic that Artaxeres first year of reign did not start until Tishri 1, 464 BC. So who is right? We will look for further information. A second document recovered from the Elaphantine community was *AP 8* . The AP 8 papyrus is well preserved and intact. In that document the following dateline is recorded.

Kislev 21 = Mesore 1
In Year 6 of Artaxerxes Reign

Kislev corresponds to November/December on both the Babylonian and the Julian or modern Gregorian calendar. Mesore 1 is the 12th month in the ancient Egyptian calendar that was in use in Egypt at that time. Note that the Jewish regnal New Year of Tishri 1 had occurred almost two months earlier. The Egyptian New Year at that time was a month called *Thoth,* which was at least 30 days after Mesore 1. Both the Hebrews and the Egyptians counted the reign of Artaxerxes from their own New Year day. Hence, both Kislev 21 and Mesore 1 were *within year 6 of Artaxerxes reign;* but again the question arises: Which year? From AP 8, the 6th year of Artaxerxes reign is said to contain Kislev 21. The following Table illustrates the three possible occurrence of Artaxerxes 6th year using AP 6.

Year	Hebrew System: Artaxerxes in Acession Year for Less than 2 Mos....AP 6	Persian System: Artaxerxes in Acession Year Till Nisan 1, 464 BC....AP 6	Hebrew System: Artaxerxes in Acession Year Till Tishri 1, 464 BC....AP 6
1	Tishri 1, 465 BC - 464 BC	Nisan 1, 464 BC - 463 BC	Tishri 1, 464 BC - 463 BC
2	Tishri 1, 464 BC - 463 BC	Nisan 1, 463 BC - 462 BC	Tishri 1, 463 BC - 462 BC
3	Tishri 1, 463 BC - 462 BC	Nisan 1, 462 BC - 461 BC	Tishri 1, 462 BC - 461 BC
4	Tishri 1, 462 BC - 461 BC	Nisan 1, 461 BC - 460 BC	Tishri 1, 461 BC - 460 BC
5	Tishri 1, 461 BC - 460 BC	Nisan 1, 460 BC - 459 BC	Tishri 1, 460 BC - 459 BC
6	Tishri 1, 460 BC - 459 BC	Nisan 1, 459 BC - 458 BC	Tishri 1, 459 BC - 458 BC
7	Tishri 1, 459 BC - 458 BC	Nisan 1, 458 BC - 457 BC	Tishri 1, 458 BC - 457 BC
8	Tishri 1, 458 BC - 457 BC	Nisan 1, 457 BC - 456 BC	Tishri 1, 457 BC - 456 BC

Tishri 1... September/October   Nisan 1 ...... March/April

Since Kislev occurs in the month of November/December, and by AP 8 it must be in Artaxerxes 6th year of reign, then the only possible, feasible alternative is that AP 8 must be referencing the Hebrew system, and that Artaxerxes *acession year* was only the short period of time between the death of Xerxes in July/Aug of 565 BC to Tishri 1 in Sept/Oct of 565 BC.

113

While this is convincing evidence, we can show that this conclusion can be reached in another way. Using modern computer software, the calendar date for the Egyptian Mesore 1 can be calculated for the year 460 BC. In that year, Mesore 1 occurred on Nov 11. This date must coincide with Kislev 21 by AP 8. Note that the Jews living in Egypt would most certainly know what the date was for Mesore 1, and it is highly likely that being a Jewish community they would also know the correct Hebrew calendar date. On the Hebrew calendar, every new month started with a new moon. Hence, working backwards a new moon must have occurred on Kislev 1, which would be October 21. Using new modern computers and NASA software, the new moon dates far back in time can be accurately determined, since the cycle of days from new moon to new moon is a constant. One can verify that in 460 BC, the New Moon of Kislev 1 occurred in close proximity to 3:22 AM on October 21 ! Hence, using two witnesses we have shown that Kislev 21 on November 11 occurred in the 6th year of Artaxerxes reign. We then conclude that the 6th year of his reign had to be from Tishri 1, 460 BC to Tishri 1, 459 BC...using non inclusive recogning on Tishri 1 in 459 BC. The 7th year of his reign is determined to be Tishri 1, 459 BC – Tishri 1, 458 BC. Using this information relative to AP 6, it is concluded that the broken/missing segment of the AP 6 document should read *In the first year of Artaxerxes reign*, and not *in the acession year of Artaxerxes reign*. We also conclude that Ezra was using the Hebrew regnal, accession year system as did Nehemiah. The table on the right shows the first 10 years of Artaxerxes reign.

	Regnal Years of Artaxerxes
1	Tishri 1, 465 BC - 464 BC
2	Tishri 1, 464 BC - 463 BC
3	Tishri 1, 463 BC - 462 BC
4	Tishri 1, 462 BC - 461 BC
5	Tishri 1, 461 BC - 460 BC
6	Tishri 1, 460 BC - 459 BC
7	Tishri 1, 459 BC - 458 BC
8	Tishri 1, 458 BC - 457 BC
9	Tishri 1, 457 BC - 456 BC
10	Tishri 1, 456 BC - 455 BC

The 7th year of Artaxerxes Reign was Tishri 1, 459 BC to Tishri 1, 458 BC

Ezra left Babylon on Nisan 1, 458 BC
Ezra Arrived in Jerusalem 5 months later
Daniel's 70 Week Prophecy started on Tishri 1, 458 BC.
Tishri 1, 458 BC -Tishri 1, 457 BC was a Sabbatical Year

To summarize: We have established with reasonable evidence..... including ancient documents double dated from a Jewish community in Egypt (AP 6 and AP 8) ..... that Ezra wrote his records from a Hebrew perspective, and that the first year of Artaxeres reign was Tishri 1, 465 BC – Tishri 1, 464 BC. Starting from that date, the 7th year of Artaxeres reign is Tishri 1, 459 BC to Tishri 1, 458 BC. Artaxerxes acession year was a short time between when Xerxes was murdered in July/Aug of 465 BC to Sept/Oct of 465 BC (Tishri 1).

We know that Ezra the scribe left Babylon in the seventh year of Artaxerxes reign (Ezra 7:7) on first day of the first month (Ezra 7:9),which was Nisan 1, 458 BC. This date was likely April 8, 458 BC as confirmed by Finnegan. He arrived in Jerusalem on the first day of the fifth month.....both in the seventh year of Artaxerzes reign. (Ezra 7:8). We will now show that these conclusions perfectly fit a 5 BC birth date for Christ and a 30 BC crucifixion date for Christ.

THE DECREE OF ARTAXERXES

We have spent a great deal of detective work to prove that the first year of Artaxerxes reign referenced by Ezra the scribe was between Tishri 1, 458 BC and Tishri 1, 457 BC. The following statements have been substantiated using Biblical records supported by archeological and historical documents.

➤ The decree which started the 70 Weeks of Daniel's prophecy (490 years) was that of Artaxerxes I in his 7th year of reign (Ezra 7)

➤ The Decree was issued sometimes just before Nisan 1 of 458 BC in the 6th year of Artaxerxes' reign. The most likely date was April 8, 458 BC.

➤ Ezra left Babylon with a decree that authorized hum to rebuild the temple (Ezra 1:1-4). It should be noted that in the 20th year of Artaxerxes, he (Nehemiah) was given permission to rebuild the walls. This second decree of Artaxerxes was not a completely new decree: it only reinforced the one given to Ezra, which in turn was

115

originally given by Cyrus. The decree given to Ezra certainly implied that Ezra thought that the Temple had to be protected by a new wall, and that the city inside had to have dwellings for the men and their families.

➤ Ezra left after Nisan 1 in 458 BC (March/April), and arrived before Tishri 1, 458 BC (Sept/Oct).

➤ After Ezra arrived, he gathered the people and declared a fast. He then established the judicial system, organized the exiles, reinstated Levitical temple service and corrected intermarriage problems. The entire decree had *gone forth* by Tishri 1, and Daniels first week of years began on Tishri 1, 458 BC.

➤ The first year of Daniel's 70 week prophecy was therefore Tishri 1, 458 BC – Tishri 1, 457 BC.

To this may be added (Pickle):

1. Daniel 9:25 specified two things for the decree that must be used for the beginning of the prophecy: 1) "restoring" and 2) "building" Jerusalem.

2. It was prophesied of Cyrus that he would command Jerusalem to be built: "*That saith of Cyrus, He is my shepherd, and shall perform all my pleasure: even saying to Jerusalem, Thou shalt be built; and to the temple, Thy foundation shall be laid*" (Is. 44:28; cf. 45:13).

3. It was also prophesied by Isaiah that God would "*restore*" Jerusalem's judiciary: "*And I will restore thy judges as at the first, and thy counselors as at the beginning: afterward thou shalt be called, the city of righteousness, the faithful city*" (Is. 1:26).

4. While Cyrus' decree of Ezra 1:2-4 and Darius' decree of Ezra 6:1-12 called for building, it is only in Artaxerxes' decree from his 7th year, as recorded in Ezra 7:12-26, that we find a call for restoring the judges.

5. The decrees of Cyrus, Darius, and Artaxerxes' 7th year are referred to in Ezra 6:14 as if they are but one decree. It is as if Cyrus began the decree and Artaxerxes finished it, which explains why Daniel 9:25 speaks of one "*commandment to*

restore and build." Once this commandment process was complete, the 70 weeks could begin.

6. Daniel's prophecy implies that the earthly ministry of Jesus Christ would begin *immediately after* 483 years have elapsed, and that He would be crucified in the midst of Daniel's 70th week (the last 7 years).

Starting in Tishri 1, 458 BC, 483 Solar/Julian years would elapse on Tishri 1, 26 AD. Note that 458 BC to 26 BC appears to be 484 years. This is because there is no year zero, and when passing from BC to AD, one extra year must be added. Jesus Christ came to Jordan River to be baptized when he was *about 30 years of age*. We have presented much evidence which indicates that Jesus Christ was born on March 23 in 5 BC. If this is true, then Christ was *about 30 years of age* (Luke 3:23)....actually 30.5 years old... when He came to be baptized at the River Jordan. We know this because if Christ was crucified on Nisan 14, the Feast of Passover, in 30 AD, April 5; He would be baptized in the month of Tishri (September/October) in 26 AD.

The prophecy of Daniel also predicted that Jesus Christ would be *cut off* or crucified *in the midst of the 70th week.* If the duration of Christ's ministry was 3.5 years, and ended on Nisan 14, 30 AD on the cross of Calvary, then everything fits perfectly.

THE CRUCIFIXION OF OUR LORD JESUS CHRIST

According to the prophecy of Daniel (Dan 9:26), *after threescore and two weeks* (after 483 total years) had been completed, Christ would be *cut off* (crucified). Exactly when this would occur can now be determined. According to Dan 9:27; Christ was prophesied to be killed *in the midst* of the 70th and (last) week. This is perfectly consistent with the known 3.5 year ministry of Christ. The midst of this last week was on *Nisan 14, April 5, 30 AD* on a *Wednesday;* which is the *Feast of Passover.* The offered chronology points to this date, but is there other evidence that this is the correct year? The answer is, *YES.*

117

- The apostle Paul was converted on the road to Damascus by Jesus Christ, who appeared in his risen body shortly after he was crucified; which we have just shown was in 30 AD. Fourteen (14) years after his conversion, Paul records in Gal. 2:1 that he, Barnabus, and Titus journeyed to Jerusalem. While Paul, Barnabus, and Titus were in Jerusalem, King Herod Agrippa died. This date is known to be during or shortly after the Passover Feast of 44 BC (March/April). The apostle Luke records that John the Baptist came to the Jordan River baptizing and preaching repentance in the 15th year of Tiberius Caesar (Luke 3:1-3). Tiberius was the successor to Augustus Caesar, who became the Emperor of Rome on Jan 13, 27 BC after the assassination of Julius Caesar. The last five years of his life (AD 10-14) were untroubled by war or disaster. Augustus was aging fast, and was more and more disinclined to appear personally in the senate or in public. Yet in AD 12 he consented, reluctantly we are told, to yet one more renewal of his imperial reign for ten years. Roman emperors were appointed in January, and officially conferred

March/April		March/April	Year
12 BC	to	13 BC	1
13 BC	to	14 BC	2
14 BC	to	15 BC	3
15 BC	to	16 BC	4
16 BC	to	17 BC	5
17 BC	to	18 BC	6
18 BC	to	19 BC	7
19 BC	to	20 BC	8
20 BC	to	21 BC	9
21 BC	to	22 BC	10
22 BC	to	23 BC	11
23 BC	to	24 BC	12
24 BC	to	25 BC	13
25 BC	to	26 BC	14
26 BC	to	27 BC	15

The 15th year of Tiberius Reign was Spring of 26 AD to Spring of 27 AD. Christ came to the river Jordan to be baptixed in the Fall of 26 AD

in March. He consented with a demand that his stepson, *Tiberius*, now over fifty years of age, should be equated with himself, both in power and authority, in the administration of the empire. He retreated to an island villa and hardly ever appeared again in public between 12 AD and his death in 14 AD. Augustus died on Aug 19, 14 AD and Tiberius became sole ruler. If Luke measured the 15 years from the co-reign of Tiberius starting in the spring of 12 BC, the 15th year would be the spring of 26 AD to the spring of 27 AD. Christ was baptized by John in September of 26 AD. There is no reason to think that Luke would not have counted the reign of Tiberius from 12 BC. Jerusalem was effectively under the iron boot of Tiberius between 12 AD-14 AD, when the death of Augustus occurred.

- Just before the first Passover of Christ's ministry (John 2:13), following his baptism at the Jordan River, Christ foretold of his death and resurrection in three days.

Destroy this temple (his body) and in three days I will raise it up
John 2:1

But the Jews thought that Christ was referring to Herod's temple and replied:

Forty and six years was this temple in building, and wilt thou raise it up in three days?
John 2:20

In the Works of Josephus (Book XV: 11:1), he records that construction on the temple was begun in the 18th year of King Herod's reign, which was 20 BC-19 BC. Leaping forward 46 years, we come to 27 AD-28 AD. The first Passover in Jesus ministry was in March/April of 27 BC.

- Shortly before the last Passover of Christ's ministry, Jesus was delivering the Olivet Discourse to his disciples. At that time, He prophesied that Herod's Temple would be destroyed and when the destruction would take place.

Verily I say unto you, this generation shall not pass till all these things be fulfilled.
Matthew 24:34

119

This prophecy was given in the spring of 30 AD the night before He suffered on the cross of Calvary. Almost all biblical scholars agree that based upon the Exodus account, the entire generation of Hebrews who left Egypt would perish (die) within a 40 year period of time. This clearly indicated that a biblical generation was 40 years in duration. Adding 40 years to the spring of 30 AD, we arrive in the spring of 70 AD. This was precisely the point in time when Herod's temple was destroyed. Only a 30 AD crucifixion renders this destruction in exactly one generation.

TERMINATING DANIEL'S 70TH WEEK

We have proposed and presented reasonable arguments to support a Nisan 14 (Wednesday; April 6, 30 AD) crucifixion date for Jesus Christ. This demands a 5 BC birth date for the Messiah. The year 30 AD falls in the *middle* of Daniel's 70th week, that is after 486.5 years had elapsed since the 490-year prophecy started. Clearly, this leaves 3.5 years to finish the prophecy. Many modern prophecy teachers allow the 70-7's to expire on Tishri 1 (Sept/Oct) of 33 AD. The event designated to end the prophecy is proposed to be the *stoning of Stephen* in Acts 6. Proponents of this theory (rightly so) identify this event as the final act of rejection of Jesus Christ as the promised Messiah by the corporate nation of Israel. From this point on, the message of salvation in Jesus Christ under the new covenant passed to both Gentiles and Jews. We totally reject the logic which ends Daniel's 70th week in 33 AD at the death of Stephen based upon three platforms. *First*, a careful study of the Book of Daniel will identify several things which must be completed before Daniel's 70 weeks of years expires which can only be accomplished at the second advent of Jesus Christ (such as the rise of the antichrist in the end times). This reason alone is enough to reject the *Steven hypothesis*. A *second* and more compelling reason is in the stoning of Steven. In Acts 1-2 we are told how the Holy Spirit fell on the Feast of Pentecost, 50 days after the resurrection. Chapter 3 records a post-Pentecost miracle, the healing of a lame man, followed by Peter's sermon. Chapters 4:1-6:7 are concerned with the beginning of persecutions and the preparation for spreading the gospel. Acts 6:8 records how Steven *full of faith and power* did *great wonders and miracles*. The Jewish leaders turned against him, fearing that he would *destroy this place, and change the customs*. At this point Stephen delivers perhaps the most powerful sermon ever preached (Acts 7:1-53). When he finished his discourse, the Jews *cast him out of the city and stoned him*. So, Steven became the first apostle named in the New Testament to be martyred after the day of Pentecost. The *third* concerns the conversion of Paul (Saul) is recorded in Acts 9. However, considering the sequence and duration of the events recorded in the Book of Acts, his conversion on the road to Damascus was likely within a year after Christ was crucified. If this is true, then it is impossible that the stoning of Steven took place 3.5 years after the crucifixion.

We therefore conclude that there has been a *gap* of almost 2000 years since the midpoint of Daniel's 70th week. The termination of Daniel's 70th week will not occur until the second coming of Jesus Christ at the end of the great tribulation period. This analysis clearly shows that there are only 3.5 years left in the 490 year prophecy given to Daniel. This shows that the Great Tribulation described in the Book of Revelation is only 3.5 years long and not 7 years as modern prophecy teachers maintain. The fact that the tribulation period described in the book of Revelation is only 3.5 years in duration and not 7 years as is commonly taught is not a large leap of faith. In either case, there is a gap in time which represents the church age. For a more detailed discussion of this conclusion see Phillips (*Revelation: Mysteries Revealed: Second Edition*).

SUMMARY AND CONCLUSIONS

This chapter has spent a great deal of time investigating when the 490 year Messianic prophecy given to Daniel the prophet while he was in Babylonian exile. It has been shown that that Jesus Christ was crucified and died in 30 AD on Nisan 14, April 7, on the Feast of Passover. This is a strong confirmation that both the determined reign of King Herod is correct, and that

Christ was indeed born during the Passover season of 5 BC. Accepting this as being correct, Christ was born on the first day of the Feast of Unleavened Bread (Nisan 15) in 5 BC, and died on the Feast of Passover (Nisan 14) in 30 AD exactly 34 years later; inclusive reckoning.

NOTES AND THINGS TO REMEMBER:

CHAPTER 8

THE 3.5 YEAR MINISTRY OF JESUS CHRIST AND THE LAST WEEK

An interesting characteristic of the Holy Scriptures is the lack of information concerning the life and times of our Lord Jesus Christ between when He was born in Bethlehem and returned from Egypt with Joseph and Mary. It has been suggested from other historical writings that Joseph and Mary remained in Egypt for 6 months to two years. We do know that when Herod died, an angel appeared to Joseph and told him that Herod was dead, and that he could return to his home in Nazareth (Matthew 2:18-21). We now know that Joseph, Mary and the babe were likely in Egypt for less than a year, depending upon when the angel appeared to Joseph. We also know that Joseph was afraid of Archaleus, who was the successor of Herod the Great; and Joseph did not return to Jerusalem, but went to his hometown of Nazareth.

There is an equally puzzling fact that almost nothing is known about the activities of Christ between when He returned from Egypt as a young child and when He came to start his 3.5 year ministry. The lone exception is that we are told that Jesus at age 12 disappeared and was found in the synagogue teaching during the Feast of Passover (Luke 2: 41-52). This is quite remarkable, for a teacher of the word was called a *rabbi* and a Jew would generally have to wait until the age of 30 to teach in public. After this incident, we do not know anything of Christ until He came to the River Jordan to be baptized by John at *about the age of 30* (Luke 3:23).

THE 3.5 YEAR MINISTRY OF JESUS CHRIST

We have found that Christ was likely born on the first day of the Feast of Unleavened Bread, on Nisan 15, March 23 in 5 BC. By careful analysis of the 490 year prophecy given to Daniel the prophet, it was determined that Christ began His ministry in the month of Tishri in 26 AD After being baptized, Christ was driven into the wilderness of Judea where he was tempted of the devil for 40 days and 40 nights. Returning from His ordeal, Christ began his 3.5 year ministry. Although the gospel accounts are often confusing, it appears that the following things occurred in pretty much the chronological sequence shown. We are extremely grateful to *Gordon Smith* for unrestricted use of his chronology; with which we agree (*http://www.ccel.org/bible/phillips/cn160_travels.htm*). Each portion of His ministry is cross referenced to a map which shows the cities and places that Jesus Christ visited. The numbers next to each city and location on each map correspond to the sequence of events as they chronologically occurred as described in the synoptic gospels; and they correspond to the order of discussion.

JESUS' FIRST 6 MONTHS:
TISHRI, 26 AD TO NISAN, 27 AD

1. Jesus, six months after having turned 30 years old (Lk 3:23) travels from his home-town of Nazareth in Galilee to be baptized by John.

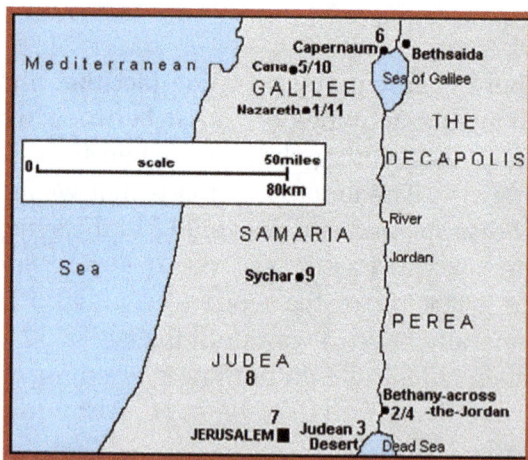

2. At the River Jordan, possibly near Bethany-across-the-Jordan, he is baptized by John the Baptist (Mt. 3:13; Mk. 1:9)

3. He goes into the Judean Desert or wilderness where He is tempted by Satan for 40 days and 40 nights. (Mt. 4:1; Mk. 1:12; Lk. 4:1)

4. At the River Jordan near Bethany-across-the-Jordan, or Bethabara (Jn. 1:28), and according to John's Gospel, Jesus calls his first five disciples (Jn. 1:35). These include Philip, Andrew, and Simon Peter, who are all from Bethsaida in Galilee (Jn. 1:44)

5. Jesus returns north to Galilee with his disciples (Jn 1:43), and attends a wedding in Cana, changes the water into wine - his first recorded miracle (Jn. 2:1). He asks for this event to remain secret.

6. He continues on to Capernaum, on the northern shore of the Sea of Galilee with his mother, brothers and disciples, and stays there a short time (Jn. 2:12)

Travels And Acts of Jesus: *Nisan 27 AD to Nisan 28 AD*

7. Jesus travels south to Jerusalem for the Passover - the first one mentioned in the Gospels (Jn. 2:13). There he drives the money-changers from the Temple for the first time (Jn. 2:14). He also meets the Pharisee, Nicodemus (Jn. 3:1)

8. Jesus leaves for the countryside of Judea where his disciples baptize believers (Jn. 3:22)

9. Jesus and his disciples continue northwards from Judea (Jn. 4:3), passing through the territory of Samaria (Jn. 4:4). Near Sychar, Jesus meets the Samaritan woman at the well (Jn. 4:5). Many Samaritans believe in him (Jn. 4:39), after which he continues on to Galilee (Jn. 4:43)

10. He reaches Galilee (Mt. 4:12; Mk. 1:14; Lk. 4:14; Jn. 4:45), and in Cana heals the official's son who lays sick in Capernaum (Jn. 4:46)

11. Jesus returns to his home-town of Nazareth, and preaches in the synagogue (Lk. 4:16). He is rejected for the first time (Lk. 4:28).

TRAVELS AND ACTS OF JESUS:
NISAN 28 AD TO NISAN 29 AD

FIRST PREACHING TOUR OF GALILEE

1. Jesus goes to Capernaum (Mt. 4:13; Mk. 1:21; Lk. 4:31).

   Mediterranean Sea

   1/3/7/11 6 Capernaum • Bethsaida • Gergesa? Sea of Galilee Region of the 10 Gerasenes

   GALILEE 2/5/9 Nazareth • Nain • 8 Gadara

   THE DECAPOLIS River

   SAMARIA Jordan Sychar •

   PEREA

   JUDEA Bethany-across -the Jordan JERUSALEM ■ 4 Dead Sea

   0 scale 50miles 80km

   According to the Synoptic Gospels, Jesus calls his disciples to full-time service (Mt. 4:18; Mk. 1:16; Luke 5:1). In Capernaum he heals the madman in the synagogue (Mk. 1:23; Lk. 4:33) and Peter's mother-in-law of her fever (Mt. 8:14; Mk. 1:29; Luke 4:38)

2. Jesus stays in Capernaum (Mt. 4:13; Mk. 1:21; Lk. 4:31). According to the Synoptic Gospels, Jesus calls his disciples to full-time service (Mt. 4:18; Mk 1:16; Lk. 5:1). In Capernaum he heals the madman in the synagogue (Mk. 1:23; Luke 4:33) and Peter's mother-in-law of her fever (Mt. 8:14; Mk. 1:29; Luke 4:38)

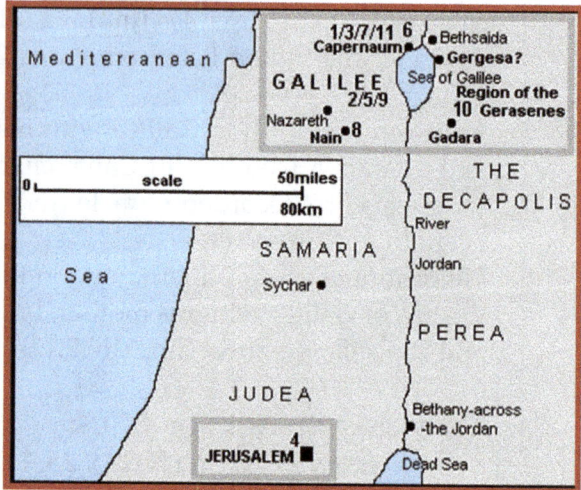

3. Jesus travels throughout Galilee, preaching and healing (Mt 4:23; Mk 1:39), including the leper (Mt. 8:2; Mk. 1:40; Luke 5:12).

4. Returning to Capernaum (Mk. 2:1) a paralyzed man is healed (Mt. 9:2; Mk. 2:3; Lk. 5:18) and Jesus calls Matthew (or Levi) the tax-collector to be a disciple (Mt 9:9; Mk. 2:14; Luke 5:27)

5. Jesus travels from Galilee south to Jerusalem for a Jewish festival - possibly the Second Passover identified in the

Gospels (Jn. 5:1). At the Pool of Bethesda he heals the crippled man (Jn. 5:2)

6. Returning north to Galilee, Jesus heals the man with the withered hand (Mt. 12:9; Mk. 3:1; Luke 6:6) and many others (Mt. 12:15; Mk. 3:7)

7. On a hillside in Galilee, probably near Capernaum, he selects his twelve apostles (Mt. 10:1; Mk. 3:13; Luke 6:12) and delivers the Sermon on the Mount (Mt 5:1). In Luke's report Jesus comes down from a hillside to give the Sermon (Lk. 6:20)

8. Back in Capernaum, (Mt. 8:5; Luke 7:1) Jesus heals the Roman centurion's servant (Mt 8:5; Luke 7:2)

SECOND PREACHING TOUR OF GALILEE

9. Jesus continues preaching and healing in Galilee, and in Nain brings the widow's son back to life   (Luke 7:11).

10. Accompanied by the twelve apostles and some of his women helpers, Jesus continues his second Galilee tour (Luke 8:1).

11. He sails across the Sea of Galilee (Mt. 8:18; Mk. 4:35; Luke 8:22) and calms a storm (Mt. 8:24; Mk. 4:37; Luke 8:23); making land in the region of the Gedarenes (Mk 5:1; Luke 8:26, Mt. 8:28) in the Ten Towns or Cities of Decapolis, Jesus heals the madman inhabited by demonic swine (Mt. 8:28; Mk. 5:2; Luke 8:27).

12. Sailing back across the Sea of Galilee (Mk. 5:21); Jesus lands at *his own town* of Capernaum (Mt. 9:1). Here he raises Jairus' daughter from the grave

TRAVELS AND ACTS OF JESUS:
NISAN 29 AD TO NISAN 30 AD

1. Jesus travels from Capernaum to Nazareth (Mk. 6:1)
2. In Nazareth, he is rejected for a second time (Mt. 13:54; Mk. 6:1)
3. He continues through Galilee (Mt. 13:58; Mk. 6:6) and sends out the twelve apostles to preach the Gospel (Mt. 10:5; Mk. 6:7; Luke 9:1)
4. The Twelve return to Capernaum, (Mk. 6:30, Luke 9:10), possibly to rest.
5. From Capernaum, they go off by boat with Jesus to a quiet place (Mk 6:32) near Bethsaida (Luke 9:10). Here he feeds the 5,000 (Mt 14:14; Mk 6:33; Luke 9:11; Jn 6:5)
6. The disciples return across the Sea of Galilee (Mt. 14:22; Mk. 6:45), Jesus walks on the water to join them (Mt. 14:25; Mk. 6:48; Jn. 6:19). They land near the Plain of Gennesaret and Jesus heals many people there (Mt. 14:34; Mk. 6:53).
7. From Gennesaret, they make their way back to Capernaum (Jn. 6:24) and Jesus teaches that He is the true Bread of Life (Jn. 6:26)

128

Jesus Preaches and Heals in Syrian-Phoenicia; Ituria and Trachonitis

8. Jesus retires from Galilee to the region of Tyre and Sidon in Syrian-Phoenicia (Mt. 15:21; Mk. 7:24) where he heals the daughter of the Gentile Syrophoenician woman (Mt. 15:22; Mk. 7:25) .
9. He leaves Syrian-Phoenicia via Sidon for Galilee (Mt. 15:29) but travels through the Decapolis (Mk. 7:31)
10. In the Decapolis he heals the deaf and mute man (Mk. 7:32) and feeds the 4,000 (Mt. 15:32; Mk. 8:1)
11. Reaching the Sea of Galilee, he crosses by boat to   the Magadan / Dalmanutha region (Mt. 15:39; Mk. 8:10). There the Pharisees and Sadducees ask for a sign from heaven   Mt. 16:1; Mk. 8:11
12. Continuing to Bethsaida, a blind man is healed (Mk. 8:22)
13. Jesus now travels from Galilee, north to Caesarea Philippi in Iturea and Trachonitis, where Peter confesses that Jesus is the Christ. (Mt. 16:13; Mk. 8:27)
14. Continuing on from Caesarea Philippi possibly further north towards Mount Hermon, three of the disciples see Jesus Transfigured in the presence of Elijah and Moses (Mt. 17:1; Mk. 9:2; Luke 9:28). On his return, Jesus heals the boy with epilepsy (Mt. 17:14; Mk. 9:14; Luke 9:37). (Other traditions place the Transfiguration to the south, on Mount Tabor). The epileptic boy would then have been healed in the area of Galilee.
15. In Galilee (Mt. 17:22; Mk. 9:30), in Capernaum (Mk. 9:33), Jesus pays the Temple Tax with a fish! (Mt. 17:24). Then to avoid the dangers in Judea, he remains in Galilee. (Jn. 7:1)

Last Ministry in Judea

16. Jesus leaves Capernaum and Galilee for the last earthly time (Mt. 19:1; Mk. 10:1) and heads for Jerusalem (Luke 9:51; Jn. 7:10). Travelling by Samaria, he heals the ten

lepers (Luke 17:11) but is rejected in a Samaritan village (Luke 9:52)

17. Arriving in Jerusalem for the Feast of the Tabernacles in the autumn of 29 AD (Jn. 7:10), Jesus forgives the woman caught in adultery (Jn. 8:2) and heals the blind man who is taken before the Sanhedrin (Jn. 9:1)

18. During his travels in Judea, Jesus visits Martha and Mary in Bethany (Luke 10:38), returning to Jerusalem for *Hanukkah*, the Jewish Feast of Dedication in December, 29 AD (Jn. 10:22)

THE LAST FEW MONTHS: 30 AD

19. Jesus withdraws to Bethany-across-the-Jordan (or Bethabara), and into the province of Perea, and stays for a while (Jn. 10:40)

20. Following the death of Lazarus, Jesus returns to Bethany near Jerusalem, and raises him (Lazarus) from the dead after 3 days. This is a shadow and type of His own death (Jn. 11:1)

21. Because of threats to his life, Jesus withdraws to Ephraim to the north of Jerusalem (Jn. 11:54)

22. Jesus crosses the River Jordan and works in Petra (Mt. 19:1; Mk. 10:1). There he blesses the little children (Mt. 19:13, Mk. 10:13; Lk. 18:15) and speaks to the rich young man (Mt. 19:16; Mk. 10:17; Luke 18:18)

THE FINAL JOURNEY TO JERUSALEM

23. Jesus travels towards Jerusalem for the last time (Mt. 20:17; Mk. 10:32; Lk. 18:31). Passing through Jericho he heals two blind men (Mt. 20:29; Mk. 10:46; Luke 18:35) and then converts Zacchaeus the tax collector (Luke 19:1). Jesus Spends the night in Jericho.

24. Jesus Reaches Bethany (Jn. 12:1) and stays at the home of Lazarus, Mary and Martha for two nights. He spends all day in the Temple and being assaulted verbally by the Pharisees and Sadducees.

25. During the last 3 nights of his life, Jesus returns to the Mount of Olives where He teaches his disciples and prays (Mt. 21:17-18; Mk. 11:11-12:19; Luke 21:37).

The first two nights are uneventful, but on the third night (then Wednesday, Nisan 14) He is betrayed by Judas.

THE LAST FEW DAYS

We will now focus on what transpired between when Christ first came to Bethany (Friday) before the last Sabbath (Saturday) of His earthly ministry, and when He rose from the dead after three days and three nights in the grave (Sheole). We steadfastly maintain that Christ was crucified on the Feast of Passover, Nisan 14, April 5 (Julian Date) in 30 BC. He rose from the grave just as the weekly Sabbath day (Saturday) passed into the next day (Sunday) at exactly 6:00pm.

Crucifixion
Feast of Passover
Nisan 14
Wednesday,
April 5

The events which transpired during the last week of Christ, often called the *Passion Week*, have been chronologically presented in many ways by many biblical scholars. The timing and position of the final events which occurred is greatly influenced by the day that Christ was assumed to be crucified. There are many opinions, but only three dominate common beliefs. The *first* is to assume that Christ was crucified on a *Thursday* in 32 AD. Those who hold to this date are generally influenced by Sir Robert Anderson and his published study called *The Coming Prince*. The *second* position is to propose a *Friday* crucifixion in 33 AD. Modern theologians hold to this day because of two main influences: (1) The Roman Catholic Church officially recognizes Friday as the crucifixion day and has since the late 4th century BC. (2) Perhaps equally influential have been the work of Dwight D. Pentecost and one of his doctoral students named Harold H. Hoehner, who showed that the work of Anderson was flawed; but they corrected his error and conducted a subsequent study that led to a Friday crucifixion in 33 AD. Their work depended upon a 1 BC death of Herod, which was shown to be possible in a detailed study by Filmer. The *third* opinion, and the one which is presented in this book, is that Christ was crucified on a *Wednesday*, April 5 (Julian Date) in 30 AD.

All three positions agree that the Hebrew calendar date of the crucifixion was **Nisan 14**: The day of **Passover**. The sequence of events between Thursday, Nisan 9 and Sunday, Nisan 18 are described in the synoptic gospels of Matthew, Mark, Luke and John. Unfortunately, all are not described in sequence in any one gospel. The gospel writers seem to have chosen events that they personally witnessed; were told to them by those who were there; or simply seemed appropriate to the basic message of each gospel. Since the work of God is divinely inspired, there can be no doubt that every event described did take place, but the chronological sequence is not only difficult to determine but also open to debate. Based upon our belief that Christ was crucified on Wednesday, Nisan 14; and after intensely studying the gospel accounts; we have chosen some key events and attempted to put them in the correct chronological sequence. In a sense, it might not make any difference.

Each event described by Matthew, Mark, Luke and John *did happen* just as described. The exact sequence is only important to theological researchers. What is important is that Christ was crucified, dead and buried: he rose again after 3 days and 3 nights in the grave (Sheole). He was the *Firstfruit Harvest* of all those who would believe upon His name; and that by him and through Him by grace, all who would believe on His name will inherit eternal life. However, to fulfill the types of the Feast of Passover, the Feast of Unleavened Bread, The Feast of Firstfruits and the Sign of Jonah.... We will show that a Wednesday crucifixion is (arguably) the only logical choice.

RECONSTRUCTING THE LAST WEEK OF CHRIST

The events which transpired during the last week of Jesus Christ's ministry can only be reconciled by considering three key facts: (1) Christ was the son of God who spent 33.5 years in a mortal body. He was the only mortal man who ever completely fulfilled the letter of the law. Anything that Christ did during the last week of His life had to follow, confirm and fulfill the law. (2) Christ willingly went to the cross where He suffered and died for our sins. He was identified by John the Baptist as *our Passover Lamb*... the Lamb of God. That meant that Christ in type completely fulfilled the sacrificial requirements of the Feast of Passover, the 7 day Feast of Unleavened Bread and the Feast of Firstfruits (3) Christ was approached by the Sadducees and Pharisees *to prove who He was*.... They asked for a sign. Christ responded that neither miracles, healings nor scriptural interpretations would confirm His claim to be the Son of God; but only the *Sign of Jonah* would he give. That sign, upon which He based the credibility of His entire ministry, was that he would be in the grave for *3 days and 3 nights*. Before we fully discuss the implications of these three key observations, it will be helpful to recount the events which occurred during the last few days of Jesus Christ; His crucifixion and burial; and His triumphant resurrection from the grave. The days which will be recreated are Thursday, Nisan 8 to Sunday Nisan 18. This would have been between March 30 and April 9 in 30 AD.

30 AD										
Nisan 8	Nisan 9	Nisan 10	Nisan 11	Nisan 12	Nisan 13	Nisan 14	Nisan 15	Nisan 16	Nisan 17	Nisan 18
Thursday	Friday	Saturday	Sunday	Monday	Tuesday	Wednesday	Thursday	Friday	Saturday	Sunday
March 30	March 31	April 1	April 2	April 3	April 4	April 5	April 6	April 7	April 8	April 9
		Weekly Sabbath	Palm Sunday				Passover	Feast of Unleavened Bread		Feast of Firstfruits

We now reiterate that Jewish days begin at 6:00pm and not at midnight as in the Western world and those who use the modern Gregorian calendar. For the sake of discussion and to avoid confusion, we will include the entire evening and night of any one day as part of that day.

DAY 1: THURSDAY, NISAN 8

Jesus has come to the end of his 3.5 year earthly ministry and now turns toward Jerusalem to attend the Jewish Feast of Passover. As he enters the city of Jericho, He passes by a sycamore tree and He calls out Zacchaeus. Zacchaeus was a short man, and he had climbed into the tree to better see Jesus. Jesus calls him down, and then follows him to his house in Jericho where He spends the night... it is now Nisan 9.

DAY 2: FRIDAY, NISAN 9

As He leaves Jericho early Friday morning, He has compassion upon two blind men and restores their sight (Matthew 20:30).
Jesus leaves Jericho and travels to Bethany; a distance of 16-18 miles. Great crowds hear of his coming and they go out to meet Him as he travels with some of His disciples. He arrives in Bethany (Which means *House of Affliction*), which is only about 2 miles from Jerusalem. That evening (Nisan 10) He spends the night in the home of Mary, Martha and His friend Lazarus (John 11:18).

The evening of Nisan 9, after 6:00pm now Saturday Nisan 10, He eats supper with his disciples, Mary, Martha, Lazarus and Miriam. Miriam anoints Jesus with oil. This is not just an act of adoration, but one which fulfills the Law of Moses (God). God commanded that on Nisan 10 a male lamb without spot or blemish is to be brought into the house and anointed for its sacrificial death on Nisan 14. This is the anointing of Jesus Christ as the perfect Passover Lamb. John foretold of this day when he saw Jesus Christ coming to be baptized: *Behold the Lamb of God who comes to take away the sins of the world.* Christ is the only acceptable sacrifice to God, without spot or blemish (sin). Christ was slain on the cross, just as the other sacrificial Passover lambs were slain. But this is not atonement (which means *covering*) for sins; it is for *forgiveness* of sins. This is *six days before Passover* (John 12:1). The anointing of Christ by Miriam fulfills in type the Passover lamb, which once selected (anointed) is then examined for 4 days for any spot or blemish. Christ will enter the Temple every day for the next 4 days (Nisan 10-11-12 and 13), and be verbally assaulted by the Pharisees and Sadducees who will seek to destroy His claim to be the Son of God. He spends the night in Bethany.

DAY 3: SATURDAY, NISAN 10 (THE JEWISH SABBATH)

Jesus now leaves the house of Martha and Mary; having been anointed the Lamb of God who must suffer and die for the sins of the world. The word has spread that He is near Jerusalem, and throngs of people are now waiting for His arrival. Knowing this, Jesus stops in Bethpage, about 1.5 miles from Jerusalem just east of the Mount of Olives. He sends for a donkey to ride, fulfilling the ancient prophecy of Hosea. He arrives in Jerusalem to thousands of people waving palm branches and singing *Hosanna to the Son of David* (Matthew 2:15). This is called *Palm Sunday* by Christians all over the eastern and western world; but it was not on a Sunday but on a Saturday. Jesus rides to the temple, dismounts and enters. He teaches all the Sabbath day in the temple. That evening, He again returns to Bethany to spend the night.

DAY 4: SUNDAY, NISAN 11

Jesus arises early on Sunday and again returns to Jerusalem. This entry into Jerusalem is celebrated as *Psalm Sunday*. There are great throngs to greet Him, and some are again waving Psalm leaves. This is His second triumphal entry into Jerusalem As He nears the temple, He is hungry and stops by a fig tree, but the fig tree is barren of fruit. Jesus now curses the fig tree for not bearing fruit. Here is a remarkable event which is not always fully understood by lay Christians. It is common to assume that in His earthly temple Christ was hungry, and turning to a fig tree finds it barren and curses (rebukes and condemns) the fig tree. This was not because Christ was hungry and the tree had no figs; this is a prophetic and important act by the Messiah. Throughout the Bible, Israel is symbolically referred to as a fig tree. Hosea 9:10 says, *When I found Israel, it was like finding grapes in the desert; when I saw your fathers, it was like seeing the early fruit on the fig tree.* The fig tree symbolically represented the corporate Nation of Israel who was God's chosen people... *the apple of His eye.* The tree which was symbolically (Israel) had apostatized: It was bearing no *fruit of righteousness.* The consequence was not that God was going to turn His back on Israel....God forbid... but that the time had come for the Levitical sacrificial system; temporary atonement for sins; and the long years that Israel had waited for their promised Messiah to come to an end. It was now time that the Law would not be written on tablets of stone, but that it would be written in the heart. Make no mistake about it: This was one of the most significant events ever to occur in the history of mankind. As people pressed to him, He enters the temple. Before He begins to teach, a remarkable thing occurs; one which would arouse much hatred in the Jewish establishment.

> *And Jesus went into the temple of God, and cast out all them that sold and bought in the temple, and overthrew the tables of the moneychangers, and the seats of them that sold doves: And said unto them, It is written, My house shall be called the house of prayer; but ye have made it a den of thieves.*
> Matthew 21: 12-13

Jesus is so offended by these practices that He (obviously) forcibly overthrew tables and physically removed many from the Holy Temple. This event also confirms that Christ... all God... was also all man. He experienced pain, sorrow, temptations and feelings of mortal man. This should be comforting to all Christians: Our Lord and Savior has experienced all of the same emotions that we have experienced... He knows... He understands... This also fully addresses one of the reasons why Christians often do not stand up for the gospel message. *Judge not lest you be judged* is a tremendous cop-out for

136

most Christians. It is acceptable and required that when you see someone purposely and clearly violating God, praying to idols, worshipping strongholds... it is your duty and calling to reject and condemn both the practice and those who practice such things. It is not sitting in judgment when you back up your opinions and beliefs with Holy Scripture. That is why every Christian must earnestly seek a bible toting, full gospel, non-compromising church. But we digress...

After cleansing the temple, many sick, blind and lame press to see Him... and they were all healed (Matthew 21:14). The reaction of the chief priests and scribes were unbelievable. Instead of praising and worshipping Him; *they were sorely displeased.* He is now standing as the chosen sacrificial Lamb of God, perfect and acceptable. Following ancient Jewish law (Exodus 12:5-6), he now stands each day for four days to be fully and completely examined for *blemishes and defects.* This is key to understanding why Christ exposed Himself publically until the night he was arrested. He returns to Bethany to spend the night. This is His last night spent in Bethany. At 6:00 pm on the evening of Nisan 11; the Jewish day of Monday, Nisan 12 begins.

DAY 5: MONDAY, NISAN 12

Sunday having now passed, Jesus returns to Jerusalem the next day. As the disciples pass the fig tree that Jesus had rebuked the previous day, the disciples wondered in amazement at how quickly the tree had withered away. The disciples did not yet fully understand what was about to happen... This fig tree (Israel) had been withering away for hundreds of years! The mantle of salvation would now pass unto the gentiles. Jesus again speaks to His disciples in parables, but they still fail to completely understand. During this day He teaches in the temple and is continuously assaulted by the scribes, Pharisees and Sadducees... the *could not sees* and the *would not sees....* but they could find no fault in Him. Jesus said; *I am the way, the truth and the life...* no one could find fault or blemish; so hatred continued to grow.

137

The evening of Nisan 12...now Nisan 13... He would not return to Bethany. He stops on the Mount of Olives and gathers His disciples to Him. They have now begun to understand what is happening, but still cling to the belief that Christ will vanquish all foes; declare Himself as the long awaited Messianic King of the Jews; and establish an earthly kingdom with no end. As He relines, the disciples ask three questions: (1) Tell us, when shall these things be? (2) What shall be the sign of thy coming and (3) when will be the end of the world? The answers to these questions are the famous *Olivet Discourse*. After the Olivet Discourse, Jesus announces that He would be betrayed by one of His disciples in two days. Now having been taken over by Satan, Judas leaves.... accepts 30 pieces of silver for his betrayal... and returns as if nothing happened. Jesus and His disciples spend the night on the Mount of Olives.

DAY 6: TUESDAY, NISAN 13

Jesus returns to the temple to preach and teach early Tuesday morning. Near the end of this day, He tells His disciples to prepare for a Passover meal that evening. Jesus instructed them to *go into the city and find a man*....Jesus said: *I will keep the Passover at his house*. The disciples did as instructed and prepared for the Passover meal that evening. This action by Christ has prompted thousands of commentaries by biblical scholars. The problem arises as to why Christ would hold a Passover meal on the night of Nisan 13, when it is crystal clear that the Passover Lamb would not be slaughtered until the afternoon of Nisan 14, and consumed on the evening of Nisan 15 after 6:00pm. Why did Jesus hold a Passover meal with His disciples on Tuesday evening (Nisan 14) instead of on the evening of Nisan 14 (Nisan 15)? Why is there so much controversy over the Lord's Last Supper?

The answer comes in two different ways. *First,* the Essene community (Dead Sea Scroll authors) had completely broken with the Sadducees and Pharisees over many religious commands. One of these was when the Passover supper was to be held. The Essene community observed Passover on the evening of Nisan 13; which we believe was clearly wrong. The Passover Lamb would have had to be slain on the afternoon of Nisan 13, and not the next day on the afternoon of Nisan 14. Some have recently suggested that Christ's last supper was served in an Essene house. It is likely that the house in which the Passover meal of Christ was to be held was not an Essene house, because there was no meat/lamb at the Lord's last supper. Since all agree that Christ was nailed to the cross at 9:00 am on Nisan 14, and that He died at 3:00pm on Nisan 14, the sacrificial death of Jesus Christ completely settles the issue. But, why would Christ want to hold a Passover meal on the evening following the daylight of Nisan 13? Christ was the perfect Passover Lamb. He knew that he would die the next day. He knew that the sacrificial lamb and the Passover meal were to be eaten on the evening of Nisan 14 (Nisan 15) to commemorate and remember how His Father had rescued Israel from Egyptian bondage that very night.

The Passover meal that Christ and His disciples had on the evening of Nisan 13 was *not* the traditional Jewish Feast of Passover. Note what John the beloved said about this supper.

> *Now **before** the Feast of the Passover, when Jesus knew that His hour was come that He should depart out of this world unto the Father, having loved His own which were in the world, He loved them onto the end.*
>
> John 13:1

This should settle the issue; John clearly says that the Lord's last supper was NOT the Passover meal. Christ made the following statement:

> *With desire I have desired to eat **this** Passover (meal) with you before I suffer.*
>
> Luke 22:15

It is important that this issue is settled with spiritual understanding and intellectual certainty. Christ knew that he could not partake of the Passover Lamb on the evening of Nisan 14 (Nisan 15). He also fully understood that he was the perfect sacrificial lamb, without fault or blemish: Fully acceptable to God His Father. His sacrificial death would end the slaughter and sacrifice of the Old Testament Passover lamb forever.

A *traditional* Passover meal could never be called a Passover meal without the lamb. It should now be clearly understood that Christ would abolish the entire Jewish religious system at His death. No Christian after His death, including those today, would ever be required to observe any Feast of Israel or any Fast day except in remembrance of Him. Several well-meaning Christian religious groups insist that Christians should still observe every feast at their appointed time. In fact, to do so is crucifying Christ all over again. The death of Christ brought the Levitical sacrificial system with all of its rituals to an end. To continue, the purpose of what we call the Lord's Last Supper was to institute a new and different Feast of Passover without ritualistic sacrifices for the atonement of sins. It is interesting to note that at the Lord's last supper there was *no meat*... no lamb. He instituted this new Feast in a remarkable way. He initiated the Lord's Last Supper with the ancient practice of washing feet. This was a common practice in all Jewish houses as guests arrived. There were no full leather boots... everyone wore sandals. Feet would get very dirty from the dusty roads they traveled, and as part of the social greeting a host would wash the feet of a visitor. But Christ was not simply repeating this ritual, He was clearly showing everyone there that every believer was to be humble and a servant... a point He made on several occasions. He then took the cup and said...

> *Drink ye all of it; for this is my blood of the new testament, which is shed for many for the remission of sins.*
> Matthew 26:28

Clearly, this cup initiated a new testament... a new covenant... which was ratified by the shedding of His own blood on the cross of Calvary. After this cup, He took the bread, broke it, and gave thanks to them saying:

> *This is my body, which is given for you: this do in remembrance of me.*
>
> Luke 22:19

This is the *New Testament Passover meal*. It replaces the Old Testament Passover meal forever. There are no more animal sacrifices, the body of Christ is now of what we partake. When we take communion, we experience a wonderful new substitutionary process when we eat the bead; which represents the body of Christ: He was beaten and abused for everyone who believes upon His holy name. And when we drink the wine, we receive the cleansing power of the blood of Christ which conquered sin and the eternal wages of sin: Forgiveness of sin was fully accomplished on the cross of Calvary when Christ shed His precious blood. Further, Christ said that this was to be done:

> *Do this in remembrance of me as often as you will*
>
> Luke 22:19

Please note that no mortal man has to be specifically ordained, anointed or trained to allow any Christian the opportunity to partake in communion. The act of communion is between you and Jesus Christ: It affirms your faith in Him and accepts by grace the forgiveness of sins and eternal life in Him. Each time you partake in communion, it should be a life-changing experience: A confirmation of what Christ fully accomplished on the cross of Calvary: Christ said: *Do this as often as you will.*

Christ next announces once again that He would be betrayed, but this time identifies the traitor as one of His disciples. Judas leaves to join the Roman soldiers who would arrest Jesus. Turning to Peter, Christ says a remarkable thing. Evidently,

Satan has requested to test Peter's faith; just as He requested God to tempt Job over 3000 years previously.

> *And the Lord said, Simon, Simon, behold, Satan hath desired to have you, that he may sift you as wheat: But I have prayed for thee, that thy faith fail not: and when thou art converted, strengthen thy brethren. And he said unto him, Lord, I am ready to go with thee, both into prison, and to death. And he said, I tell thee, Peter, the cock shall not crow this day, before that thou shalt thrice deny that thou knowest me.*
>
> Luke 22:31-34

He tells Peter that He will deny Him three times, each time at the crow of a rooster. This is the same Peter that Christ once pointed to and said:

> *And I say also unto thee, that thou art Peter, and upon this rock I will build my church; and the gates of hell shall not prevail against it.*
>
> Matthew 16:18

This should be an object lesson to all Christians. We have all sinned and fallen short of the glory of God, but still we march on. Paul was told; *My grace is sufficient for thee: for my strength is made perfect in **weakness*** (II Corinthians 12: 9)

After his last supper, Christ returns to the Mount of Olives to await His betrayal. It is now nearing 10:00 PM on the evening of Nisan 13, which in Jewish minds is Nisan 14. Many things will transpire that night of nights.

- They reach a place called the Garden of Gethsemane
- Jesus prays that *this cup would be taken from me...* but nevertheless, *thy will be done*
- Jesus retreats to pray on His own, asks His disciples to pray for Him
- He returns to find them all asleep.

142

- Christ again retreats to prayer, and again returns to find everyone asleep.
- He wakes them, and immediately Judas appears. In a final act of defiance and hate, the priests, scribes and elders all appear wielding swords.
- Judas kisses Jesus to identify Him. The betrayal is complete.
- One of Jesus' followers arises and cuts off an ear of a priest's servant.
- Jesus is arrested, and taken to Annus, an ex high priest, who questions him with a group elders.
- After midnight, Jesus is next taken before Caiaphas, who was the third son of Annus an ex high priest..

Jesus now condemns Himself by speaking the truth about who He was and that He would return again. The high priest shouts out: *Are you the Son of God?*

> ...*and Jesus said,* **I am:** *and ye shall see the Son of Man sitting on the right hand of power (God), and coming (again) on the clouds of heaven.*
>
> Mark 14:62

No mortal man could make this statement... only the Son of God. To the Jew, this is blasphemed which brings death by stoning. The people wanted Christ to die; and the only way that this could occur is to have the death penalty placed upon Christ by the Roman Magistrate or Governor. This can only be done by convicting Christ of insurrection against Rome... an act of treason punishable by death.

- The high priest spat upon him, and declared him to be guilty of blasphemy against God.
- Peter is spotted in the crowd... denies he knows Christ three times to the cock of a rooster
- Jesus is beaten and cast in a rocky prison cell for the night.

Day 7: Wednesday, Nisan 14 (Passover)

- Early the next morning He is taken before the Sanhedrin; who was the "supreme court" of the Jews. The Sanhedrin does not accuse Christ of blaspheme; but of **treason** against Rome. They then takes Him to Pontius Pilate (the governor of Judea) to be sentenced to death.
- After extensive questioning, Pilate finds no fault in Jesus! In the ensuing discussion, Pilate is told that Jesus is from *Galilee* (Luke 23:6-7). Pilate now has a way out: Herod Antipas is Governor over the area called Galilee, so Pilate has Jesus taken to Herod Antipas who has come to Jerusalem to attend Passover and is staying in the Temple complex.
- Herod is only amused by Jesus. He commands Jesus to perform a miracle, but Jesus does nothing and remains silent. After a short time he sends Him back to Pilate.

In the morning hours of Nisan 14 around 8:00 AM, Christ was brought before Pontius Pilate for the second time. Pilate was the Roman prefect or governor of all Judea. It was the duty of a Roman prefect to interpret and enforce the law. Pilate had been appointed by Tiberius Caesar in 26 BC. He had the *Gloria Patria*...the power over life and death.

- Pilate questions Jesus, but can find no fault in Him. The people are on the verge of insurrection, but Pilate does not wish to condemn Jesus to death. He seizes upon a way out. Jewish custom allowed that on the Feast of Passover one man condemned to die could be pardoned provided that another man take his place. A man named Barabbas, who had been condemned to die for heinous crimes, was brought before the people and Pilate asked the people which one they would choose to free. The chief priests and the people pointed at Jesus Christ, and in a final act of rejection cried out ... *Crucify Him, Crucify Him!!* .... The final die had been cast.

- So Barabbas was released and Christ was chosen to be executed. But Christ was not found guilty of treason against Rome, so why was he condemned to die on the cross? The answer is interesting and shows us how God can control all human events if He chooses to do so. Note that Christ took the place of Barabbas, and Barabbas was set free. When Christ replaced Barabbas He also inherited the death penalty ascribed to Barabbas! So, in a tremendous miscarriage of justice, Christ was not sentenced to death by either Pilate or Herod; but He would die by crucifixion.

- Christ was condemned to be executed by nailing Him to a cross. This barbaric form of Roman execution was reserved for only the most despised and hardened criminals. It was a cruel, slow and tortuous death: *for it is written, **Cursed** is every one that hangeth on a tree* (Gal 3:13).

- Christ was removed to a hall called Pretorium, where he was clothed in a purple robe, and a crown of thorns was placed upon His head. The frenzied crowd spit upon Him, smote him repeatedly about the head and mocked Him as *King of the Jews.*

- They stripped Christ naked, beat Him, put His clothes back on Him and led Him out to be crucified.

- They brought Him to a place called Golgotha (The place of the skull). Before nailing Him to the cross, they offered him wine mixed with myrrh (very bitter), but He refused.

- At *the third hour,* which is 9:00 AM on Nisan 14, they nailed Him to the cross, stripped Him naked, and cast lots for His garments.

- He is crucified with two thieves: One seeks forgiveness and Christ saves him. The other does not.

- Jesus cries out: *I thirst* (John 19:28). He is offered a sponge with vinegar and hyssop. Jesus receives the liquid and said, *It is finished.* This was more than just a cruel and tortuous act; it was also a fulfillment of Old Testament shadow and type. At the first Passover, God instructed the people of Israel to slaughter a lamb without spot or blemish, collect the blood, and then using a hyssop plant cover the lintel of the door of the house with that blood. This would cause the angel of death to pass over that house at midnight on Nisan 15 (Exodus 12). What a beautiful picture of the sacrificial death of Jesus Christ as He hung on the cross.

- Darkness falls upon the face of the earth for several hours. Notice that scholars have called this a solar eclipse; but a solar eclipse cannot occur at the time of a full moon (Nisan 14). This is a supernatural event, and cannot be explained by natural phenomena.

- Christ dies at the 6th hour (3:00 pm). The Vail of the temple was rent from top to bottom...another supernatural event... and there was a great earthquake. The first covenant has now passed away....a new covenant had been initiated. It has been confirmed by blood....the blood of our Lord Jesus Christ.

*And almost all things are by the law purged with blood; and without **shedding** of blood is no remission (of sin)*
Hebrews 9:10

Now we must examine key facts that provide convincing evidence that all of these things happened on Nisan 14, a Wednesday. Confusion arises because the Gospel of Mark clearly states that:

*And now when the even was come, because it was the preparation (day); that is the **day before the Sabbath**.*
Mark 15: 42

Everyone acknowledges that the Jewish Sabbath day is Saturday and that Friday is used to prepare for the Sabbath; on which no work or travel more than a Sabbath days distance could take place. Friday is commonly called the *day of preparation* for the Sabbath day. Since Saturday is the weekly Jewish Sabbath day, the Roman Catholic Church seizes upon this verse to identify Nisan 14 as falling on Friday; and institutionalized this belief. It was then declared that the crucifixion of Christ took place on

Friday. In the last chapter, we addressed this error but now we will destroy this belief again. It is true that the Jewish Sabbath is Saturday; so on the surface the record of Mark seems to create an open and shut case. Christians who have *not studied* Jewish Feast days, Fast days and ordained days of rest cannot find a solution to this dilemma. The apostle John provides the information that will lead us to the truth. The apostle John recorded the following:

> *The Jews, therefore, because it was the **preparation** (day), that the bodies should not remain upon the cross on the Sabbath day (for that Sabbath day was a **HIGH day**).*
>
> John 19: 31

What is a *high day*? In addition to the weekly Sabbath (Saturday), there are 7 other sabbaths ordained by God. These are called *Sabbatons* or *High Sabbaths*, and they are observed with the same rules that a weekly Sabbath must follow. The day before any Sabbath day is a day of preparation. However, some are also *fast* days. The seven Sabbatons are designated in relation to the Seven Feasts of Israel.

The first and seventh days of the Feast of Unleavened Bread; The Feast of Pentecost, The Feast of Trumpet (Rosh Hashanah in Hebrew), The Feast of Atonement (Yom Kippur), the first day of Tabernacles (Succoth), and the Last Great Day of Tabernacles (which is the 8th day) are all *Sabbatons* or High Sabbaths. The first three occur in the spring, and the last four in the fall. The high day of which John was speaking was one of the three spring holy days, and since Jesus crucifixion took place on the day of Passover (Nisan 14 on the Hebrew calendar), the high day of which he speaks must be the first day of Unleavened Bread, which falls the day after the Passover (Nisan 15).

Because the Hebrew calendar is lunar-solar, Passover can fall on either Wednesday or Friday, but not Thursday. Nisan 14 in 30 AD fell on a Wednesday, and the *High Sabbath*, clearly identified by the apostle John, fell on Nisan 15, Thursday in 30 AD. This is why the Jewish followers of Christ were so anxious to get Christ removed from the cross and placed in a tomb before the next day, Nisan 15; which started at 6:00 pm on Nisan 14. The next day was the 1st day of the Feast of Unleavened Bread and a High Sabbath day. Realizing that the Sabbath day (Nisan 15) which followed the crucifixion day (Nisan 14) was a *high holy day* explains the urgency to get Christ into the tomb before 6:00 PM. It would be unlawful (work on the Sabbath) to remove the body of Christ from the cross after 6:00 PM on Nisan 14. Knowledge that Nisan 15 fell on a high Sabbath day not only explains how Christ could be crucified on a Wednesday, but it also speaks strongly against a Friday crucifixion. If Christ was crucified on a Friday, Nisan 14; then Nisan 15 would fall on a Saturday. This would mean that a Saturday Nisan 15 would be both a high Sabbath and a Jewish weekly Sabbath. The high priests sought to avoid this situation when they set each year but it did occur in 33 BC. Hence, 33 BC is a year that is commonly accepted as the year that Christ died. The question of how Christ could spend 3 days and 3 nights in the grave using a Friday crucifixion will be addressed later in this chapter.

DAY 8: THURSDAY, NISAN 15 (A HIGH SABBATH DAY)
Day eight, Thursday Nisan 15, was a *high Sabbath* as we have previously verified. When Christ suffered on the afternoon of the previous day, we know that *Mary Magdelene and Mary the mother of James* was there (Mathew 27:56). When Christ expired, there was no place to put His body. As the evening was approaching, a rich man of Arimathaea (a small town about 20 miles north of Jerusalem) named Joseph, who was a disciple of Jesus, went to Pilate and asked for the body of Jesus. Pilate commanded the body be given to Joseph. (Luke 23:53). Joseph took the body, wrapped it in linen and laid it into a tomb hewed out of solid rock. It is obvious that this tomb was not in Armathaea but was in Jerusalem; likely only a short distance from where Christ was crucified. A great stone was rolled over the entrance to the tomb, and those that were there departed. The urgency to get Christ into the tomb before 6:00 PM dictated that the body of Jesus could not be anointed with oil and spices, properly wrapped and prepared for burial on the dame day

that He died. By the time that Christ was laid into the tomb and the stone rolled in place, it was now after 6:00 PM on Thursday, Nisan 15. This was both a high holy day and the 1st day of the Feast of Unleavened bread. Being a Sabbath day (high Sabbath), no stores would be open to purchase burial supplies. Even if there were, preparing the oils and spices constituted work which was forbidden on a Sabbath day. Nisan 15 passed and Friday, Nisan 16 arrives.

DAY 9: FRIDAY, NISAN 16 (DAY OF PREPARATION)

On this day, the women probably purchased the necessary burial supplies, and prepared them to anoint Jesus. This is the only day that this could be done, since Nisan 15 (Thursday) and Nisan 17 (Saturday) were Sabbath days.

> And **when the Sabbath was past**, Mary Magdalene, and Mary the mother of James, and Salome, **had bought sweet spices**, that they might come and anoint him. And very early in the morning the **first day** of the week, they came to the sepulcher at the rising of the sun.
>
> Mark 16: 1-2

When the Sabbath was passed was a high holy day (Thursday). They purchased the sweet spices and other needed supplies on that day. The next day being the weekly Sabbath day (Saturday), the women would have waited until early Sunday morning to come to the tomb. Notice carefully that Mark says it at the *rising of the sun*. The sun had not yet burst forth, but it was very close to that time (John 20:1). This clearly establishes when they came to anoint Christ for burial. Friday, Nisan 16 now passes into Saturday, Nisan 17...the weekly Sabbath.

DAY 10: SATURDAY, NISAN 17 (JEWISH SABBATH DAY)

The weekly Sabbath (Nisan17) is over at 6:00 PM, but they chose to wait until the next morning as just discussed (Mark 16:1-2). Here we have a difficult time accurately predicting what happened next. The synoptic gospel accounts record that there was definitely two visits to the tomb by the women, one by a few disciples and possibly even a 3rd by the women. We offer the following believable scenario for the events which transpired next.

DAY 11: SUNDAY, NISAN 18 (STARTS AT 6:00PM, NISAN 17) THE WOMEN VISIT THE TOMB

The following is a likely chronological sequence of the four gospel accounts of the women's visit to the tomb after the end of the Sabbath. It is taken from B. L. Cocherel with whom we agree.

After the Sabbath day; which was Saturday, Nisan 17; and just as the sun was rising on the first day of the week (Sunday, Nisan 18), many women who were followers of Jesus came to the tomb to anoint his body with spices and ointments (See Matt.28:1; Mk.16:1-2; Lk.23:56, 24:1-2; Jn.28:1). We repeat the account of Mark.

> *And when the Sabbath was past, Mary Magdalene, and Mary the mother of James, and Salome, had bought sweet spices, that they might come and anoint him. And very early in the morning the first day of the week, they came to the sepulcher at the rising of the sun*
>
> Mark 16: 1-2

And when the Sabbath was passed... This Sabbath referred to by Mark is Saturday, Nisan 17... They (the Women) **had bought sweet spices** (on Friday, Nisan 16)......Observed the weekly Sabbath on Saturday... and very early the next morning (Sunday, Nisan 18) they came to the tomb.

> *"Now on the first day of the week, very early in the morning, they came to the sepulcher, bringing the spices which they had prepared, and **certain others with them.**"*
>
> Luke 24:1

> *"The first day of the week cometh Mary Magdalene early, when it was yet dark, to the sepulcher..."*
>
> John 20:1

It is not completely certain from all four gospel accounts that these narratives all refer to the same group of women, and that they all occurred just before the light of dawn on Sunday morning. However, we believe that this is true.

Standing before the tomb, the women asked; *Who is going to open the tomb for us?* (Mk.16:3). Remember that the tomb had been sealed and guards were sent to prevent someone from stealing Jesus' body (Matt.27:62-66). The guards had been stationed by Pilate for 3 days and 3 nights.

As the women stood before tomb, wondering how they were going to get it open so that they could anoint the body, there was a great earthquake and an angel appeared in a blazing light and rolled back the stone that covered the entrance to the tomb (Matt.28:2-4; Mk.16:4; Lk.24:2; Jn.20:1).

> *And, behold, there was a great earthquake: for the angel of the Lord descended from heaven, and came and rolled back the stone from the door, and sat on it. His countenance was like lightning, and his raiment white as snow: And for fear of him the keepers did shake, and became as dead men.*
>
> Matt.28:2-4

> *And when they looked, they saw that the stone was rolled away: for it was very great.*
>
> Mark 16:4

> *...and see the stone taken away from the sepulcher.*
>
> John 20:1

> *And they found the stone rolled away from the sepulcher.*
>
> Luke 24:2

The stone was rolled back for the women, but not for Jesus Christ. The angel then tells the women that Jesus is not in the tomb and to come and see for themselves. No stone could keep

Him in the grave. He was already gone as is clear from the following.

> And the angel answered and said to the women, Fear not you: for I know that you seek Jesus, which was crucified. **He is not here**: for he is risen as he said. Come, see the place where the Lord lay.

> Matthew 28:5-6

All the women enter the tomb and find that Jesus' body is indeed not there (Mk 16:5-6, Mark 16:5-6; Luke 24:3).

The women now enter the tomb to see for themselves. It is possible that out of fear they did not fully enter, but paused at the entrance and looked inside. In any case the tomb was not empty. They saw another angel inside. Christ was not there as they had been told.

> And entering into the sepulcher, they saw a young man sitting on the right side, clothed in a long white garment; and they were afraid. And he said to them, Be not afraid: you seek Jesus of Nazareth, which was crucified: he is risen; he is not here: behold the place where they laid him.

> Mark 16:5-6

Now they enter the tomb as commanded. This supports the conjecture that at first they stopped and looked into the tomb without entering.

> And they entered in, and found not the body of the Lord Jesus.

> Luke 24:3

While the women are still in the tomb two more angels appear to them and begin to explain to them what had happened in the context of what Christ had already told them.

And it came to pass, as they were much perplexed thereabout, behold, two men stood by them in shining garments: And as they were afraid, and bowed down their faces to the earth, they said to them, Why seek you the living among the dead? He is not here, but is risen: remember how he spake to you when he was yet in Galilee, Saying, The Son of man must be delivered into the hands of sinful men, and be crucified, and the third day rise again. And they remembered his words.

Luke 24:4-8

The women are told to go quickly and tell Peter and the other disciples that Jesus has risen and that He would see them in Galilee (Matt.28:7; Mk.16:7).

Go quickly, and tell his disciples that he is risen from the dead; and, behold, he goes before you into Galilee; there shall you see him: lo, I have told you.

Matt.28:7

But go your way, tell his disciples and Peter that he (Christ) goes before you into Galilee: there shall you see him, as he said to you.

Mk.16:7

All the women now leave the tomb to tell Peter, John and the other disciples what has happened. (Matthew 28:8; Mark 16:8; Luke 24: 8-9).

And they departed quickly from the sepulcher with fear and great joy; and did run to bring his disciples word.

Matthew 28:8

And they went out quickly, and fled from the sepulcher; for they trembled and were amazed: neither said they anything to any man; for they were afraid.

Mark 16:8

153

This does not contradict the accounts in either by Luke or John. It simply says (quite naturally) that they would tell no one else except the disciples as they were commanded to do.

> *And they remembered his* (the angels) *words, and returned from the sepulcher, and told all these things to **the eleven, and to all the rest.***
>
> Luke 24:8-9

It is obvious from Luke that during this visit, none of the disciples are with the women, It is also clear that Christ sent the women to tell the disciples and to ***all the rest*** that He had risen and He would meet them all in Galilee. How many is all the rest? We are not told, but as we shall see it was enough to split the women into two groups. The followers of Christ were likely widely spread and still sleeping. Other accounts mention only two of the disciples, but that is not necessarily in conflict with Dr. Luke's account. This is confirmed as follows.

MARY MAGDALENE TELLS PETER AND JOHN

At this point Mary Magdalene runs by herself to tell Peter and John, who are sleeping together. The other women hurry to tell the other disciples and *others* what they have just experienced and that Jesus is not in the tomb:

> *Then she (Mary Magdalene) runs, and comes to Simon Peter, and to the other disciple, whom Jesus loved (John), and said to them, 'They have taken away the Lord out of the sepulcher, and we know not where they have laid him.*
>
> John 20: 2

Upon hearing what Mary told them; Peter, John, and Mary run to the tomb. Peter and John immediately arise to see for themselves. John outran Peter. And was the first to arrive at the tomb. He stops outside. When impulsive Peter arrives, he rushes past Peter and enters the tomb.

Peter therefore went forth, and that other disciple, and came to the sepulcher. So they ran both together: and the other disciple did outrun Peter, and came first to the sepulcher. And he stooping down, and looking in, saw the linen clothes lying; yet went he not in. Then cometh Simon Peter following him, and went into the sepulcher, and sees the linen clothes lie, And the napkin, that was about his head, not lying with the linen clothes, but wrapped together in a place by itself. Then went in also that other disciple, which came first to the sepulcher, and he saw, and believed. For as yet they knew not the scripture, that he must rise again from the dead. Then the disciples went away again to their own home.

John 20: 3-18

Then arose Peter, and ran to the sepulcher; and stooping down, he beheld the linen clothes laid by themselves, and departed, wondering in himself at that which was come to pass.

Luke 24: 12

It is interesting that in all the gospels Christ revealed that He would be crucified, dead and buried but that He would rise after 3 days and 3 nights; but Peter and John did not recall this important prophecy by Jesus. Just like every Christian today, we must listen carefully to those soft, sweet words that the Holy Spirit whispers to us or we might miss something extremely important.

After examining the tomb and wondering what had happened, Peter and John leave and go back from where they came: But Mary Magdalene...either exhausted or simply being overcome with grief.....stays behind.

MARY MAGDALENE STAYS BEHIND

After Peter and John leave the tomb, Mary Magdalene stays behind weeping. Jesus suddenly appears to her and tells her that he is about to ascend to appear before his heavenly Father. Only one thing needs to be accomplished before the greatest act ever performed by mortal man has been accomplished. Christ, the sacrificial Passover lamb, must be fully accepted as the final redeeming sacrifice. The Father was surely waiting! Mary is probably weeping uncontrollably, and Christ now pauses to comfort her. Do not miss the impact of this event. Christ is so compassionate and so full of love He turns to Mary and comforts her before He ascends to His Father. Oh what compassion! What love that our Shepherd has for His sheep!!!!

> Mary stood outside the tomb crying. As she wept, she bent over to look into the tomb and saw two angels in white, seated where Jesus' body had been, one at the head and the other at the foot. They asked her, 'Woman, why are you crying?'
>
> John 20:11-13.

> They have taken my Lord away, and I don't know where they have put him. At this, she turned around and saw Jesus standing there, but she did not realize that it was Jesus. 'Woman, he said, why are you crying? Who is it you are looking for?' Thinking he was the gardener, she said, 'Sir, if you have carried him away, tell me where you have put him, and I will get him.' Jesus said to her, 'Mary' She turned toward him and cried out in Aramaic, 'Rabboni!' (which means teacher)
>
> John 20:14-16.

> Jesus said, 'Do not hold on to me, for I have not yet returned to the Father. Go instead to my brothers and tell them, I am returning to my Father and your Father, to my God and your God.
>
> John 20:17-18.

Jesus' instruction to Mary not to touch him is important, because it shows that he is about to leave the earth and appear before his Father; to be accepted as the perfect sacrifice for the sins of humanity. Jesus now ascends and is accepted by His Father. Concerned for His followers, He immediately returns. He is accompanied by *many* from the depths of *Sheole* (Hell), where he has just spent 3 days and 3 nights preaching to the inhabitants there. He has *set the captives free*, those who believed upon His Holy name (Ephesians 4: 8-10).

JESUS MEETS THE OTHER WOMEN

While the *other women* are still on the way to tell the other disciples what the angels have told them, Jesus meets them and tells them to tell the disciples he will meet them in Galilee:

> *And as they went to tell his disciples, behold, Jesus met them, saying, All hail. And they came and held him by the feet, and worshiped him. Then said Jesus to them, Be not afraid: go tell my brethren that they go into Galilee, and there shall they see me.*
>
> Matthew 28:9-10.

Jesus undoubtedly gave specific instructions as to where and when He would meet 49 days later. Notice that the women touched Jesus. This assures us that our previous scenario is correct: Between the time that Jesus spoke to Mary Magdalene and forbid her to touch him, and his meeting this group on women on their way to find the other disciples; he had ascended to his Heavenly Father, been accepted as the perfect sacrifice for the sins of humanity, and had returned to earth. While the women were still on their way to tell the other disciples what had happened, some of the men who were guarding the tomb informed the chief priests of the events that occurred at the tomb. Mary Magdalene and the other women now tell of their experiences at the tomb and their meeting Jesus, but they do not believe them.

> *Mary Magdalene came and told the disciples that she had seen the Lord, and that he had spoken these things to her.*
>
> John 2:18.

> *Now when Jesus was risen early the first day of the week, he appeared first to Mary Magdalene, out of whom he had cast seven devils. And she went and told them that had been with him, as they mourned and wept. And they, when they had heard that he was alive, and had been seen of her, believed not.*
>
> Mark.16:9-11.

157

It was Mary Magdalene, and Joanna, and Mary the mother of James, and other women that were with them, which told these things to the apostles. And their words seemed to them as idle tales, and they believed them not.

Luke 24:10-11.

Taking all the scriptural accounts as a single reliable narrative by 4 different disciples (none of them were there); the following is a plausible chronology of the events concerning the visits to the tomb by the men and women involved:

1. Jesus is nailed to the cross at 9:00 AM on Nisan 14, and dies at 3:00 PM that same day (Wednesday)
2. Pilate grants permission for his men to remove Jesus' body from the place of crucifixion and deliver it to Joseph (late Nisan 14).
3. Joseph places the body of Jesus in the tomb wraps it in linen, just before the High Sabbath day arrives at 6:00 PM.
4. The next day is a Sabbaton... a High Sabbath (Nisan 15, Thursday).
5. The women likely purchased spices and prepared them on the day following (Nisan 16, Friday) the high Sabbath (Nisan 15, Thursday). They observe the normal weekly Sabbath the next day (Nisan 17, Saturday), and made plans to visit the tomb early on Sunday morning (Sunday, Nisan 18) just before sunrise.
6. The women arrive at the Tomb on the first day of the week (Nisan 18, Sunday) just as the sun was rising but it was still dark: They see that the tomb is sealed, and ask who will roll back the stone at the entrance.
7. While they are standing in front of the tomb, there is an earthquake, and an angel descends from heaven that rolls back the stone from the tomb's entrance.
8. As the women stand there in fear, the angel comforts them and tells them that Jesus is not in the tomb, but that he has risen. He had in fact risen at exactly 6:00

PM exactly as Saturday Nisan 17 passed into Sunday, Nisan 18. One foot in the tomb at a fraction of a second just before 6:00 PM, and the other foot out of the tomb just a fraction of a second after 6:00 PM. This is to fulfill His own words: *I will rise on the third day*, and *I will rise after 3 days and three nights in the grave*. How can we be sure that this happened as we say it did? This has to be the truth, since to stay in the tomb any part of Sunday, Nisan 18 would make the very words of Christ untrue. The women are told to go into the tomb and see for themselves. There they encounter two more angels, and then a third.

9. A *mighty angel* explains what has happened and tells the women to go and tell the disciples.

10. They all depart to tell the disciples, and they split into *two groups*. We are told that Mary goes to tell Peter and John, and the other women go to tell the rest of the disciples. Peter and John are sleeping together... the rest are scattered somewhere.

11. Peter and John are told... They arise quickly and run to the tomb with Mary Magdalena lagging behind. Peter and John arrive; look in the tomb: and find it empty. Probably not understanding what has just happened, they go back to where they came from.

12. Mary Magdalene stays at the tomb. Possibly she is tired and need to rest; possibly she tarries there to pray; suddenly, Jesus appears to her. Mary grasps at Jesus feet but is told not to cling to Him.

13. Jesus then leaves Mary, and then goes to meet the other women on their way to inform the other disciples. He has ascended to the Father; He has been accepted as the perfect Passover sacrifice; and returned.

14. Jesus intercepts the other women. The other Mary and her companions now worship Jesus and touch His feet.

15. Jesus departs: Mary Magdalene and the other women tell the disciples of their meeting Jesus, and that he is alive; but no one believes them.
16. Later that day, Jesus meets two Jewish males and talk to them.
17. 49 days later on the Day of Pentecost Jesus meets the disciples and others in the Upper Room. The Holy Spirit falls on all believers.

There have been hundreds of attempts to rationalize the four different gospel accounts. I agree with Brother B. L. Cocherel that this is a reasonable and believable scenario.

THE SIGN

Why is it so important to identify whether Christ was crucified on a Wednesday or on a Friday? I believe that it is of paramount importance if we are to follow after Christ in spirit and in truth. Christ was being questioned by the Pharisees and the scribes who wanted Him to prove by *a sign* that He was the Son of God.

> *Then certain of the scribes and of the Pharisees answered, saying, Master, we would see a sign from thee. But he answered and said unto them, An evil and adulterous generation seeketh after a sign; and there shall no sign be given to it, but the sign of the prophet Jonas: For as Jonas was three days and three nights in the whale's belly; so shall the Son of man be three days and three nights in the heart of the earth. Then certain of the scribes and of the Pharisees answered, saying, Master, we would see a sign from thee. But he answered and said unto them, An evil and adulterous generation seeketh after a sign; and there shall no sign be given to it, but the sign of the prophet Jonas: For as Jonas was three days and three nights in the whale's belly; so shall the Son of man be three days and three nights in the heart of the earth.*
>
> Matthew 12:38-40

Close examination of these verses yield three very important facts:

(1) The scribes and Pharisees demanded a sign from Christ. They were not satisfied that He turned water to wine, healed the lame, restored sight to the blind or even raised the dead. What were they expecting to see?

(2) Christ responded that only an adulterous and evil generation would ask for a greater sign(s).

(3) He concluded the inquiry by declaring that the only sign he would give would be the *Sign of Jonah.*

The *Sign of Jonah* was well known to all Jewish believers (Jonah 1:2, 3:4). Jonah refused to obey God's command to go to Nineveh and preach repentance, and after trying to flee from God he was swallowed by a *great fish*…. it does not say a whale! Jonah was in the belly of the great fish for three days and three nights.

Carefully reading the account, Jonah was clearly drowned with seaweed covering his head. Jonah had to die and then be brought back to life to fulfill what God had in store for him to do, which was to preach to the wicked people at Nineveh. This is a perfect shadow and type of Christ and his ascension to be our High Priest and intercessor before God. Christ was clearly saying that He would also die (be crucified), and that He would lie in the grave for three days and three nights. After that time, He too would rise from the dead. Let us admit that Christ did not equate 3 days and three nights to 72 hours. This is a key omission which is central to determining how three days and three nights in the grave can be accomplished. Was Christ playing word games, or was He simply stating in the plainest terms that He would be in the grave (Sheole) for a normal and full 3 days and 3 nights (72 hours)? The following graphic might help to visualize a week in which Nisan 14 would fall on a Wednesday.

Nisan 14	Nisan 15	Nisan 16	Nisan 17	Nisan 18

Wednesday		Thursday		Friday		Saturday		Sunday
Morning	Evening	Morning	Evening	Morning	Evening	Morning	Evening	Morning

WEDNESDAY CRUCIFIXION: NISAN 14

- Christ is placed in the grave just before 6:00 PM on Wednesday , Nisan 14
- *Night 1*: 6:00pm Wednesday (now Thursday) to 6:00 AM Thursday, Nisan 15
- *Day 1*: 6:00 AM Thursday – 6:00 PM Thursday, Nisan 15
- *Night 2*: 6:00pm Thursday (now Friday) to 6:00 AM Friday, Nisan 16
- Day 2: 6:00 AM Friday – 6:00 PM Friday, Nisan 16
- *Night 3:* 6:00pm Friday (now Saturday) to 6:00 AM Saturday, Nisan 117
- Day 3: 6:00 AM Saturday – 6:00 PM Saturday, Nisan 15

Christ arises from the grave after exactly 3 days and 3 nights (72 hours) around 6:00 PM, late Saturday The following graphic depicts a week in which Nisan 14 falls on a Friday.

Nisan 14		Nisan 15		Nisan 16

Wednesday		Thursday		Friday		Saturday		Sunday
Morning	Evening	Morning	Evening	Morning	Evening	Morning	Evening	Morning

FRIDAY CRUCIFIXION: NISAN 14

- Christ is placed in the grave just before 6:00 PM on Friday ,Nisan 14
- *Night 1*: 6:00pm Friday (now Saturday) to 6:00 AM Friday, Nisan 15
- *Day 1*: 6:00 AM Saturday – 6:00 PM Saturday, Nisan 15
- *Night 2*: 6:00pm Saturday (now Sunday) to 6:00 AM Sunday, Nisan 16

Christ arises from the grave just as Saturday *dawned on* to Sunday, Nisan 18 6:00 PM (Matthew 28: 1). Christ clearly said:

162

*For as Jonas was **three days** and three nights in the whale's belly; so shall the Son of man be **three days** and three nights in the heart of the earth.*

Matthew 12:40

We must now ask: How do the proponents of a Friday crucifixion allow for the Sign of Jonah to be fulfilled if it demands a full 3 days and 3 nights in the grave? It is *impossible* to arrive at a *full three days and nights* that Christ would have been in the grave using a Friday crucifixion and a Sunday morning resurrection. The answer lies in an interpretation that any part of a day can count as a full day. We will now show that a clever application of this belief can result in a count of 3 days and 3 nights... but it stretches the imagination.

To get 3 days, we must agree that the very short time that Christ spent in the tomb of Joseph, just before Nisan 14 was changing into Nisan 15; would be counted as an entire 24 hour day. If those last few minutes of Nisan 14 counted as an entire day, by definition this included one full day and one full night!! Using those few minutes late Friday before 6:00 PM would be counted as one full day and one full night. The night of 6:00 PM Saturday-6:00 AM Saturday would count as *night2*. 6:00 AM-6:00pm on Saturday would count as *day2*. The Roman Catholic Church declared that Christ arose just before sunrise on Sunday morning. This would allow 6:00pm-6:00 AM (Sunday) to be the third night. But where is the 3rd day? Since Sunday (Jewish calendar day) starts on 6:00PM Saturday evening and ends on 6:00PM Sunday; the night of Sunday (after 6:00PM Saturday) would also count as one full day and night. This will result in 3 days and 3 nights (72 hours) being accounted for in just over 30 hours. Such an accounting scheme boggles the mind, and even suggests that Christ was being deceptive in suggesting that He would be in the grave a full 3 days and 3 nights. Did Christ understand what a Jewish day actually was? What a silly question! But we note that Christ said:

*Jesus answered, Are there not twelve **hours** in the day? If any man walks in the day, he stumbleth not, because he seeth the light of this world.*

John 11:9

This should certainly settle the issue. Incidentally, Pilate was approached by the Jews to place a set of guards in front of the tomb for a full 3 days and a full 3 nights to make sure that no Christian or disciple would steal the body of Jesus and claim that He had risen. It is clear that both the Jews that requested the guards be placed at the tomb, and Pilate, certainly believed that Christ meant what He said. There is a good reason why Pilate did that. A Jewish historical belief was that once a person died. The soul would be allowed to return to the body for 3 days, and after that time the soul would be taken to Sheole. Pilate wanted to make sure that the body of Christ would not be stolen during that period of time and claim that He had risen. Recall that when Lazarus died, word was sent to Christ to come quickly. However, Christ waited 2 days before departing and did not arrive until the 4th day. Christ then declared to His disciples that Lazarus is dead: then He commanded Lazarus to come forth from the tomb. This narrative fits the ancient Jewish custom that after 3 days and 3 nights, there is no return from the dead. Christ might have known this and to demonstrate his deity and authority over death, he waited until the 4th day to raise Lazarus (John 11:1-43)

Although it might be conceded that there are times in the Holy Scriptures where a portion of a day was counted as a full day, it stretches my imagination too far. If Christ banked the validity of His entire 3.5 year ministry on this *sign*; and His assertion that He was the only begotten Son of God; and His assertion that He would be in the heart of the earth for 3 days and 3 nights was based upon such unusual and clever accounting: I think that He would have said so.

There are some other biblical clues that Christ was crucified on a Wednesday...all agree it was on Nisan 14.

164

If Nisan 14 fell on a Wednesday, and Christ rose early Sunday evening Nisan 18......a full 3 days and three nights is assured. First, we will shortly look at the Messianic, 490 year prophecy of Daniel. In Daniel 9:27, Gabriel told Daniel that Messiah would be *cut off in the middle of the 490th week*. This clearly meant after 3.5 years had elapsed in the final 7 year period of time, but this phrase might possibly have a double meaning. The middle of a week is on Wednesday, not Friday. This might be interesting but not very convincing.

Second, let's go back to Genesis and visit Noah. It is generally held that the ark is a *type* of Jesus. The ark saved Noah and his family from the wrath of God's judgment upon the evil world. Jesus offers salvation to all those who trust in Him, sparing them from judgment for their sins. The type is clear. The ark rested, or finished the work of saving Noah's family on a significant day. The ark rested in the seventh month, the seventeenth day of the month, on the mountains of Ararat (Genesis 8:4).

God did not institute a calendar change until after the Exodus, and the seventh month of Nisan became the first month. When the flood occurred, the first month was not Nisan but Tishri. So in the Genesis account of the flood, It turns out that the same day the ark rested, which is the 17th day of Nisan, just happens to be three days and three nights after the 14th of Nisan. This might mean that in a prophetic illustration, God caused the ark to rest from the flood (His wrath on an evil world) on the same day that Jesus would rise from the dead to save mankind from the future wrath of God upon a sinful world. Coincidence? Maybe, but if this is a shadow and type of Christ rising from the grave to redeem mankind, a Wednesday crucifixion and a resurrection just at 6:00 PM corresponds to when the ark rested and Noah's family was saved.

THE WORDS OF CHRIST

Before closing this biblical investigation of how long Christ was in the tomb, let us again review the words of our Lord Jesus

Christ when He taught on this subject. This principle is at the heart of when Jesus Christ was crucified.

> *Then certain of the scribes and of the Pharisees answered, saying, Master, we would see a sign from thee. But he answered and said unto them, An evil and adulterous generation seeketh after a sign; and there shall no sign be given to it, but the sign of the prophet Jonas: For as Jonas was three days and three nights in the whale's belly; so shall the Son of man be three days and three nights in the heart of the earth.*
>
> Matthew 12:38-40

We have previously discussed this passage of scripture. The scribes and the Pharisees asked for a *sign* that Christ was who He said He was... the Son of God. Christ then answered that the only sign that He would give would be the *Sign of Jonah*. Every Jew would know what this meant: Jonah was swallowed by a great fish and was in the belly of this great fish for three days and three nights. Christ said that He would be in the grave (Sheole) for this amount of time. What did Christ mean? I have looked at hundreds of commentaries on Jonah, and not one questioned the Holy Scriptures as to what period of time this actually meant. It is *always* understood to be exactly what it says... a full 3 days and 3 nights or 72 hours. It is only when one reads commentaries on the very words of Jesus is this period of time challenged, questioned and rationalized. The problem starts with the Roman Catholic Church, followed by numerous other denominations and meaningful Christians who by cleverly counting time stretch no more than 36-37 hours into 72 hours. The issue is critical to determining when Christ was crucified. It is our position that the most logical and straightforward interpretation is to believe what Christ clearly implied and said: Christ was in the heart of the earth for a full 3 days and 3 nights, or 72 hours. If Christ was crucified on a Friday, this is impossible. If Christ was crucified on a Friday, no more than 36-37 hours would elapse before His resurrection; which is claimed to be just before sunrise on Sunday morning. But there is more to this issue that needs to be presented.

166

I. Christ said that He would *rise up after 3 days*.

> *And he began to teach them, that the Son of man must suffer many things, and be rejected of the elders, and of the chief priests, and scribes, and be killed, and **after three days rise again**.*
>
> Mark 8:31

> *Saying, Sir, we remember that that deceiver said, while he was yet alive, **After three days** I will rise again.*
>
> Matthew 27:63

II. Christ also said that He would be *raised on the third day*.

> *From that time forth began Jesus to shew unto his disciples, how that he must go unto Jerusalem, and suffer many things of the elders and chief priests and scribes, and be killed, and be **raised again the third day**.*
>
> Matthew 16:21

> *And while they abode in Galilee, Jesus said unto them, The Son of man shall be betrayed into the hands of men: And they shall kill him, and **the third day he shall be raised again**.*
>
> Matthew 17:22-23

Both the Book of Acts and the Apostle Paul *confirmed* the words of Christ

> *And we are witnesses of all things which he did both in the land of the Jews, and in Jerusalem; whom they slew and hanged on a tree: Him **God raised up the third day**, and shewed him openly.*
>
> Acts 10:39-40
>
> *And we are witnesses of all things which he did both in the land of the Jews, and in Jerusalem; whom they slew and hanged on a tree: Him **God raised up the third day**, and shewed him openly.*

I Cor. 15:3-4

*And Jesus going up to Jerusalem took the twelve disciples apart in the way, and said unto them, Behold, we go up to Jerusalem; and the Son of man shall be betrayed unto the chief priests and unto the scribes, and they shall condemn him to death, And shall deliver him to the Gentiles to mock, and to scourge, and to crucify him: and **the third day he shall rise again**.*

Matthew 20:17-19

*Then he took unto him the twelve, and said unto them, Behold, we go up to Jerusalem, and all things that are written by the prophets concerning the Son of man shall be accomplished. For he shall be delivered unto the Gentiles, and shall be mocked, and spitefully entreated, and spitted on: And they shall scourge him, and put him to death: and **the third day he shall rise again**.*

Luke 18:31-33

III.   Jesus also seemed to imply that it would take ***three days to rise.***

*Then answered the Jews and said unto him, What sign shewest thou unto us, seeing that thou doest these things? Jesus answered and said unto them, Destroy this temple, and **in three days** I will raise it up. Then said the Jews, Forty and six years was this temple in building, and wilt thou rear it up in three days? But he spake of the temple of his body.*

John 2:19-21

At this point, I want to assert that I am a *Bible Literalist.* That is. I believe that the words of the Holy Scripture are God inspired, that they are infallible and that there is no ambiguity or confusion in the scriptures. So, it appears that I have painted myself into a corner from which there is no escape. From the words of Christ, He said that (1) ***I will rise again after 3 days*** (2) ***I will rise again on the third day*** and (3) ***It would take 3 days to rise.*** Many biblical expositors have avoided the actual words of Christ by either

168

omission, commission or by crying out *scribal error*. Can there possibly be a way to explain these 3 positions? The answer is YES.

First, we will re-assert the belief that Christ meant what He said and He said what He meant…. He would be in the tomb for a full 3 days and 3 nights. I believe that the Christ was placed in the tomb of Joseph and the tomb was sealed at exactly 6:00 PM; just as Nisan 15 began, as required by Levitical law. Christ satisfied every jot and tittle of the law. His body remained in the tomb exactly 72 hours, and that period of time would elapse at exactly 6:00 PM on Sunday, Nisan 17. At one second before 6:00PM, one holy foot of Jesus Christ was in the tomb; at exactly 6:00 PM He left the tomb: and at 1 second after 6:00 PM His other foot was set on the ground outside of the tomb. *He rose on the third day; He rose after exactly 3 days and 3 nights as He said He would; and He arose after 3 days.* Incredible as it might seem, in one moment of time Christ fulfilled His destiny which was preordained since time began.

I am quite sure that many well-meaning Christians will fail to accept this scenario; to them I have an humble and sincere reply. First, my God created man by His command, called the earth and universe into existence, and by an eternal, divine and perfect plan has sent His only Son to save my miserable, sinful soul certainly can orchestrate a scenario which exactly satisfies everything that Jesus Christ said. Second, if there is an alternative explanation can be found that can satisfy all Holy Scripture, I am perfectly willing to believe that scenario. May God speak to anyone with an ear to listen.

SUMMARY AND CONCLUSIONS

We have carefully examined biblical clues and the Gospel accounts of Matthew, Mark, Luke and John to arrive at a justifiable, reasonable and believable account of what transpired during the last week of our Lord Jesus Christ upon this earth. We believe that evidence demands a verdict.

- Christ was Crucified and buried on Nisan 14, 30 AD. This happened to fall on the Julian calendar day of Wednesday, April 5.
- Christ was placed in the tomb just before 6:00PM on Nisan 14 and te tomb was sealed at exactly 6:00 PM. He was now entombed. The day of Nisan 15 (6:00 pm, Nisan 14 - 6:00 PM Nisan 15 began the first day of the seven day Feast of Firstfruits (Thursday, Nisan 15 - Wednesday, Nisan 21).
- The day of Nisan 15 was a *high Sabbath day*, as commanded by God.
- Christ remained a full 3 days and 3 nights in the grave, just as he told His disciples He would.
- Christ rose from the depths of Sheole at exactly at 6:00 PM; as Saturday, Nisan 17 passed into Sunday; Nisan 18 in 30 AD.

This ends our summary and exegesis of what likely occurred during the last week of Jesus Christ. Perhaps other biblical investigators can either confirm or modify these accounts.

CHAPTER 9

EVIDENCE DEMANDS A VERDICT

The purpose of this book has been to examine all available biblical facts and supporting evidence to determine the answer to two important and long debated and important questions: (1) When was our Lord Jesus Christ born? (2) When did our Lord Jesus Christ die? These two questions are so closely tied to one another that to answer one demands an answer to the other. Using all available information, we propose that the following conclusions be accepted as true.

1.0 Jesus Christ was born in 5 BC on March 23, Nisan 15 which was the first day of the Feast of Unleavened bread.

2.0 Jesus Christ died on Nisan 14, April 5 in 30 AD on the Feast of Passover. Christ lived exactly 34 Jewish years.

3.0 Herod the Great, King of the Jews, died between Nisan 1 and Nisan 15 in 4 BC

4.0 Daniel the prophet received a 490 year (70-7's) prophecy from the Archangel Gabriel sometime during his 70 year exile by King Nebuchadnezzar in Babylon. Perhaps the most important Old Testament prophecy recorded, it revealed to Daniel a timeline which once initiated predicted the first and second coming of Jesus Christ. The prophecy *went forth* and was initiated on Tishri 1 in 457 BC. The first year and month of Christ's 3.5 year ministry was accurately determined to be in 26 AD on or near the Feast of Atonement, Tishri 10 when He came to be baptized by John who was preaching redemption. The prophecy also accurately predicted that He would be cut off or crucified on Nisan 14 in 30 AD on the Feast of Passover.

Can we show that Christ was crucified in 30 BC using other scriptures and historical events? The answer is: YES.

CONFIRMING FACTS

This study has shown that the day and year of Jesus' birth was March 23, 5 BC, which demands that Christ would have turned 30 years old on March 23, 26 BC. He was crucified on the Feast of Passover, April 5, Nisan 14 in 30 AD. Christ would have begun a 3.5 year ministry on or near the Feast of Tabernacles in 26 BC, when He came to the River Jordan to be baptized by John. Both the birth and death of our Lord Jesus Christ occurred exactly 34 Jewish years apart. This has been confirmed using biblical, historical, and astronomical data. Other studies have suggested that his death ranged from 27 A.D. to 34 A.D. We have shown that Christ was crucified on Nisan 14 in 30 AD, but can we confirm a 30 AD crucifixion by a second witness? The following are several biblical, historical, and astronomical proofs that strongly suggest that the crucifixion of Christ occurred in 30 A.D.:

PAUL AND HEROD AGRIPPA

Paul mentions that Barnabas and Titus went with him to Jerusalem 14 years after his conversion (Gal. 2:1). This could only be the trip that he took to Jerusalem with food supplies and money that is mentioned in Acts 11:30. While Paul, Barnabas, and Titus were at Jerusalem, King Herod Agrippa died. His death is well documented to have occurred in 44 A.D. If we subtract 14 years from 44 A.D., this brings us to 30 A.D

THE CONVERSION OF PAUL

Paul was converted on the road to Damascus shortly after the death of Christ. The scriptures say he was breathing fire and preparing to execute all the Christians he could reach by orders from Rome. There is little doubt that Paul's conversion and the year of Jesus death are one and the same.

Agrippa, who was a friend of Caligula the Emperor of Rome, was made king of the Tetrarchy of his uncle Philip Techoritis only a few days after Caligula's ascension to power in March of 37 A.D.. Agrippa went to his lands in 39 A.D., and almost immediately returned to Rome to bring accusations against his uncle Antipas to Caligula in 39 A.D. Upon the assassination of Caligula on January, 24, 41 A.D., Agrippa encouraged Claudius to accept the rulership of the Empire. Very early in his reign, probably shortly after March 15 in 41 AD, Claudius conferred to Agrippa the jurisdiction of the land Caligula had made to him, and added to them the rest of the kingdom of Herod the Great. This gave him total dominion over Israel. Josephus says that after having reigned for 3 years (41-44 A.D.), Agrippa died. (*Antiquities XIX 8.2*) Agrippa's death is also described in the book of Acts.

> *On the appointed day Herod, wearing his royal robes, sat on his throne and delivered a public address to the people. They shouted, 'This is the voice of a god, not of a man.' Immediately because Herod did not give praise to God, an angel of the Lord struck him down, and he was eaten of worms and died.*
>
> Acts 12:21-23

Notice that at this time Paul and Barnabas were in Jerusalem:

> *When Barnabas and Saul had finished their mission, they returned from Jerusalem, taking with them John, also Mark.*
>
> Acts 12:25 NIV

Paul's trip to Jerusalem, which is noted in Acts 12: 21-25, is the same one mentioned in Galatians 1:22 and 2:1.

> *I was personally unknown to the churches of Judea that are in Christ. They only heard the report: the man who formerly persecuted us is now preaching the faith he once tried to destroy. And they praised God because of me. Fourteen years later I went up again to Jerusalem, this time with Barnabas. I took Titus also along.*
>
> Galatians 1:22 NIV

This trip to Jerusalem took place 14 years after Paul's conversion (Acts 9: 1-22), which we have proposed was in 30 BC. Paul's *first* trip to Jerusalem was three years after his conversion (Gal. 1:18;

Acts 9: 23-30). This information clearly points out that Paul's *second* trip to Jerusalem was well after his conversion and likely occurred in 44 A.D. Therefore the year of Paul's conversion and Jesus' death was 30 A.D. This is all shown in the graphic below:

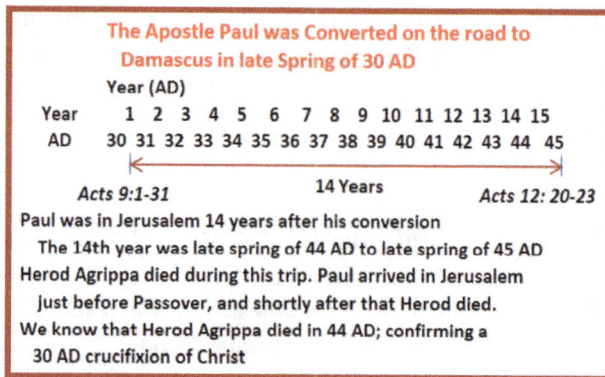

The Apostle Paul was Converted on the road to
Damascus in late Spring of 30 AD
Year (AD)

| Year | 1 2 3 4 5 6 7 8 9 10 11 12 13 14 15 |
| AD | 30 31 32 33 34 35 36 37 38 39 40 41 42 43 44 45 |

Acts 9:1-31   14 Years   Acts 12: 20-23

Paul was in Jerusalem 14 years after his conversion
  The 14th year was late spring of 44 AD to late spring of 45 AD
Herod Agrippa died during this trip. Paul arrived in Jerusalem
  just before Passover, and shortly after that Herod died.
We know that Herod Agrippa died in 44 AD; confirming a
  30 AD crucifixion of Christ

THE FIFTEENTH YEAR OF TIBERIUS CAESAR

Now, in the fifteenth year of the reign of Tiberius Caesar, Pontius Pilate being governor of Judea, and Herod being tetrarch of Galilee, and his brother Philip tetrarch of Ituraea and of the region of Trachonitis, and Lysanias the Tetrarch of Abilene, Annas and Caiaphas being the high priests, the word of the Lord came to John the son of Zachrias in the wilderness. And he came into all he country about Jordan, preaching the baptism of repentance for the remission of sins.

Luke. 3:1-3

The following facts are known about Augustus Caesar and Tiberius Caesar.

AUGUSTUS CAESAR (GAIUS JULIUS OCTAVIANUS)
- Born on September 23, 63 B.C.
- Nephew of Julius Caesar
- Julius Caesar assassinated March 15, 44 B.C.
- Made Emperor (essentially) on January 13, 27 B.C.

TIBERIUS CAESAR (TIBERIUS CLAUDIUS NERO)

- Born on November 16, 42 B.C.
- Adopted by Augustus and named Tiberius Julius Caesar
- On becoming Emperor, he was named Tiberius Julius Caesar Augustus
- Began co-regency over eastern provinces in 12 A.D.
- Became Emperor upon Augustus' death August 19, 14 AD
- Confirmed as Emperor by Senate on September 17, 14 AD
- Died March 16, 37 AD
  (Confirming Source: 1963 *Encyclopedia Americana*: Anchor Bible Commentary

In 12 AD Augustus Caesar retreated to his island villa off the coast of Italy, and was never seen in public again. Before leaving, he appointed his son Tiberius as co-emperor. From this point on, Tiberius was the de-facto reigning emperor with autonomous powers. The fact that Augustus Caesar was still alive was almost academic; the people were being ruled by Tiberius from 12 BC until his death in 37 BC. So, Tiberius began to as co-regent in 12 AD and as sovereign Emperor in 14 A.D. If Luke's reference to the 15th year of Tiberius' reign is calculated from 12 AD, the beginning of Christ's ministry would be 26 AD, and again we find that 30 A.D. is a consistent date with other sources as the year of Jesus' death.

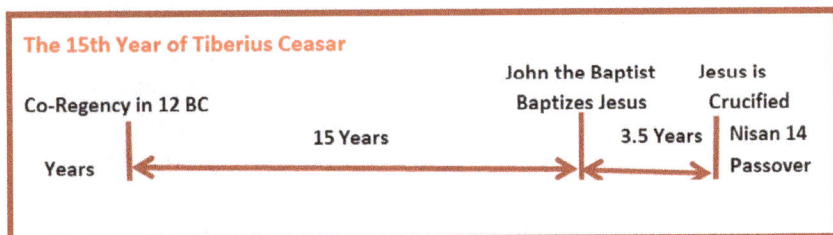

The 15th Year of Tiberius Ceasar

Co-Regency in 12 BC — 15 Years — John the Baptist Baptizes Jesus — 3.5 Years — Jesus is Crucified / Nisan 14 Passover

Years

FORTY SIX YEARS BUILDING THE TEMPLE

During the first Passover of Christ's ministry in 27 BC, the Jews stated that the Temple had been 46 years in building (John 2: 20).

And now Herod, in the eighteenth year of his reign (that is, the eighteenth in Jerusalem, but the twenty-first year from his coronation in Rome)... undertook a very great work that is to build of himself the Temple to God.

Antiquities 15:11:1

The 18th year of Herod's Jerusalem reign was 20 BC to 19 BC, which was the first year of building the Temple. Moving forward 46 years we come to 27 AD which was the first Passover in Christ's 3.5 year ministry.

Finally, there are other interesting events that were recorded by Jewish Rabbis concerning events which transpired between 30 AD and 70 AD, when Titus and his Roman legions completely destroyed Herod's temple on Av 9 in 70 AD.

DESTRUCTION OF THE TEMPLE

Jesus left the temple and was walking away when his disciples came up to him to call his attention to its buildings. 'Do you see all these things?' he asked. 'I tell you the truth, not one stone here will be left on another; everyone will be thrown down.'

Matthew 24: 1-8, Luke 21: 5-6.

Herod's Temple was completely destroyed and burned to the ground in 70 AD. That is forty years after the year 30 AD. Forty is the scriptural number for trial and testing. It appears that God gave the priests forty years to repent and seek forgiveness for their part in the crucifixion which occurred in 30 AD. They did not repent and the Temple was destroyed; right on schedule, forty years later. The only year that Christ could have been crucified to fulfill his own prophecy was 30 AD.

THE WITNESS OF THE JEWISH *TALMUD*

We read in the Jerusalem Talmud:

For forty years before the destruction of the Temple, the western light went out, the crimson thread remained crimson, and the lot for the Lord always came up in the left hand. They would close the gates of the Temple by night and get up in the morning and find them wide open.

Jacob Neusner, The Yerushalmi, P.156-157.

Herod's Temple was destroyed on Av 9 in 70 BC. A similar passage in the Babylonian Talmud states:

Our rabbis taught: During the last forty years before the destruction of the Temple the lot ['For the Lord'] did not come up in the right hand; nor did the crimson-colored strap become white; nor did the western most light shine; and the doors of the Hekel [Temple] would open by themselves.

Soncino version, Yoma 39b.

What are these passages talking about?

ATONEMENT FOR THE SINS OF THE PEOPLE

On the Feast of Atonement (Tishri 10) a ceremony took place which was ordained by God at Mt. Sinai (Leviticus 16). The Jewish Mishnah records that two goats were brought before the high priest. One goat would be placed on his right; the other on his left. He would have two pieces of gold exactly alike, one inscribed with the words *La Addnai* (for the Lord) and the other *La Azazel* (the scapegoat). The two golden pieces would then be cast into an urn and shaken. The high priest would then reach into the urn and grasp one in his right hand, and the other in his left hand. He then placed his right hand upon the goat to his right; and his left hand upon the goat on his left. The fate of each goat was determined by the inscription on the golden piece in each hand. The *La Addnai* was sacrificed and the goat's blood

177

would be taken into the Holy of Holies and sprinkled on the mercy seat.

> *And almost all things are by the law purged with blood; and without shedding of blood is no remission* (of sins).
>
> Hebrews 9:22

The high priest would then lay both of his hands on the *Azazel* goat, *confess over it all the iniquities of the children of Israel, and all of their transgressions and all of their sins: The Azazel goat would then be driven into the wilderness by the hand of a suitable man* (Lev 16: 5-22). The disposition of the Azazel in the wilderness is a matter of debate. Some say that it was released in the wilderness to die; others say it was driven over a steep cliff.

During the Temple Period (Exodus to destruction of Herod's Temple in 70 AD) it was considered to be a good omen if the left hand of the High Priest produced the gold amulet with the inscription *La Addnai* (for the Lord). It is recorded in the Levitical historical records that for *40 straight years* between 30AD and 70 AD, the La Addnai was selected by the *right hand!!*

The odds against this happening are astronomical (2 raised to the 40th power). In other words, the chances of this occurring are 1 in approximately 5,479,548,800 or about 5.5 billion to one! The selection for La Addnai in the left hand, contrary to all the laws of chance, came up 40 times in a row from 30 to 70 AD! This was considered a dire event and signified something had fundamentally changed the Yom Kippur ritual. Unknown and unrecognized by the Jews was that when Christ died the Jewish sacrificial system ended. This amazing sequence of events is also accompanied by yet another miracle which will now be described.

THE MIRACLE OF THE RED CLOTH

The second miracle concerns the crimson strip or cloth tied to the Azazel goat. A portion of this red cloth was removed from the scapegoat and tied to the Temple door. Each year on the Feast of Yom Kippur, the red cloth on the Temple door turned white as if to signify that this atonement for the sins of Israel was acceptable to the Lord. This happened *every year* until 30 AD, when the cloth remained *crimson* each year to the time of the Temple's destruction in 70 AD. This undoubtedly caused much stir and consternation among the Jews. This traditional practice is linked to Israel confessing its sins and ceremonially placing this nation's sin upon the Azazel goat. The sin was then removed by this goat's death. Sin was represented by the red color of the cloth (the color of blood). But the cloth remained crimson that is, Israel's sins were not being atoned and the cloth *made white*.

As God told Israel through Isaiah the prophet:

> *Come, let us reason together, saith the LORD: though your sins be as scarlet [crimson], they shall be white as snow; though they be red like crimson, they shall be as [white] wool.*
>
> Isaiah 1:18

The clear indication is that the whole Jewish community had lost atonement for sins. In the Old Testament, the word atonement meant *covering*. When Christ died for our sins, the *covering* of sins was over; the permanent forgiveness of sins was now possible through His sacrificial death. Although not mentioned in the Scriptures, long before 30 AD during the 40 years Simon the Righteous was High Priest, a crimson thread which was associated with his person always turned white when he entered the Temple's innermost Holy of Holies. The people noticed this. Also, they noted that the *lot of the LORD* (the white lot) came up for 40 straight years during Simon's priesthood. They noticed that the "lot" picked by the priests after Simon would sometimes be black, and sometimes white, and that the crimson thread would sometimes turn white, and sometimes not. The Jews came to believe that if the crimson thread turned white, that God approved of the Day of Atonement rituals and that Israel could be assured that God forgave their sins. But after 30 AD, the crimson thread never turned white again for 40 years, till the destruction of the Temple and the cessation of all Temple rituals!

What did the Jewish nation do in 30 AD to merit such a change at Yom Kippur? On April 5, 30 AD, the 14th of Nisan on Passover; the Messiah put Himself to death as a sacrifice for sin. Atonement (sacrificial covering for sins) was no longer necessary. Permanent forgiveness of sin has now come. Like an innocent Passover lamb, the Messiah was put to death even though no fault was found in Him! But unlike Temple sacrifices or the rituals of Yom Kippur, where sin is only covered over for a year, the Messianic sacrifice came with the promise of forgiveness of sins through grace given by God to those who accept a personal relationship with Messiah. The permanent forgiveness of sin occurred in 30 AD for both Jews and Gentiles alike.

THE MIRACLE OF THE TEMPLE DOORS

The next miracle which was recorded by Jewish Rabbis was that after being locked, the doors to Solomon's Temple swung open every night of their own accord for forty years in a row, beginning in 30 AD. The leading Jewish authority of that time, Yohanan ben Zakkai, declared that this was a sign of impending doom, and that the Temple itself would be destroyed. The Jerusalem Talmud states:

> Said Rabban Yohanan Ben Zakkai to the Temple, 'O Temple, why do you frighten us? We know that you will end up destroyed. For it has been said, 'Open your doors, O Lebanon, that the fire may devour your cedars.'

> Zechariah 11:1

Yohanan Ben Zakkai was the leader of the Jewish community during the time following the destruction of the Temple in 70 AD, We might speculate that the doors began to open in 30 AD to

180

signify that all may now enter the Temple, even to its innermost holy sections. The evidence supported by the miracles described above suggests the Lord's presence had departed from the Temple. This was no longer just a place for High Priests alone, but the doors swung open for all to enter the Lord's house of worship.

The Miracle of the Temple Menorah

The fourth miracle involved the Menorah, which was to perpetually burn in the Holy place. Starting in 30 AD following the crucifixion of Christ, the main lamp of the Temple lampstand (menorah) went out of its own accord every night for 40 years (over 12,500 nights in a row) no matter what attempts and precautions the priests took to safeguard against this event! Ernest Martin states:

> In fact, we are told in the Talmud that at dusk the lamps that were unlit in the daytime (the middle four lamps remained unlit, while the two eastern lamps normally stayed lit during the day) were to be re-lit from the flames of the western lamp (which was a lamp that was supposed to stay lit all the time it was like the 'eternal' flame that we see today in some national monuments)...
>
> This 'western lamp' was to be kept lit at all times. For that reason, the priests kept extra reservoirs of olive oil and other implements in ready supply to make sure that the 'western lamp' (under all circumstances) would stay lit. But what happened in the forty years from the very year Messiah said the physical Temple would be destroyed? Every night for forty years the western lamp went out, and this in spite of the priests each evening preparing in a special way the western lamp so that it would remain constantly burning all night!"
>
> The Significance of the Year CE 30, Ernest Martin, Research Update, April 1994)

Again, the odds against the lamp going out every night for 40 years in a row are astronomical. Something out of the ordinary was going on. The light of the Menorah represented contact with God and His Presence: these had departed from the temple when Christ was crucified.

It should be clear to any reasonable mind that there is no natural way to explain all these four signs which started in the year 30 AD. The only possible explanation has to be supernatural. When we take an objective look at these events which occurred between 30 AD and 70 AD when Herod's Temple was completely destroyed by the Roman General Titus and his forces, who can doubt that 30 AD was indeed the true year of the crucifixion and resurrection of the true Messiah God sent to Israel? Who can deny that He is the one and only true Messiah? Who else has fulfilled all the prophecies of the Old Testament?

CHAPTER 10
SUMMARY AND CONCLUSIONS

This book has investigated the Birth and Death of Jesus Christ. These two events were perhaps the most important in the history of the world. God created man in his own image, and placed Adam and Eve in a perfect dwelling place called the Garden of Eden. Man was created to commune with God; walk in His glory; and be an earthly companion. Instead of living in everlasting light and a sinless coexistence with God, Adam and Eve fell from grace by listening to Satan and committing sin. From that moment on, the curse of Adam fell upon every man and woman who would ever live. So God created an alternate plan. He would choose to bring to Himself a chosen people, a special people called the *Hebrews* or the *Children of Israel*.

The Hebrew people were given laws to *regulate* the nation. They were given Abraham, Isaac, Jacob and Moses to be great men of God who would *lead* the nation. God *gave them* the Promised Land, and led them to victory after victory over their enemies. But this was not enough: In time, man once again failed God. Israel did not want divine leadership… they wanted to be led by a King just like every other nation. They wanted to follow a man and not God. So the Nation of Israel corporately fell into idolatry, wickedness and iniquity. The Levitical priesthood apostatized and the nation became insidiously wicked. No amounts of sacrifices were enough, no atonement was sufficient, and no redemption by acts of man complete.

In the fullness of time, God in His mercy instituted a new plan: He sent His only begotten Son to save man. Jesus Christ was born of the Virgin Mary by divine conception; He lived among man for 34 years; He came to the River Jordan at *about age 30* (Luke 3:23) to be baptized and anointed by the Father to proclaim salvation and redemption for 3.5 years. In complete obedience to God the Father, Christ had one last mission to fulfill: He willingly had to go to the cross of Calvary, suffer and

183

die for the sins of man, and be resurrected from the dead: The Firstfruit of all who would believe in His Holy name. The *Old Covenant* had passed away; the *New Covenant* replaced the old. Christ our Passover Lamb suffered and died for our sins. He was the perfect sacrifice; sinless, unblemished and fully acceptable to the Lord. Through Him and by Him all old things passed away. The gift of eternal life and total forgiveness of sins was now proclaimed to all who would believe upon His name and confess Him as their Lord and Savior. Salvation has now come to Jews and Gentiles alike; Not by fulfilling the law but by faith and grace.

Hence, the Birth and death of our Lord Jesus Christ are the two most important events ever to occur in the history of mankind. The importance of these two events demand that they be fully understood and clearly confirmed. That was the mission and goal of this biblical study. The Holy Bible must be the final, accurate, and divinely inspired word of God; this is where all biblical studies must begin and end. While the Holy Bible frames and establishes the birth, death and works of Christ in the flesh, for reasons only known to God the Father the Holy Scriptures sometimes fail to provide exact dates and occurrences of key events. Hence, it is necessary to carefully examine extra-biblical sources of confirming data. All archeological findings and ancient writings are potential sources of supporting and confirming data. However, all sources must be examined and weighed against Holy Scripture. If archeological and historical revelations agree with the Holy Scriptures, they should be considered. If not, they must be discarded. This measure of truth must always be carefully applied in any study of God's word. Of course, some measure of subjectivity must always be used. It is certain that the full and perfect truth will never be known until we can sit with our Lord and Savior and have Him tell us the full meaning of all things. This study presents a carefully researched and documented result of dedicated and honest interpretation of accumulated facts. These results are sure to be accepted by some; challenged by many; and rejected by others.

THE BIRTH AND DEATH OF JESUS CHRIST

We have presented evidence that our Lord and Savior Jesus Christ was born on March 23 in 5 BC. The cosmic sign that heralded this historic event was the sudden and dramatic appearance of a spectacular comet as seen in the east and southeast from Babylon, Persia and China. The Chinese kept accurate records of all heavenly signs for thousands of years. In particular, the Chinese book *Han shu* (***Book of Han, Hanshu*** or ***History of the Han Dynasty*** from 206 BC to 25 AD). The following record appears in this manuscript.

> *A suibsing (comet) appeared during the second month of   the second year's reign of Ch'in-niu of the Chien-p'ing reign period: (5 BC, March 9-April 6), and lasted over 70 days.*

As detailed in Chapter 3, this was the last in a series of heavenly signs that spectacularly appeared between 7 BC and 5 BC. In an amazing coincidence, the first day of the Feast of Unleavened Bread fell on Nisan 15, March 23, 5 BC. This is in perfect agreement with Chinese astrological records. This is a most appropriate time for Christ to be born... He is the bread of life, bread without leaven (sin). We believe that Jesus Christ was born in Bethlehem on this day. If Christ was born on the first day following Passover in 5 BC (Nisan 15), then He would have turned 30 on the same Hebrew calendar day in 26 AD (Remember one year must be added as 1 BC crosses into 1 AD) and He would die exactly 34 Hebrew calendar years later on the Cross of Calvary. Christ would have likely been baptized on or near Tishri 15 (Feast of Tabernacles), while John was preaching *repentance* (Mark 1:4). He was *about 30 years old* (Luke 3:23).... 30 years and 6 months.

After a 3.5 year ministry starting in the Fall of 26 AD, Christ was crucified on Wednesday, April 5, Nisan 14 in 30 AD. Christ would remain in the *heart of the earth... in* Sheole...(Matthew 12: 40) for 3 days and 3 nights. This doctrine was so important, that Christ placed the validity of His entire ministry upon the *Sign* of

Jonah. Christ would remain in the grave for a full 3 days and 3 nights, just as Jonah was in the belly of a great fish for 3 days and 3 nights. A Nisan 14 Wednesday crucifixion is the ONLY day that Christ could have been nailed to the cross to fully satisfy the very words of Christ. All agree that Nisan 14 (Passover) fell on Wednesday, April 5 (Julian date) in 30 AD.

At the death of Jesus Christ, a series of supernatural events took place which cannot be explained as natural phenomenon. For three hours before He died darkness fell even though it was only mid afternoon. When Christ said *it is Finished* and He *gave up the ghost,* the veil in the temple which separated the holy Place from the Holy of Holies was rent (torn) from top to bottom and there was an earthquake. Surely this man was the Son of God who died for the sins of the world. The following graphic summarizes key events between 457 BC and 70 AD, when Herod's temple fell to Titus and his Roman army.

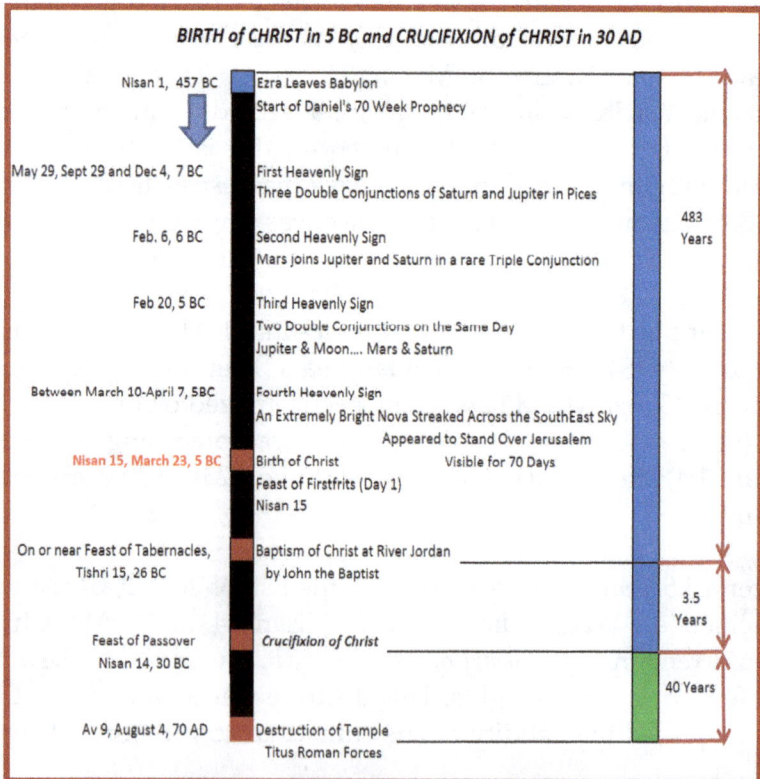

BIRTH of CHRIST in 5 BC and CRUCIFIXION of CHRIST in 30 AD

Nisan 1, 457 BC	Ezra Leaves Babylon Start of Daniel's 70 Week Prophecy	
May 29, Sept 29 and Dec 4, 7 BC	First Heavenly Sign Three Double Conjunctions of Saturn and Jupiter in Pices	483 Years
Feb. 6, 6 BC	Second Heavenly Sign Mars joins Jupiter and Saturn in a rare Triple Conjunction	
Feb 20, 5 BC	Third Heavenly Sign Two Double Conjunctions on the Same Day Jupiter & Moon.... Mars & Saturn	
Between March 10-April 7, 5BC	Fourth Heavenly Sign An Extremely Bright Nova Streaked Across the SouthEast Sky Appeared to Stand Over Jerusalem	
Nisan 15, March 23, 5 BC	Birth of Christ Visible for 70 Days Feast of Firstfrits (Day 1) Nisan 15	
On or near Feast of Tabernacles, Tishri 15, 26 BC	Baptism of Christ at River Jordan by John the Baptist	3.5 Years
Feast of Passover Nisan 14, 30 BC	*Crucifixion of Christ*	
Av 9, August 4, 70 AD	Destruction of Temple Titus Roman Forces	40 Years

186

THE REIGN OF KING HEROD

It is impossible to separate the birth of Christ from the reign of Herod the Great in Jerusalem. The apostle Matthew clearly stated:

Now when Jesus was born in Bethlehem of Judaea in the days of Herod the King.

Matthew 2:1

So Herod was reigning as King in Jerusalem when Christ was born. The reign of Herod the Great has been the subject of much theological study and debate for over 1500 years. Various dates for the death of Herod range from 4 BC to 1 AD. Historically, a date of 4 BC has been held as the most likely. Almost all we know about Herod, his reign and his death, comes from the Jewish historian Josephus who composed an extensive history of the Jewish people called *Antiquity* and *Wars*. In this massive documentary, Josephus records much historical information related to the reign of King Herod. One of the things he records is an eclipse of the moon which occurred shortly before the death of Herod. Modern astronomy has found that an eclipse occurred on March 17, 4 BC, and from Josephus we know that Herod died before the Jewish Feast of Passover which fell on April 11 in 4 BC (Julian date). Most have historically accepted this eclipse as the one Josephus records, but several modern researchers have challenged this assumption. Josephus recounts many events which took place between when the eclipse occurred and Herod died. From the above dates, this period of time was less than 25 days; and it severely stretches the imagination to assume that this period of time was sufficient to accommodate all the things that Josephus recorded. In looking for an alternative, it was discovered that another eclipse occurred which could have been the one that Josephus mentioned... It was the total eclipse of March 23 in 5 BC. This new theory provides 6 months for the many events to occur that were recorded by Josephus. Please note that the eclipse of March 17 in 4 BC did occur; It was just not the one indicated by Josephus. The details of this analysis are found in Chapters 5 and 6 resulting in the following chronology of King Herod's reign.

Reign of Herod the Great

Herod the Great became King of the Jews by Roman Consular Appointment in early 40 BC.... No later than March 5

Herod became King of the Jews By conquest of Antigonus at Jerusalem on March 5, 36 BC . Nisan 1 fell on March 22 in 36 BC. Hence, using a non-acession year system Herod's first year was credited as Nisan 1, 37BC - Nisan 1, 36 BC

REIGN OF HEROD

Herod the Great became King of the Jews by Roman consular appointment in early 40 BC.... No later than March 15, 40 BC

Herod became King of the Jews by conquest of Antoginus at Jerusalem on March 5, 36 BC

Year of Reign Dates: 37 years	Year of Reign Dates: 34 years
By Roman Appointment	By Conquest of Artabanus
1 March, 40 BC - March, 39 BC	1 March 5, 36 BC (Adar 13) - March 22, 36 BC (Nisan1)
2 March, 39 BC - March, 38 BC	2 Nisan 1, 36 BC - Nisan 1, 35 BC
3 March, 38 BC - March, 37 BC	3 Nisan 1, 35 BC - Nisan 1, 34 BC
4 March, 37 BC - March, 36 BC	4 Nisan 1, 34 BC - Nisan 1, 33 BC
5 March, 36 BC - March, 35 BC	5 Nisan 1, 33 BC - Nisan 1, 32 BC
6 March, 35 BC - March, 34 BC	6 Nisan 1, 32 BC - Nisan 1, 31 BC
7 March, 34 BC - March, 33 BC	7 Nisan 1, 31 BC - Nisan 1, 30 BC
8 March, 33 BC - March, 32 BC	8 Nisan 1, 30 BC - Nisan 1, 29 BC
9 March, 32 BC - March, 31 BC	9 Nisan 1, 29 BC - Nisan 1, 28 BC
10 March, 31 BC - March, 30 BC	10 Nisan 1, 28 BC - Nisan 1, 27 BC
11 March, 30 BC - March, 29 BC	11 Nisan 1, 27 BC - Nisan 1, 26 BC
12 March, 29 BC - March, 28 BC	12 Nisan 1, 26 BC - Nisan 1, 25 BC
13 March, 28 BC - March, 27 BC	13 Nisan 1, 25 BC - Nisan 1, 24 BC
14 March, 27 BC - March. 26 BC	14 Nisan 1, 24 BC - Nisan 1, 23 BC
15 March, 26 BC - March, 25 BC	15 Nisan 1, 23 BC - Nisan 1, 22 BC
16 March, 25 BC - March, 24 BC	16 Nisan 1, 22 BC - Nisan 1, 21 BC
17 March, 24 BC - March, 23 BC	17 Nisan 1, 21 BC - Nisan 1, 20 BC
18 March, 23 BC - March, 22 BC	18 Nisan 1, 20 BC - Nisan 1, 19 BC
19 March, 22 BC - March, 21 BC	19 Nisan 1, 19 BC - Nisan 1, 18 BC
20 March, 21 BC - March, 20 BC	20 Nisan 1, 18 BC - Nisan 1, 17 BC
21 March, 20 BC - March, 19 BC	21 Nisan 1, 17 BC - Nisan 1, 16 BC
22 March, 19 BC - March, 18 BC	22 Nisan 1, 16 BC - Nisan 1, 15 BC
23 March, 18 BC - March, 17 BC	23 Nisan 1, 15 BC - Nisan 1, 14 BC
24 March, 17 BC - March, 16 BC	24 Nisan 1, 14 BC - Nisan 1, 13 BC
25 March, 16 BC - March, 15 BC	25 Nisan 1, 13 BC - Nisan 1, 12 BC
26 March, 15 BC - March, 14 BC	26 Nisan 1, 12 BC - Nisan 1, 11 BC
27 March, 14 BC - March, 13 BC	27 Nisan 1, 11 BC - Nisan 1, 10 BC
28 March, 13 BC - March, 12 BC	28 Nisan 1, 10 BC - Nisan 1, 9 BC
29 March, 12 BC - March, 11 BC	29 Nisan 1, 9 BC - Nisan 1, 8 BC
30 March, 11 BC - March, 10 BC	30 Nisan 1, 8 BC - Nisan 1, 7 BC
31 March, 10 BC - March, 9 BC	31 Nisan 1, 7 BC - Nisan 1, 6 BC
32 March, 9 BC - March, 8 BC	32 Nisan 1, 6 BC - Nisan 1, 5 BC
33 March, 8 BC - March, 7 BC	33 Nisan 1, 5 BC - Nisan 1, 4 BC
34 March, 7 BC - March, 6 BC	34 Nisan 1, 4 BC - Nisan 1, 3 BC
35 March, 6 BC - March, 5 BC	
36 March, 5 BC - March, 4 BC	
37 March, 4 BC - March, 3 BC	

Herod Dies between Nisan 1 (March 29) and Nisan 7(April 4) in 4 BC
Feast of Unleavened Bread started on Nisan 15, April 12, Thursday

Herod was a ruthless and cruel man, who slaughtered innocent children and even killed his own son. He was feared by all with whom he came in contact. In a paradoxical way, Herod did several remarkable things. When he deposed Antagonis and destroyed his armies he proved to be a capable military leader. Herod invested in vast building enterprises. There are many projects that could be mentioned, such as Antipatris (on the road from Jerusalem to Caesarea), Cypros (at Jericho), Phasaelis (west of the Jordan) and constructing the coastal port of Cesaria. However, his crowning achievement was when he rebuilt the Holy Temple in Jerusalem. Although he died a madman, ravened with painful physical diseases, he was in many ways a remarkable man… certainly one who will be remembered.

VISIT OF THE WISE MEN (*MAGI*)

Closely aligned with the Birth of Christ is the story of how a group of wise men called Magi left their home in the north and journeyed to Jerusalem to worship the new-born Messiah. A spectacular series of heavenly signs that occurred in 7 BC and 6 BC were undoubtedly observed and discussed by the Magi, who were ancient astrologers and astronomers. The final and convincing sign was a spectacular comet that appeared in the east as viewed from Babylon and Persia. In the spring of 5 BC it streaked across the south and eastern sky. It was visible for 70 days, and finally appeared to be stationary over Jerusalem. The 70 day visibility is perfectly in line with the time it would have taken the Magi to make the trip from Babylon; our assumed place of origin for the Magi. As presented and documented in Chapters 3 and 4, the Magi would have arrived in Jerusalem in the early summer of 5 BC. There they visited

7 BC: Triple Conjunction
- Jupiter and Saturn in Pisces
  - Happens once every ~900 years
  - Divine King to be born in Israel

6 BC: Three-way Conjunction
- Mars, Jupiter, Saturn in Pisces
  - Happens once every ~800 years
  - A mighty king would be born in Israel

5 BC: Comet appeared
- Comet Appeared in Capricorn
  - Capricorn in East in Spring
  - Third sign: Imminent, important birth
  - Consistent with OT prophesy regarding the Messiah

with King Herod, and being led by a supernatural *star* or star-like-light, they did not visit the Child in Bethlehem, but in Nazareth at the house of Joseph. There they worshiped the child, leaving gifts of gold, frankincense and myrrh. Having been told by an angel, the Magi warned Joseph and Mary that Herod sought to find and kill Jesus and they (Magi) sent them to Egypt. The Magi then returned to their own land. The following graphic summarize our findings.

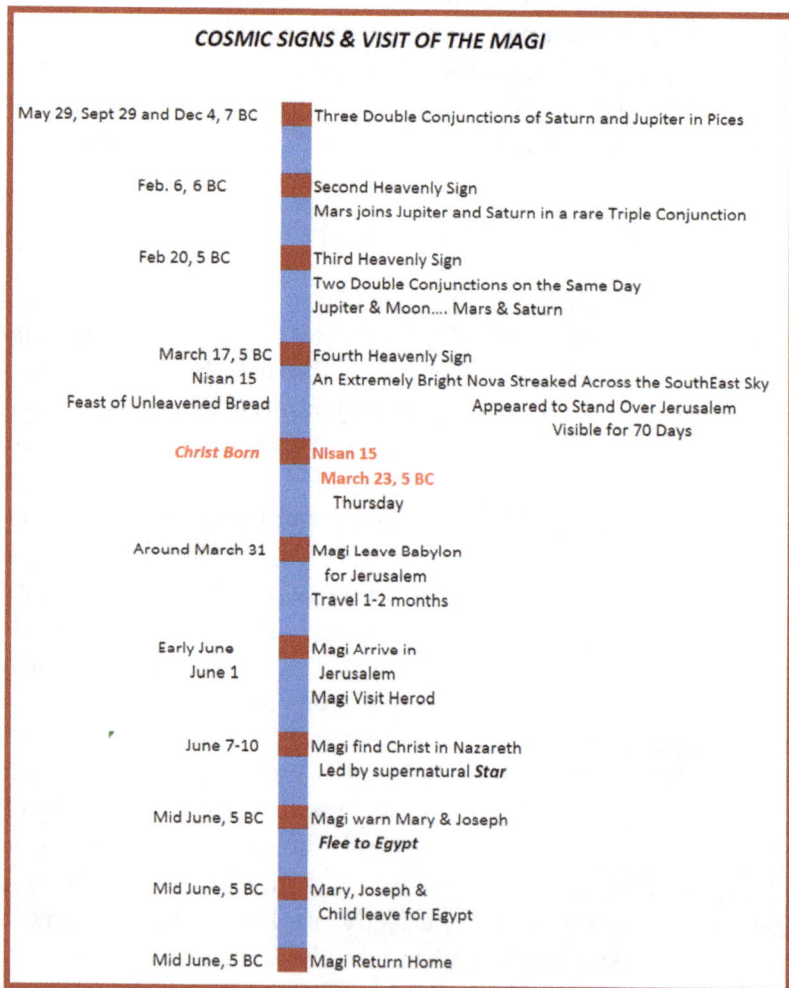

COSMIC SIGNS & VISIT OF THE MAGI

May 29, Sept 29 and Dec 4, 7 BC	Three Double Conjunctions of Saturn and Jupiter in Pices
Feb. 6, 6 BC	Second Heavenly Sign Mars joins Jupiter and Saturn in a rare Triple Conjunction
Feb 20, 5 BC	Third Heavenly Sign Two Double Conjunctions on the Same Day Jupiter & Moon.... Mars & Saturn
March 17, 5 BC Nisan 15 Feast of Unleavened Bread	Fourth Heavenly Sign An Extremely Bright Nova Streaked Across the SouthEast Sky Appeared to Stand Over Jerusalem Visible for 70 Days
Christ Born	Nisan 15 March 23, 5 BC Thursday
Around March 31	Magi Leave Babylon for Jerusalem Travel 1-2 months
Early June June 1	Magi Arrive in Jerusalem Magi Visit Herod
June 7-10	Magi find Christ in Nazareth Led by supernatural *Star*
Mid June, 5 BC	Magi warn Mary & Joseph *Flee to Egypt*
Mid June, 5 BC	Mary, Joseph & Child leave for Egypt
Mid June, 5 BC	Magi Return Home

190

THE LAST DAYS OF KING HEROD

Herod the Great was a remarkable king in many ways. He reigned for 37 years after Antony brought him before the Roman senate and he was named king in Rome. He was credited with 34 years of reign as King of the Jews after he procured Antigonus to be slain and the temple in Jerusalem fell to his army. Herod accomplished many things. He built several port cities, strengthened and defended Israel against foreign invasion, and in his most prodigious act he completely rebuilt the temple of Solomon that had fallen to Varius in 36 BC.

The finished temple was magnificent, and its presence reinstated temple worship and the Levitical sacrificial system. However, Herod himself was not of Jewish descent, and when he ascended to the throne he ended the 103 year Hasmonean dynasty in which all kings were direct descendents of King David. During the reign of Herod the Levitical priesthood completely corrupted. This continued until Titus and his Roman army completely destroyed Herod's Temple in 70 AD on Av 9, August 4 (Julian calendar date).

Herod physically and mentally slowly degenerated, and he was feared by both his family and the nation of Israel. His behavior during the last 6 months of his life was particularly unstable. Josephus says he *behaved like a madman*. For example, when Herod realized that he had been deceived by the Magi, in a rage he declared that all male children in Jerusalem and Bethlehem under the age of two must be killed. This is known as the *slaughter of the innocents.* The following events occurred after he realized that the Magi had deceived him.

5 BC						5 BC
Tishri 9 Sunday Sept 9	Tishri 10 Monday Sept 10	Tishri 11 Tuesday Sept 11	Tishri 12 Wednesday Sept 12	Tishri 13 Thursday Sept 13	Tishri 14 Friday Sept 14	Tishri 15 Saturday Sept 15
	Feast of Atonement				Herod burns Matthias During Day	Feast of Tabernacles
					Eclipse that Night ...now Day of Atonement	

- In or around late summer or early fall of 5 BC, he had a Jewish leader called Matthias burned to death and several other young men executed after they pulled down a Golden Eagle that Herod had placed over the main temple gate.
- His health rapidly failing, after he bathed in hot oil baths, his health improved and he went to Jericho. There he ordered all male Jews to come to Jericho where he shut them up in the Hippodrome; a large coliseum. Then he ordered that all be killed upon his death.
- Herod next commanded that one male from each Jewish family be slain upon his death. This was to make sure that each family mourned, and not celebrate his own death.
- Herod's son heard that his father was dead and hosted a feast; but the report was false. Upon hearing of this, Herod had him disowned from the kingly line and had him executed... his own son!
- Herod dies 5 days later. The graphic on the next page summarizes the last few months of Herod's life

Herod's Last Days

Early June-June 1	Herod talks to Magi
	Sends Magi to find Christ
Mid June-June 15	Herod realizes he has been decieved
	Herod orders the "Slaughter of the Innocents
	All male chilldren 2 years and younger
Summer of 5 BC	*The Golden Eagle Incident*
	Herod erects a large Golden Eagle over the Temple entrance
	Matthias and Judas lead a group which pulls down the Eagle
	.... Matthias is a high priest & Judas is his assistant
	Both are arrested with 40 other young men
Total Lunar Ecipse:	All are taken to Jericho for trial
Sept 15, 5 BC	Herod is lenient as a large crowd gathers
	The Matthias Incident
	Matthias service comes around, but the night before
	he has a "sedition" which makes him ritually unclean
	Herod denies Matthias and Joseph (called the other
	Matthias by Josephus) from serving.
Tishri 10, Sept 11, 5 BC	**** The exact date is the Feast of Atonement****
	Tishri 10, Monday September 11, 5 BC
Day of Tishri 13, September 14	Herod has Matthias put to death
Total Eclipse	There is an eclipse of the moon that night
Night of Tishri 14	Tishri 15, September 15, 5 BC
Now Tishri 15	
	Herod's health fails rapidly…. He will be dead in 6 months
Tishri 15, Sept 15	* He has distemper
	* His feet become diseased
	* His privates putrify
	* He eats constantly: fat and bloated
	Herod travels "beyond River Jordan" for hot baths
	He rests in "hot oils" and rallies
	He goes to Jericho
	* Contracts cholera
	* Behaves like a "madman"
	* Issues a royal command… All male Jews must come to Jericho
	* Failure to comply…Death penalty
6 Months Time	* The men gather… Herod shuts them up in the "Hippadrome"
	* Herod sends for his sister in Bethlehem
	* He orders that upon his death, all males in Hippadrome
	be put to death
	* Herod next proclaims that upon his death, one member
	from each family must die.
	Herod becomes so sick. He tries to kill himself with a knife
	while eating an apple.. He is discovered and stopped
	A false report goes out.."Herod is dead".. His son Antipater
	celebrates; thinking he is now king. Herod hears of this,
	and condemns Antipater to be executed.
Adar II, March 13	Partial eclipse of the moon (not the ecyise recorded in Josephus)
4 BC	
	Antipas is executed as Herod commanded
	5 days later, Herod dies between Nisan 1 and Nisan 15, 5 BC

193

THE LAST WEEK OF JESUS CHRIST'S LIFE ON EARTH

It is important to accurately determine the sequence of events that took place from when Jesus Christ began to journey to Jerusalem for the Feast of Passover and when He rose from the grave. Most Christians do not realize that everything which happened during that final week was a fulfillment of Old Testament types and prophecies. The key to understanding exactly what happened and when it happened is to understand that Christ had not only come to save sinful man from eternal damnation, but to satisfy the first four (spring) feasts of Israel. The fulfillment of each feast was a step in God's eternal plan of salvation.

THE FEAST OF PASSOVER
Nisan 14.... Christ is Crucified; our Passover Lamb

THE FEAST OF UNLEAVENED BREAD
Nisan 15-21...Christ is the bread of life; no leaven (sin)

THE FEAST OF FIRSTFRUITS
First Sunday after the first Jewish Sabbath during the Feast of Unleavened Bread... Begins the count of 50 days to Pentecost. Christ rose from the grave on this day as this day begins, the *firstfruit* of all who will follow

THE FEAST OF SHAVUOT (PENTECOST)
50th day after the Feast of Firstfruits begins, the Feast of Pentecost is held to celebrate the giving of the Law to Moses and the Jewish people on Mt. Sinai. On this very same day, the Holy Spirit fell on all believers. Christ said he would not leave us without a comforter.

THURSDAY, NISAN 8
Jesus Christ begins His final week. He arrives at Jericho on Thursday. As He enters the city, he was walking with the crowd and was hard to see. A man named Zacchaeus climbed up into a sycamore tree so that he might be able to see Jesus. When Jesus

reached the tree, he looked up into the branches; addressed Zacchaeus by name; and told him to come down. He then told him that he intended to visit his house that night.. The crowd was shocked that Jesus, a Jew, would associate with Zacchaeus, who was a hated tax collector. Zacchaeus came down and prepared supper for Jesus at his house. Jesus spends the night with Zacchaeus in Jericho.

FRIDAY, NISAN 9
It is now 6 days before Passover (John 12:1) Christ leaves Jericho and travels 16-18 miles to Bethany. Hearing that He was coming, great crowds began to gather in His path. He is accompanied by His friend Lazarus. That evening He eats in the house of Martha and Mary. It is now Sabbath evening, Nisan 10. After the evening meal, He is anointed by Miriam to fulfill His destiny as the perfect Passover Lamb (Exodus 12:1-3). He is both the sacrifice and the sacrificer.

SATURDAY, NISAN 10
Jesus arises early and sends for a donkey to ride to fulfill prophecy (Zechariah 9:9). He rides into Jerusalem among throngs of people waving palm branches and crying *Hosanna in the highest*. He enters the temple and begins to teach. As He teaches, the Sadducees and Pharisees try to discredit Him, asking difficult questions. Christ is now fulfilling the Law of the Sacrificial Lamb, who is brought into the *house* 4 days before it is to be killed on Nisan 14 as the Passover sacrifice. Christ will teach in the temple (House of God) and be examined for the next 4 days for *fault and blemish,* but none will be found. Christ is the perfect Passover lamb without spot or blemish, fully acceptable to God as the last and permanent sacrifice for sin. He returns to Bethany to spend the night.

SUNDAY, NISAN 11
Christ arrives from Bethany, having been joined by some of His disciples. He is hungry, and pausing by a fig tree to get some fruit He finds the tree barren. He curses the fig tree and it immediately starts to wither. The disciples are unaware that this

act is symbolic of the Nation of Israel: They had been given every opportunity to serve God, but time and again they turned aside. Now they would finally reject their long awaited messiah, being blinded to His offer of eternal life to all who would believe upon His name. The *tree* of Israel had failed to bring forth fruit, and now God would turn aside from them. Jesus prophesied of this moment this moment 3.5 years earlier when He was baptized by John: *And now also the axe is laid unto the root of the trees: therefore every tree which bringeth not forth good fruit is hewn down, and cast into the fire* (Matthew 3:10). Salvation would now come through the gentiles and by grace. The Law would be written not on tablets of stone, but on the heart. Christ enters the temple and in a rare moment of physical display, He turns over the tables of the money changers and runs them out of the temple. These money changers were selling sacrificial lambs for profit; the holy temple was now only an empty religious edifice. In 40 years there would not be one stone left standing. After teaching all day, He returns to Bethany. This will be His last night of rest in a house.

MONDAY, NISAN 12

Christ Leaves Bethany and returns to the temple. Along the way, the disciples are shocked as they pass by the fig tree that Christ had rebuked: They were amazed to see it so soon fully withered and without leaves. They still failed to understand what was about to happen. The mantle of salvation would now pass from the Jews to the gentiles. A new entity called the church would rise from the grave with our Lord Jesus Christ. Jesus arrives at the temple and teaches all day. That evening He does not retire to Bethany, but walks to the Mount of Olives where He will speak with His disciples and pray. He reveals to them that one of His own would betray Him in two days. Judas leaves and now having been taken over by Satan he accepts 70 pieces of silver for what he is about to do. The disciples continue to fail to discern the full impact of what is about to happen. They inquire of Christ when He will establish His eternal kingdom and what will be the signs. Christ responds by delivering the magnificent Olivet Discourse, His most powerful and complete prophecy of

196

His second coming. He remains on the Mount of Olives for the night, praying for strength to endure the cross that looms before Him.

TUESDAY, NISAN 13

In the morning, Jesus returns to the temple for the 4th straight day to fulfill Old Testament law. He is the New Testament sacrificial lamb who is taken into the house (the temple) and examined (questioned) for spot or blemish for 4 days; but none is found. That afternoon while He is teaching and revealing the scriptures, he instructs his disciples to go to a man and prepare for His last meal. This is the Passover for Christ, and it initiates a new covenant: It is called the *Lord's Last Supper*. Jesus teaches His disciples to be humble and to be a servant by washing the feet of those that are there. He then initiates the remembrance ceremony of Him by serving the bread and the wine, symbolic of His own body and His own blood. This is what we now call *Holy Communion*. Jesus now announces that one of His disciples would betray Him later that night. Judas leaves to join the Roman centurions who will arrest Jesus. Jesus returns to the Mount of Olives where He prays and strengthens Himself. Judas arrives with the soldiers, kisses Jesus to identify Him; and Christ is arrested. He is taken before Annus...then Caiaphas. To fulfill the words of Jesus, Peter denies Christ 3 times while the cock crows each time. Christ spends the night in custody.

WEDNESDAY, NISAN 14

In the early morning hours of Nisan 14, Christ is taken before the Sanhedrin and is accused of blaspheme when He declares that He is the Son of God. Jesus is now a real threat to Pharisees, the Sadducees and the corrupt Priesthood. They seek to kill Him, and the Sanhedrin now accuses him of treason against Rome: A charge which would carry death by crucifixion. But, only the Roman governor can pass a death sentence, so Christ is taken before Pilate to be formally accused and sentenced. Pilate questions Christ, and being warned by his wife who had a prophetic dream, Pilate can find no reason to condemn Christ to death. However, the crowd is angry and demands the death of

197

Christ. As the crowd nears insurrection, Pilate hears that Christ is from Galilee. Galilee is south of Jerusalem and falls under the rule of Herod Antipas; son of Herod the Great. Christ is hastily taken to Herod Antipas, who is in Jerusalem for the Feast of Passover. Pilate is amused by Christ and commands Him to perform a miracle... but Christ remains silent. After questioning Christ, Pilate can also find no fault in this man. So, he returns Christ to Pilate. Imagine the fear of Christ when he sees Jesus returning to him with the angry crowd. Pilate seeks a way out, and invokes an ancient Jewish law: A single prisoner condemned to death can be pardoned on Passover. Pilate brings forth Barrabas and asks the crowd to select either him or Jesus Christ to be pardoned. In a final and complete act of rejection, the people curse Jesus and yell... *Crucify Him! Crucify Him!!!* And so the crowd frees Barabbas, a murderer. Jesus is now condemned to death. The soldiers take Him away; they strip Him naked and beat Him; they then give him a purple robe and place a thorn of crowns upon His head. Christ is now beaten, stripped of His clothes and taken to Calvary, where at 9:00 am on Nisan 14 He is nailed to the cross with two other men; one on each side of Him. One asks for forgiveness, the other is silent. Christ forgives him of his sins. This is symbolic of the Jews and Gentiles. In a final poignant act of grace, He then turns to those who have placed Him on the cross and says; *Father forgive them for they know not what they do.* Jesus suffers and dies at 3:00 PM, the same time that the Jewish Passover lamb is being slain in the temple.

The Levitical sacrificial system has ended forever. Jesus is our perfect Passover lamb; the sacrifice is final and acceptable to God. At this same moment, the veil which separates the holy place (the Jewish people) from the Holy of Holies (God) is rent from top to bottom. This is symbolic of our new access to God the Father through His son, Jesus Christ. Christ had previously stated: *I am the way, the truth and the life... no man cometh unto the Father except by me.* All who will accept Jesus Christ as their savior will now have access to the very presence of God through His Son.

A follower of Christ called Joseph of Aramathea goes to Pilate and requests His body, so that Christ can be placed in his (Joseph) own tomb. Christ is hastily taken from the cross, and is quickly placed in a tomb just as Nisan 14 passes into Nisan 15 at 6:00 PM. Nisan 15 is both a Jewish Sabbath day, and the first day of the Feast of Unleavened Bread. Christ is the true *Bread of Life* who declared: *He who eats of this bread will never die.* The symbolism of the Feast of Passover and the Feast of Unleavened Bread has now become reality. Only the Feast of Firstfruits and the Feast of Pentecost remains.

THURSDAY, NISAN 15

Nisan 15 is the first day of the 7 day Feast of Unleavened Bread. It is a *high holy day*, a *Sabbath day*. Herod secures the tomb for three days with guards, being afraid that some Jews might remove His body and claim that He is risen as He said He would. Roman guards are placed at the tomb for 3 days and 3 nights to prevent anyone from stealing the body and declaring that Christ had risen: So one could approach the tomb for three days and three nights, again confirming that the time that would pass between burial and resurrection was a full 72 hours, and nothing less.

FRIDAY, NISAN 16

The scriptures are silent as to anything that happened on this day. There is actually nothing to report, but we can assume that since Nisan 15 and Nisan 17 are Jewish Sabbath days the women probably purchased the necessary supplies to prepare burial oils, spices and garments for Jesus on this day, and prepared for the burial ceremony.

SATURDAY, NISAN 17

This is the weekly Jewish Sabbath day. Just as 6:00 pm arrives, which ends Nisan 17, Christ arises from *Sheole* in the *heart of the earth*. His own mortal body is then resurrected from the tomb; the Firstfruit of all who would follow him into eternity. It has been 3 days and 3 nights, just as Christ said it would.

Behold, I shew you a mystery; We shall not all sleep, but we shall all be changed, In a moment, in the twinkling of an eye, at the last trump: for the trumpet shall sound, and the dead shall be raised incorruptible, and we shall be changed.

I Corinthians 15: 51-52

SUNDAY, NISAN 18

All 4 gospels document between 2 and 3 visits to the tomb by the women, and one concurrently by Peter and John. Christ is not in the tomb, He has risen. This fulfills the ancient Feast of Firstfruits. No crops can be picked and consumed until the Firstfruit Harvest is picked and taken to the High Priest, where it is presented before God. Christ is the *Firstfruit* of all who will follow. He instructs the women to tell His disciples to wait for Him in an upper room in Jerusalem, where He will meet with them 50 days later on the Feast of Shavuot (Pentecost).

On the Feast of Pentecost, the Holy Spirit fell on all who believed in Him. This fulfills the shadow and type of the Feast of Pentecost. All four spring feasts had become completely fulfilled by Christ our Lord and Savior. For those who might be interested, the last three (fall feasts) will also be fulfilled at the second coming of Christ. A detailed treatment of this subject is in *Phillips: The Book of Revelation: Mysteries Revealed.* The graphic on the following page summarizes the last week of Jesus Christ.

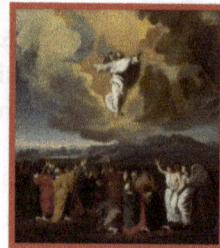

THE PASSION WEEK
Thursday, Nisan 9 to Sunday, Nisan 18
30 AD

Nisan 9, Friday, March 31
Jesus leaves house of Zaccheus in Jerico
Travels 16-18 miles to Bethany
Great crowds begin to gather

Matthew 26:6-13
Eats supper with Marha and Mary that evening

Mark 14:3-9
now Nisan 10

John 12:1-11
Miriam annoints Jesus as the Passover Lamb
to be slain for our sins (Exodus 12:1-3)
Six days before Passover (John 12:1)
Spends night with Mary, Martha and Lazarus

Nisan 10, Saturday, April 1
Jesus sends for a donkey to ride into Jerusalem
to fulfill prophecy (Zachariah 9:9)

Matthew 21:1-11
Jesus enters Jerusalem to throngs of people waving

Mark 11:1-11
Psalm branvhes and crying Hosannah to the King

Luke 19:28-40
He visits Temple & teaches

John 12:12-19
This is the first of 4 days He is examined for "spot or blemish" (Exodus 12:3-6)
...our Passover sacrifice (I Cor 5:7)
Spends night again at Bethany

Nisan 11, Sunday, April 2
Jesus arrives from Bethany
Curses fig tree
Chases money changers from temple
Religious leaders seek to discredit him with questions
Returns to Bethany for 3rd night

Nisan 12, Monday, April 3
Jesus returns to Bethlehem
Disciples see fig tree withered & barren

Matthew 21:20-25
Jesus now teaches to disciples in parables

Matthew 21:26, 23:39, 26:1-16
Confronted in temple by Saducees & Pharacees

Mark 11: 20-27, 28
Retires to the Mount of Olives

Mark 12:44
Jesus predicts His bertrayal and death in two days

Luke 20-21-22
Judas accepts 70 pieces of silver to betray Christ
Jesus spends night on Mount of Olives teaching disciples
Jesus delivers the *Olivet Discourse*

Nisan 13, Tuesday, April 4
Jesus returns to temple...Teaches all day...answers questions
Jesus instructs disciples to *His Passover Meal.. The Last Supper*

Tuesday evening
New Passover Meal is observed that evening
It is now
Christ institutes Bread & Wine as a Memorial to Him
Wednesday,
After Meal, Jesus tels disciples one of them will betray Him
Nisan 14
Judas leaves to join Roman Centurians
Evening
(1) Jesus goes to Garden of Gethsemane
(6:00pm-6:00am)
(2) Prays alone & suffers in agony
(3) Judas betrays Jesus
(4) Jesus taken to Annus
Then Caipaphas
(5) Peter denies Christ 3 times... Cock crows 3 times
(6) Christ kept in custody

Feast of Passover
Early morning... Christ is taken before Pilate
Wednesday, Nisan 14, April 5
Pilot finds no fault in Him
Crowd cries... "Crucify Him !!!"
Crowd chooses to free Barrabus and not Christ
Jesus is given Crown of Thornes and driven to Calvary
Jesus is nailed on the cross at 9:00 AM
Jesus dies at 3:00 PM... Same hour Priest is killing
Passover Lambs
Christ is placed in the Tomb just before 6:00 PM

Feast of Unleavened Bread
Nisan 15 is a "High Holy Day".... A Sabbath Day
Thursday, Nisan 15, April 6
John called it a "High Sabbath" (John 19:31, Exodus 12:16))
Herod secures tomb for 3 days with guards
Jesus said: **"I will spend 3 days and 3 nights in the grave... then**
I will rise"

Friday, Nisan 16, April 7
The Scriptures are silent on thisday
but the women probably bought buriel clothes
spices and myrr to annoint Jesus. They prepare
for annointing but the weekly Sabbath starts at 6:00 PM

Saturday, Nisan 17, April 8
Jesus arises from the grave just as Saturday, Nisan 17 passes into
Sunday, Nisan 18.
Jesus is 3 days and 3 nights in the grave as He stated in all 4 gospels

Sunday, Nisan 18, April 9
Meets two men on Road outside Jerusalem

DANIEL'S 70 WEEK (490 YEAR) PROPHECY

In order to confirm that Christ began his 3.5 year ministry in the month of Tishri, 26 AD and that Christ was crucified on Nisan 14 in 30 AD, an extensive investigation of the 490 year prophecy given by the archangel Gabriel to Daniel the prophet was undertaken in Chapter 7. It was shown by using the biblical records and archaeological evidence that Ezra the scribe left Babylon in the spring of 458 BC after Artaxerxes found the original command issued by Cyrus to rebuild the temple, and added to it that the temple and the city could be restored. Ezra left on Nisan 1, and the command went forth to the people on Tishri 1, 458 BC. This started Daniels 490 year prophecy which accurately predicted that Jesus Christ would begin His 3.5 year ministry in the month of Tishri in 26 AD, and that He would be cut off or crucified on Nisan 14; which was the Feast of Passover on April 5, 30 AD. Daniel's prophecy completely supports and aligns with a 5 BC and a 30 AD death of Jesus Christ. It should be noted that Daniel's 490 years was interrupted by the death of Christ with 3.5 years remaining to fulfill the prophecy. This chronology is shown on the following page.

The remainder of Daniels 70th week (3.5 years) has been divinely reserved for the **Great Tribulation Period** described in the Book of Revelation. A complete treatment of this subject can be found in Phillips: *The Book of Revelation: Mysteries revealed*.

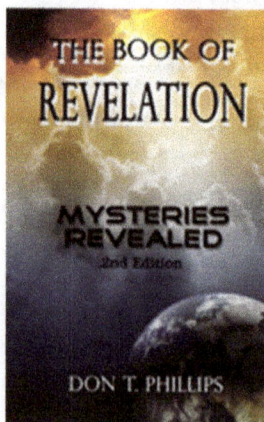

DANIELS 70 WEEK PROPHECY

	605 BC	Daniel is deported to Babylon
	Between 605 BC-537 BC	Daniel is given a 70 week prophecy (490 years)
	Nisan 1, 458 BC	Ezra leaves Babylon for Jerusalem
	Tishri 1, 458 BC	Ezra arrives in Jerusalem Prophecy is initiated
486.5 Years	483 Years	
	Month of Tishri 26 AD near Feast of Atonement	Jesus comes to the River Jordan to be baptized....starts His 3.5 year ministry
	Nisan 14, Wednesday. April 5 Feast of Passover	Jesus is "cut off" or crucified "in midst " of 70th week
	Unknown Period of Time Now almost 2000 years	Daniel's 490 year prophecy is interrupted and suspended
3.5 Years	Great Tribulation Period described in the Book of Revelation ends	Great Tribulation Period Starts Lasts 3.5 years
		End of Daniel's 70th week End of Church Age
		1000 year Millennial kingdom

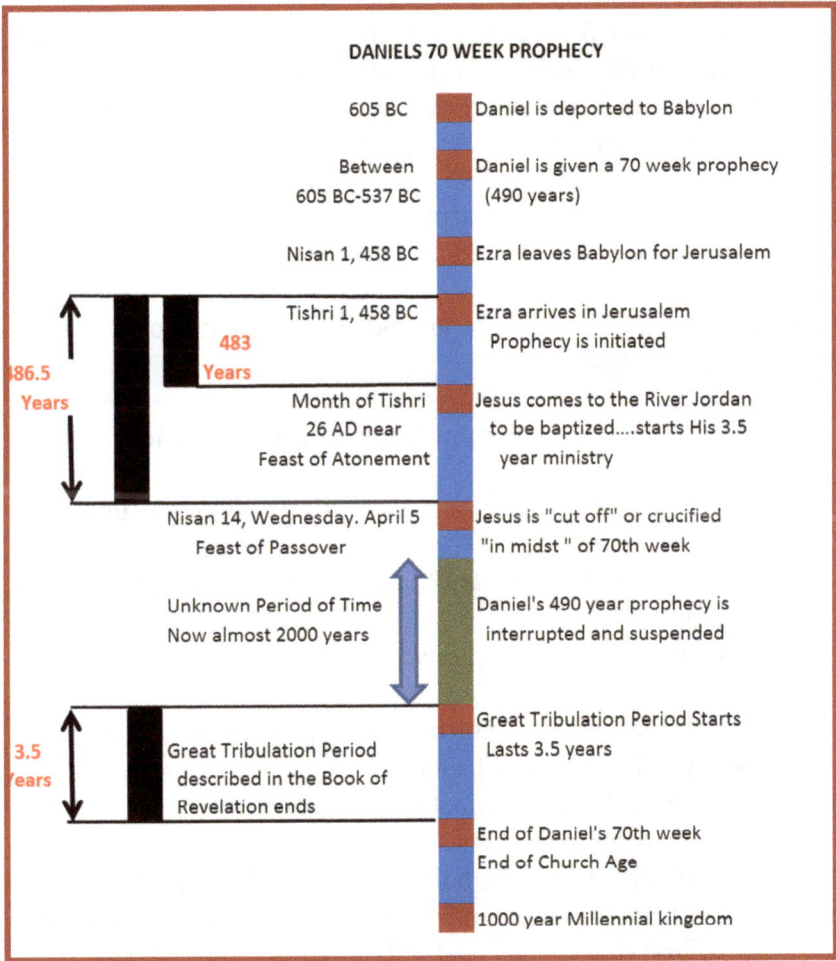

SUMMARY AND CONCLUSIONS

This investigation has presented strong evidence that Christ was born on March 23, 5 BC on Nisan 15; which was the first day of the Feast of Firstfruits. Christ was crucified on Nisan 14 on the Feast of Passover, April 5 (Julian calendar date) in 30 AD. We have also spent a great deal of time and effort to verify that the 490 year prophecy given to Daniel the prophet by the Archangel Gabriel substantiates these conclusions. Daniel's 70 week prophecy (70 weeks of 7 years) does indeed show that Christ started His earthly ministry in the fall (Tishri) of 26 AD, and that

He was crucified 3.5 years later on Nisan 14, which was the Jewish Feast of Passover on Wednesday, April 5 in 30 AD (Julian calendar date). Christ was crucified halfway through the last week of 7 years of Daniel's 490 year prophecy... just as Daniel was told by Gabriel (Daniel 9:27). A 30 AD crucifixion demands a 5 BC birth, so by the testimony of multiple witnesses, our findings seem to be confirmed and fit like a glove.

Our long journey has come to an end. This book has proposed to do *four* main things:

(1) Determine the day, month and year in which Jesus Christ was born
(2) Determine the day, month and year in which Jesus Christ was crucified.
(3) Determine the start, end and duration of King Herod the Great
(4) Correct long standing misconceptions of:

- The nativity and birth of Jesus, Joseph and Mary
- The last week of Jesus Christ
- The role and characterization of the Magi who came to worship the Christ
- When Christ was born and when Christ died
  Christ was born in 5 BC on March 23, Nisan 15 on the First day of the Feast of Firstfruits
  Christ died in 30 AD on April 5, Nisan 14 on the Feast of Passover
- Christ rose from the grave a full 3 nights and 3 days later, just as Saturday Nisan 17 turned into Sunday, Nisan 18, at 6:00pm
- Christ sent the Holy Spirit as He promised on the Feast of Pentecost, 50 days later.

It is certain that (1) Christ was not born on December 25 and that (2) Christ did not rise from the grave early in the morning or on what we now call *Easter Sunday*. The results of this study are verifiable, logical and defensible.

We want to make one thing crystal clear: This does not negate or take anything away from the fact that most of the world celebrates the birth of Christ on December 25, and celebrates his resurrection from the grave at sunrise on Easter Sunday. What is important is that these celebrations are no doubt held at the wrong time, but that they do celebrate that Christ was born of a virgin called Mary, and that 34 full Jewish years later Christ was crucified, dead and buried. He rose from the grave after a full 3 days and 3 nights. He is now our heavenly High Priest, who sits on the right hand of God the Father and continually intercedes for us. His shed blood both justifies and sanctifies all who will believe upon His name. *Every person who believes that Jesus Christ suffered and died for their sins will be forgiven of those sins and receive the gift of eternal life.* Each will be joined with Christ after the great tribulation period described in the Book of Revelation.

Christ is the Firstfruit of all who will rise from the grave...and who will be with him for all eternity. So we celebrate these two great events at the wrong time, but for the right reason. It is only important that we know the truth, for Christ said that *the truth will set you free.* May God richly bless you and keep you.... May His light shine upon you... and May you be free from the ravening wages of sin. Hold on to all that is good, righteous and Holy in the sure belief that since Christ Jesus has risen from the grave and ascended to heaven, that He will return again and receive us to Him also..... and so we will be with Him forever.

AMEN... Let it be so

Peter proceeded to speak and said:

"You know what has happened all over Judea,
beginning in Galilee after the baptism
that John preached,
how God anointed Jesus of Nazareth
with the Holy Spirit and power.
He went about doing good
and healing all those oppressed by the devil,
for God was with him.
We are witnesses of all that he did
both in the country of the Jews and in Jerusalem.
They put him to death by hanging him on a tree.
This man God raised on the third day and granted that he be visible,
not to all the people, but to us,
the witnesses chosen by God in advance,
who ate and drank with him after he rose from the dead.
He commissioned us to preach to the people
and testify that he is the one appointed by God
as judge of the living and the dead.
To him all the prophets bear witness,
that everyone who believes in him
will receive forgiveness of sins through his name."

ACTS 10:34A, 37-43

BIBLIOGRAPHY

Africanus, Julius. *Chronographies*. Grand Rapid, Michigan: 1978 reproduction of 1867 version.

Agee, M. J. *The End of the Age*. New York, NY: Avon Books, 1994.

Albright, W. F. *The Chronology of the Divided Monarchy of Israel*. American School of Oriental Research: 1945.

Anderson, Sir Robert. *The Coming Prince*. 1882.

Anderson, Sir Robert. *The Coming Prince*. Grand Rapids, Michigan: Kregel Publications, 1988.

Anstey, M. *The Romance of Biblical Chronology*. London, England: Marshall Brothers, 1913.

Archer, Gleason, *A Survey of the Old Testament*, Chicago, Illinois: Moody Press, 1974.

A Summary of Edwin Theil's Work. http://www.olive-tree.net, 2007.

Babylonian Talmud, Rosh Hashana and Arakin Tract.

Barnhouse, Donald Grey. *Revelation*. Grand Rapids, Michigan: Zondervan Publishing House, 1871.

Booker, Richard. *Jesus in the Feasts of Israel*. Shippinsburg, Pennsylvania: Destiny Image Publishers, 1987.

Bright, J. *A History of Israel*. Chicago, Illinois: Westminister Press, 1959.

Bullinger, E. W. *The Companion Bible* Grand Rapids, Michigan: Kregal Publishing Co., 1990.

Finis Jennings Dake. *Dake's Annotated Reference Bible*. Lawrenceville, Georgia: Dake Bible Sales, Inc., 1974.

DeHaan, M.R. *Daniel the Prophet*. Grand Rapids, Michigan: Zondervan Publishing House, 1947.

Dewitt, Roy Lee. *Teaching From the Tabernacle*. Grand Rapids, Michigan: Baker Book House, 1991.

Encyclopedia Judaica. Jerusalem, Israel: Keter Publishing House, 1971.

Finnegan, Jack. *Handbook of Biblical Chronology.* Revised ed. Peabody, Maryland: Hendrickson Publishing Co., 1998.

Faulstich, Eugene. http://biblechronologybooks.com/

Fuchs, Daniel. *Israel's Holy Days.* Neptune, New Jersey: Loizeaux Brothers, 1985.

Galil, Gershon. *The Chronology of the Kings of Israel & Judah.* New York, New York: E. J. Brill Publishing Co., 1996.

Gaster, Theodore H. *Festivals of the Jewish New Year.* New York, New York: Morrow Quill Paperbacks, 1978.

Glaser, Zhava and Mitch Glaser. *The Fall Feasts of Israel.* Chicago, Illinois: Moody Bible Institute, 1977.

Good, Joseph. *Rosh Hashanah and the Messianic Kingdom to Come.* 3rd ed. Port Arthur, Texas: Hatikva Ministries, 1970.

Hales, William. *A New Analysis of Chronology.* 2nd ed. London, England: 1830.

Hislop, Alexander. *The Two Babylons.* New Jersey: Loizeaux Press, 1916.

Hoehner, Harold W. *Chronological Aspects of the Life of Christ.* Grand Rapids, Michigan: Zondervan Press, 1977.

Horn, H. H., and Wood, L. H. *The Chronology of Ezra 7.* 2nd ed. TEACH Services, Inc., 1970. www.TEACHServices.Com.

Ice, Thomas. http://www.pre-trib.org/

Ironside, Henry A. *Daniel.* Oakland, California: Loizeaux Brothers Inc., 1920.

Jeffrey, Grant R. *Armageddon: Appointment with Destiny.* Toronto, Canada: Frontier Research, Inc., 1988.

Jones, Floyd Nolan. *The Chronology of the Old Testament.* Master Books, Third Printing, May 2007.

Josephus, Flavius. *The Works of Josephus.* Hendrickson Publishing Company, 1987.

Lahaye, Tim. *Revelation.* Grand Rapids, Michigan: Lamplighter Books and Zondervan Publishing House, 1975.

Larkin, Clarence. *The Greatest Book on Dispensational Truth in the World.* Glenside, California: The Clarence Larkin Estate, 1918.

Lenski, R. C. H., *Lenskie's Commentary on the New Testament*, Augsbury Fortress Press, 1964.

Levitt, Zola. *The Seven Feasts of Israel*. P. O. Box 12268, Dallas, Texas, 75225: Zola, 1979.

Lindsay, Gordon. *16 Volume Revelation Series*. Dallas, Texas: Christ for the Nations, 1982.

Lindsey, Hal. *The Late Great Planet Earth*. Grand Rapids, Michigan: Zondervan Publishing Company, 1970.

Lukenbill, D.D. *Ancient Records of Assyria and Babylon*. New York, New York: Greenwood Press, 1968.

Newton, Sir Issac. *The Chronology of Ancient Kingdoms*. London, England, 1728.

McDowell, Josh. *Prophecy: Fact or Fiction*. San Bernadino, California: Here's Life Publishing Company, 1981.

McFall, Leslie. http://www.btinternet.com/~lmf12/

McGee, J. Vernon. *Daniel*. Nashville, Tennesee: Thomas Nelson Publishers, 1975.

Morris, L.C. *The Gospel According to Luke*. Grand Rapids, Michigan: William B. Eerdmans Publishing Company, 1982.

Nee, Watchman. *Come Lord Jesus*. New York, New York: Christian Fellowship Publishers, 1976.

Pentecost, Dwight D., *Parables of Jesus*. Grand Rapids, Michigan: Zondervan Publishing, 1973.

---. *Things to Come*. Grand Rapids, Michigan: Zondervan Publishing, 1973.

Phillips, Don T. *The Book of Revelation: Mysteries Explained*. Revised Ed. College Station, Texas: Virtualbookworm.com Publishing Co., 2012.

Phillips, John. *Exploring Revelation*. Chicago, Illinois: Moody Press, 1987.

Pickle, Bob. http://www.pickle-publishing.com/papers/

Pink, A. W. *The Antichrist*. Grand Rapids, Michigan: Kregel Publishing, 1988.

Pratt, John P. *Divine Calendars Testify of Abraham, Isaac and Jacob.* Meridian Magazine, 11 September 2003.

Prideaux, Humphrey. *The Old and New Testament: History of the Jews.* 25th ed. London, England: 1858.

Rawlinson, George. http://en.wikipedia.org/wiki/George_Rawlinson

Rice, John R. *The King of the Jews (Matthew).* Murfreesboro, Tennessee: Sword of the Lord Publishers, 1971.

Rice, John R. *The Son of Man (Luke).* Murfreesboro, Tennesee: Sword of the Lord Publishers, 1971.

Ritchie, John. *Feasts of Jehovah.* Grand Rapids, Michigan: Kregel Publications, 1982.

Rosenthal, Marvin. *The Pre-Wrath Rapture of the Church.* Nashville, Tennessee: Thomas Nelson Publishers, 1990.

Ryrie, Charles C. *Ryrie Study Bible, King James Version.* Chicago, Illinois: Moody Press, 1978.

---. *Ryrie Study Bible, New King James Version.* Chicago, Illinois: Moody Press, 1985.

Salerno, Donald A. *Revelation Unsealed.* College Station, Texas: Virtualbookworm.com Publishing Co., 2004.

Sedar Olam. New York, New York: Roman & Littlefield Publishing Company, 2005.

Shea, William H. Andrews University Seminary Studies, Summer 1988, Vol. 26, No. 2, 171-180.

Shepard, Coulso. *Jewish Holy Days.* Loizeaux Brothers Publishing Co., 1961.

Shodde, George H. *The Book of Jubilees.* Artisan Publishers, 1980.

Spurgeon, Tommie. *The 7 Spirits of God.* http://www.americaisraelprophecy.com/thesevenspiritsofgod.html

Strauss, Lehman. *God's Prophetic Calendar.* Loizeaux Brothers Publishing Co.,1987.

Strong, James. *Strong's Concordance of the Bible.* Iowa Falls, Iowa: World Bible Publishers, 1986.

Thiele, Edwin R. *The Mysterious Numbers of the Hebrew Kings*. Grand Rapids, Michigan: Zondervan Press, 1983.

Thiele, Edwin R. *A Summary of Edwin Thiele's Work*. http://www.olive-tree.net

Thomas, Robert. *Revelation 1-7: An Exegetical Commentary*. Chicago, Illinois: Moody Press, 1992.

---. *Revelation 8-23: An Exegetical Commentary*. Chicago, Illinois: Moody Press, 1992.

Ussher, James. *Annals of the World*. London, England: Master Books, 1658.

Van Kampen, Robert. *The Sign*. Crossway Books, Inc., 1992.

Vine, W.E. *The Expanded Vines Dictionary of New Testament Words*. Minneapolis, Minnesota: Bethany House Publishers, 1994.

Wacholder, Ben Zion. *The Calendar of Sabbatical Cycles During the Second Temple and the Early Rabbinic Period, Hebrew Union College Annual*. 44 (1973), pp. 153-196

Footnote: *This manuscript has drawn heavily upon several Excellent websites found by GOOGLE. It is my intention to reference every source of information, but this information could not be found in some cases. Information used was either marked open source or not marked at all. If any author(s) see any material they want referenced, please contact me. For any unreferenced material I am grateful and God will know the source.*

Don T. Phillips
drdon@tamu.edu